D1457697

Psychology and Law
in a Changing World

Psychology and Law in a Changing World

NEW TRENDS IN THEORY, RESEARCH AND PRACTICE

Edited by

Giovanni B. Traverso

and

Lara Bagnoli
University of Siena, Italy

London and New York

First published 2001
by Routledge
11 New Fetter Lane, London EC4P 4EE

Simultaneously published in the USA and Canada
by Routledge
29 West 35th Street, New York, NY 10001

© 2001 Routledge

Routledge is an imprint of the Taylor & Francis Group

Typeset by Expo Holdings, Malaysia
Printed and bound in Great Britain by MPG Books Ltd, Bodmin

British Library Cataloguing in Publication Data

A catalogue record for this book is available from the British Library

ISBN: 0–415–27143–6

Contents

Contributors

Maria L. Alonso-Quecuty
Department of Cognitive, Social and Organizational Psychology,
University of La Laguna, La Laguna, Spain

Ramòn Arce
Department of Social Psychology, University of Santiago de Compostela,
Santiago de Compostela, Spain

Lara Bagnoli
Department of Forensic Sciences, University of Siena, Siena, Italy

Anna C. Baldry
Department of Social and Developmental Psychology, University of Rome
'La Sapienza', Rome, Italy

Astrid Birgden
CORE, The Public Correctional Enterprise, Melbourne, Australia

Thomas Bliesener
Institute of Psychology, University of Erlangen-Nürnberg, Erlangen,
Germany

Serge Brochu
International Centre of Comparative Criminology, University of
Montreal, Montreal, Canada

Laura Campos
Department of Cognitive, Social and Organizational Psychology,
University of La Laguna, La Laguna, Spain

Anne Chamandy
International Centre for Comparative Criminology, University of
Montreal, Montreal, Canada

Line Chayer
International Centre for Comparative Criminology, University of
Montreal, Montreal, Canada

Silvio Ciappi
Department of Forensic Sciences, University of Siena, Siena, Italy

Paul M. Dietze
Turning Point Alcohol and Drug Centre, Fitzroy, Australia

Francisca Fariña
Department of Social Sciences, University of Vigo, Pontevedra, Spain

David P. Farrington
Institute of Criminology, University of Cambridge, Cambridge, UK

Jósef K. Gierowski
Department of Forensic Psychology, Institute of Forensic Research, Kraków, Poland

Marc Hillbrand
School of Medicine, University of Yale, USA

Adelma M. Hills
Department of Psychology, University of Western Sydney Macarthur, Campbelltown, Australia

Mark R. Kebbell
Department of Psychology, University of Liverpool, Liverpool, UK

Arthur Kreuzer
Institute of Criminology, University of Giessen, Giessen, Germany

Helmut Kury
Max Planck Institute, Freiburg in Breisgau, Germany

Friedrich Lösel
Institute of Psychology, University of Erlangen-Nürnberg, Erlangen, Germany

Rebecca Milne
Institute of Police and Criminological Studies, University of Portsmouth, Portsmouth, UK

Isabelle Parent
International Centre for Comparative Criminology, University of Montreal, Montreal, Canada

Santiago Real
Department of Social Sciences, University of Vigo, Pontvedra, Spain

Gilda Scardaccione
Department of Psychological Medicine and Psychiatric Sciences, University of Rome 'La Sapienza', Rome, Italy

Hein-Juergen Schramke
Institute of Criminology, University of Giessen, Giessen, Germany

Reuben T. Spitz
Albert Einstein School of Medicine, Yeshiva University, New York, USA

Maciej Szaszkiewicz
Department of Forensic Psychology, Institute of Forensic Research,
Kraków, Poland

Donald M. Thomson
Charles Sturt University, Bathurst, NSW, Australia

Giovanni B. Traverso
Department of Forensic Sciences, University of Siena, Siena, Italy

Alfredo Verde
Institute of Criminology and Forensic Psychology, Genoa, Italy

Carlos Vila
Department of Social Psychology, University of Santiago de Compostela,
Santiago de Compostela, Spain

Graham F. Wagstaff
Department of Psychology, University of Liverpool, Liverpool, UK

Elmar G.M. Weitekamp
Institute of Criminology, University of Tübingen, Tübingen, Germany

David B. Wexler
College of Law, James E. Rogers Law Center, University of Arizona,
Tucson, USA

Frans W. Winkel
Department of Social Psychology, Vrije University, Amsterdam, The
Netherlands

Jósef Wójcikiewicz
Ekspertyz Sandowych Institute, Kraków, Poland

John L. Young
Department of Mental Health and Addiction Services, Connecticut Valley
Hospital, Middletown, CT, USA

Acknowledgements

The present volume contains a selection of contributions to the 6th European Conference on Psychology and Law held in Siena in August 1996.

A number of persons and institutions supported the Conference. They all earn our sincere thanks.

We wish to thank the University of Siena for funding and provision of the facilities for the meeting. We also thank our bank, the Monte dei Paschi di Siena, for funding. We wish to thank too the national and international scientific associations which co-sponsored the Conference: the Italian Society of Criminology, the Italian Society of Forensic Psychiatry, the International Society of Criminology, and the American Academy of Psychiatry and the Law.

We are very grateful to the members of the Scientific Committee of the Conference (Jànos Boros, Anna Coluccia, Gaetano De Leo, David Farrington, Uberto Gatti, Hans-Juergen Kerner, Friedrich Lösel, Gianluigi Ponti, Assunto Quadrio, Mario Reda, Nereide Rudas, and Denis Szabo) and to the members of the Scientific Secretariat (Silvio Ciappi, Anna Lida Elia, and Giulia Leone).

Personal thanks go to Professor David Farrington, Friedrich Lösel and Frans Winkel, who represent the real 'life and soul' of the European Association of Psychology and Law, who gave us continuous support, encouragement and precious advice both for the organization of the Conference and the arrangement of this volume.

Finally, we wish to express our grateful thanks to all the Staff of the Congress Office of the University of Siena for the highly valuable help and assistance in bureaucratic and administrative matters concerning the organization of the Conference.

Introduction

PSYCHOLOGY AND LAW AT THE END OF THE CENTURY

Giovanni B. Traverso and Alfredo Verde

Psychology and Law at the End of the Century follows and updates a previous contribution on the same topic (Traverso and Manna, 1990) which traced the origins and early developments in Italy of the relations between law and psychology. The goal of this book is to offer a global picture of the multifaceted discipline of Legal Psychology (*Psicologia Giuridica*) trying ambitiously to describe it and to highlight both its weaknesses and potentialities in the light of two fundemental criteria: 1) the quality of its theoretical framework, in terms of originality and relevence of conceptual contributions and theoretical constructions; and 2) the quality of empirical research.

CONCEPTS AND DEFINITIONS

First of all, we need some definitions. De Leo, in his recent *Manuale di Psicologia Giuridica* edited in collaboration with Quadrio (Quadrio & De Leo, 1995) distinguishes between the *object* of the discipline under discussion, that is:

> justice, conceived both as field in which law takes shape and expresses itself, and as organized institutional setting in which there enter problems ....which are being elaborated by a complex and diversified penal and civil judiciary activity, more and more linked to a network of personnel, either internal or external to the judiciary itself

and its *competences:* that is '*how*' the discipline handles such problems, by which approaches, and by which methods.

Hence, he distinguishes a *psychology of law* which has the aim of studying and analyzing:

> *law as text,* that is the epistemological, conceptual, linguistic, and narrative aspects of juridical concepts and texts, in order to evaluate if and how most juridical constructions are founded on, and supported by scientific principles and particularly by psychological knowledge.

Here the reference is to the old *legal psychology* of Enrico Ferri, and this reference is very important inasmuch as it allows De Leo (1995a) to single out the risk of a submission of psychology to law. As he states:

We may ask, in fact, whether judicial psychology has got a structural architecture as well as a historical vocation *to be applicative in respect to the law*, to its goals, to its judiciary, institutional operations, etc. In other words, many of us ask whether judicial psychology is a direct and linear function of the demands and needs of law, or whether it can remain autonomous with regard to this functional link. At the very end, does judicial psychology have to have as its main references (that is, it can be held responsible for) the criteria constitutive and expressive of the law, or those of psychology as a science?

This is a very serious problem, as judicial psychology risks having only an ancillary function, being called upon in areas dominated by law, by its subject matters and by its preoccupations of disciplinary control, both in the penal and the civil arena. In De Leo's words (1995a):

> In the majority of the cases, judicial psychology tended and tends to cover a reply function to precise questions formulated within a field of social reality structured by law and by its procedures.

De Leo goes back in time tracing the origin of this frame of reference, up to Sante De Sanctis (1913) and Mira y Lopez (1945); then quotes, in a different perspective, Sabaté (1979) who distinguishes between psychology 'in' the law and psychology 'for' the law, defining the former as applied psychology free from the probationary functions of an ancillary science which characterize the latter; then, he steps back from the positions held by Gulotta (1987a)—who seems to submit psychology to the exigencies of law and its procedures—assuming finally a dialectic position (De Leo 1995a):

> Even when judicial psychology does have ancillary and probationary functions (as it has in civil and penal expertises), it must have as primary reference sources (otherwise it fails twice, both as a scientific discipline and as an ancillary discipline) the scientific and methodological criteria of clinical psychology, affirming indeed its own differentiation and autonomy towards law and jurisdiction; however, in the meantime, even when it doesn't have the previous probationary functions, it *cannot do without letting itself down within the context* of the systems in which law is active and produces interactions between human beings and institutional roles, given that an applicative science which cannot 'take upon' the context in which it operates, loses, for this very same reason, scientific consciousness and can 'rave' senseless truths.

Clearly, these assertions, although reasonable, generate a series of problems which pertain to the nature of 'science' itself, and particularly to the field of 'applicative science,' that is: can applicative science exist? what is the difference between applicative science and mere technology? and, on a parallel level, 'where' can science find its own 'meaning,' producing new hypotheses, new 'truths'? In this perspective, judicial psychology, fixed in a juridical frame within which it occupies a little independent space (like the states of Lesotho, Swaziland, Bophutoswana within the Republic of South Africa in the old times of Piers Botha and of apartheid) can live its own 'autonomy' without any growth, but at the same time without breaking the kind of gentlemanly agreement which let it cohabit with its juridical counterpart.

Taking this not unambiguous perspective, De Leo (1995b) outlines the specific fields of interest of judicial psychology:

a) *psychology of judiciary activities and dynamics*: this branch embraces many sectors of interest, from the assessment of criminal responsibility and dangerousness to the psychology of testimony, the psychology of the victim, the psychology of sentencing, etc.
b) *psychology of interventions, treatments and training of personnel*, with emphasis on methods and clinical models and related problems of training personnel;
c) *psychology of risky situations in adolescence*;
d) *psychology of social maladjustment, deviance and criminal behavior.*

Following this classification, let's mention the main contibutions in the different areas.

PSYCHOLOGY OF LAW

The field of *psychology of law* (or *legal psychology*) is tremendously important, given that it represents a kind of reference ground in which psychology critically discusses its relations to law and confronts itself with its own concepts. The specific questions scholars fight to cope with in this area are represented by the scientific foundation of the juridical concepts, as well as by the reliability of typologies and expectations of behavior founded on law.

It is a field where the law is not taken for granted and, for this very same reason, it is a field not practiced by the majority of people. Making a parallel with sociology, it is the area where sociology becomes 'critical,' and reflects on its own foundations, on its own origins, on its own limits; and the same can be said if we take criminology as an example, with its 'critical' approaches (Traverso & Verde, 1981a; De Leo, 1981; Ceretti, 1992), especially directed against the correctional perspective of etiology of crime and delinquency (Bandini et al., 1991).

Interestingly, this field reflects the high profile scientific *querelles* which have recently focused the attention of many of us in Italy, centered on the issues of responsibility and punishment (both in the juvenile and in the adult criminal justice systems), and on the use or misuse of the technical-juridical tools at disposal for assessing responsibility, i.e. the psychological/ psychiatric expertise.

One major example is represented by the debate following the enforcement in 1989 of a new Procedural Penal Code, which embraces some new legal norms for juveniles, too, which in turn did not remove — as someone had envisaged — the concept of 'immaturity' linked to the notion of 'incapacity of understanding and will' due to the adolescent status (young age) of the subject. Once more, De Leo was in the middle of the *querelle,* being at the same time both a member of the National Commission for the Reform of the Juvenile Penal Procedural Code (which finally *maintained* the provision of 'immaturity'), and a scholar who had so far fought the prevalent judicial praxis of diverting minors away from the criminal justice system by considering them 'immature'(Lanza, 1982), and had on the contrary stressed (De Leo, 1989) that had the juvenile been considered 'immature' (that is 'not responsible' for his/her behavior), this would have let the juvenile himself/herself lose the actual, real meaning of his/her wrongful and unlawful behavior, forcing an unavoidable process of becoming passive towards his/her action, and not responsive, in terms of self-attribution, with regard to such action. The proper societal reaction, according to De Leo, should have been on the contrary one which, following the most recent cognitive, interactive-constructionist and ethogenic paradigms, stresses the capacity of the individual (even if minor) 'of monitoring his/her own behavior in relation to the different levels of reality, subjective, relational, symbolic, which compound the action' (Patrizi, 1995). A solution, however, not free of ambiguity given the actual danger of transforming the innovations provided for by the new accusatorial system into a mere, crude jailing of juvenile delinquents (Traverso & Manna, 1988).

Finally, within the field of psychology of law the studies on the applicability to our juridical context of the Popperian criteria of verification/ falsification (epistemology of science) should be mentioned. In this regard, the contributions by Quadrio and Castiglioni (1995), who make an overview of inferential and deductive procedures of 'pure' and 'empirical' sciences, as well as those by De Leo (1996) and De Cunzo (1996), who study the epistemology of the evaluation system of judicial proofs, taking a position in favor of a Popperian perspective, are particularly important.

PSYCHOLOGY OF CRIMINAL BEHAVIOR

The field of 'psychology of criminal behavior' is characterized by a lack of well-grounded clinical and empirical work. It is a field where rhetoric, and a propensity to tell sensational and stirring stories, with an emphasis on the moral defects of our society, dominate the (scientific) scene, something which in turn favours the reappearance of the 'monster' or, in more modern terms, using the F.B.I. classification and definition, a variety of the monster: the so-called *serial killer*.

As all of us know the monster, the guy (let us talk in masculine terms!) who kills one or more persons and performs on the body of his victims, before or after their death, a series of brutal acts, physically and sexually abusing them, mutilating them, or even eating parts of them, is *not* a new type of criminal. In fact the very birth of our discipline (forensic psychology/psychiatry) rests on the attempt by Lombroso, Kraft-Ebing, and others to classify, describe and interpret this type of criminal.

As Traverso and Manna (1992) recall, quoting Foucault (1981), it was as a consequence of the shift of interest of criminology from the study of crime to the study of the individual man, from the punishment of the offender to the protection of the social system, that psychology and psychiatry began to extend their interest to problems of crime and justice, replying to the demands of the new penal systems that, through confinement in prison, hard labor, and isolation, no longer wished to punish only individuals for the perpetration of crimes but also wanted to transform the criminal's personality, habits and motivations.

Forgetful, so to speak, of their own fathers, perhaps with a perceived feeling of having been betrayed by history, by treatment institutions incapable of doing any good for the patient, some scholars have taken the problem of the serial killer as a starting point to develop an interpretation of the criminal as a bearer of evil, as a 'bad guy' with internal malignant compulsions which he doesn't want to control or even enjoys displaying, exerting his bad and perverted fascination on others. As Ponti and Fornari (1995) point out in their book *The fascination of evil*, centered on three serial killers whom they have seen in their role as court-appointed psychiatric experts:

> Our subjects are squalid champions of a historical period -but, how many were there in the past -characterized by a weak ethical and cultural capacity, by a social destructiveness and degradation, by a sort of obscurantism of reason, by irrational pulsions, affective flattening, emotional distortion, severe reduction of respect, interest, and availability towards others. Many crimes of our days are

symptoms of the above: they are expressions of a dreadful moral defect. As testimonies of such a (moral) poverty and gloominess, they can exert a perverted fascination on who is as poor and gloomy as they are.

It is clear, through these words, that 'criminal psychology' is becoming an opportunity for pamphleting, for asserting one's own moral truths and one's own perspectives about criminal policies. Moreover, notwithstanding other, 'more scientific' contributions on this topic, like those by Fornari and Birkhoff (1996) on three famous serial killers of the past (Vincenzo Verzeni, Karl Denke and Peter Kuerten), whose psycho(patho)logical dynamics are better clarified and stressed, the real danger of this approach is the transformation of the forensic psychiatrist into someone who is engaged in writing what Ceretti (1995), quoting Girard (1982), calls 'persecution texts,' texts which, through the easy identification and punishment of the culprit, allow society at large and sometimes the culprit himself -to achieve peace, but that do not allow maintainance of the neutrality needed to transform personal opinions about mankind into scientific sentences and tested hypotheses.

INVESTIGATIVE PSYCHOLOGY

The discourse about serial killers brings us to stress another aspect which makes this type of criminal so important for some recent developments in our discipline, that is the utilization of new technologies in the criminal justice system, an approach that at least in Italy has only recently captured the attention of forensic psychologists and psychiatrists (Traverso & Ciappi, 1995).

As Traverso and Ciappi (1995) recall, since ancient times mankind has been making attempts to control criminals and their behavior. In the Positivistic Era for instance, scientific investigation focused mainly on the criminal man and on the study of somatic as well as psychological/psychiatric features of criminal personality, in search of the bio-psycho-social determinants (*biological* versus *social* determinism) of criminal behavior, and with the goal and the great hope of a strong reduction of criminality through detection and prevention.

One important direct effect of the success of such an ideology in the field of criminal justice was the birth of the effort to identify and classify criminals, especially the recidivists. Together with the monumental work by Cesare Lombroso, there is the work of Alphonse Bertillon who, in an attempt to describe the characteristics of recidivists created the so called method of *anthropometric identification*, based on some measures concerning height, arms, length of head and so forth; and that of the well known as istologist Purckinje, who in the same period (1823) worked out an impressive classification of fingerprints, anticipating the modern dattiloscopic technologies later introduced by William Hershell.

Nowadays, following the simple idea that 'if science and technology can get a man to the moon, then certainly it must have some important contributions to make in the realm of controlling crime' (Blumstein, 1988), technology has had a dramatic impact and has become extremely pervasive in the criminal justice system too, not only within the more traditional fields of investigations that each of us knows (like automated fingerprint identification methods, the use of DNA analysis, or correctional supervision and treatment, like electronic monitoring, continuously signalling system, and Depot-Provera treatments for dangerous and recidivist sexual offenders), but also in new areas of forensic psychology/ psychiatry, like the use of computer assisted testing, lie detectors, hypnosis, the phallometric method (a technique which allows the differential diagnosis of pedophilia versus surrogate choice), and finally an approach which holds promise for more immediate influence on police investigation, dealing for instance, with interpersonal and residential concommittants of the offence, and suggesting overt descriptions of the offender and his social circumstances that can generate information of direct value to police investigation (Canter, 1989). This broadly behavioral approach, which received considerable impetus by being included in FBI training (Ressler et al., 1988) assumed the name 'offender profiling,' and its rationale is represented by the following two assumptions: a) there are coherent consistencies in criminal behavior, and b) the relationship those behavioral consistencies have to aspects of an offender are important to the police in an investigation (Canter and Heritage, 1990).

We hope that this method, nowadays in its infancy in Italy, will be developed within our University Departments of Forensic Sciences in strict collaboration with the Intelligence Services of our different Police Forces (Polizia, Carabinieri, Guardia di Finanza).

Needless to say, technology has its own risks, and a series of 'technofallacies' have been identified (Marx, 1988) the major risk being that of diffusing the prison ethos into society at large (a society which becomes the functional alternative to prison), building up the so called 'maximum security society' where:

> the line betwen the public and the private is oblitered; we are under constant observation, everything goes on a permanent record, and much of what we say, do and even feel may be known and recorded by others. (Marx, 1988).

To avoid these risks, as Traverso and Ciappi (1995) have recently pointed out, the various legislations pose limitations, at various degrees and levels, to the availability of possibly dangerous scientific and technological applications in order to avoid over intrusiveness, with the consequence of a kind of cultural sterilization and intolerable alteration of the balance between privacy and social security, in favor of the latter.

Following this rationale the Italian penal procedural law strongly forbids, in the provisions of two articles (artt. 188 and 189 cpp), the utilization of any kind of device able to influence the self-determination of the individual. As art. 188 c.p.p. states: 'there cannot be utilized, not even with the subject's consent, any method or technique able to influence the freedom of self determination or to modify the capacity of recalling and evaluating facts,' while article 189 c.p.p. states: 'In case of evidence not regulated by law, the judge can admit it only if it is apt to ensure knowledge of facts and if it doesn't damage the moral liberty of the subject.'

OTHER AREAS OF INTEREST

In our overview, we will focus now on the issues of psychology applied to the study of events which are internal to the justice system. This represents one of the sectors in which psychological research can remain 'pure,' influenced neither by clinical work, nor by the implications and preoccupations of forensic praxis. For this reason, the vast majority of scholars in this field belong to the broad area of cognitive and systemic psychology. We distinguish three areas of interest:

a) a global approach to the functioning of the justice system;
b) psychology of testimony;
c) psychology of juridical procedures and of decision making processes.

The global functioning of the justice system

The first topic, namely the global functioning of the justice system, from the point of view of organizational and social action theories, has been approached by Di Federico and his colleagues (see Di Federico et al., 1993; Mestitz, 1995): the justice system is viewed as a complex, disorganized, conformist, formalist, rigid and over-regulated organization, with obsolete recruitment procedures, and a weak propensity to technological innovations.

By analyzing the juvenile justice system, especially in the civil area ('voluntary jurisdiction'), we see great differences in the interventions of the different juvenile Courts, with particular reference to the concrete source of intervention: in one Court, the responsibility for initiating the civil action was something which was the responsibility of the District Attorney, whilst in another Court the social services of the City directly approached the competent judge, who in turn asked the District Attorney to take up the civil action. Mestitz (1992) shows that, in the latter case, the judge was heavily influenced by welfare personnel in his/her choices.

Another still ongoing piece of research on the functioning of the juvenile district attorney's offices after the enforcement of the new procedural penal law, shows great oppositions and delays, partly due to the fact that both the general organization and the information services are behind the times (Cocchini & Nicoli, 1993, 1994).

Psychology of testimonies

Another area of interest, actually the first, historically speaking, to be investigated by Italian scholars (Gulotta, 1987b), is that of the psychology of testimony. Notwithstanding the great bulk of literature produced on this topic by previous researchers (Cabras, 1996a), good empirical research is lacking. One important contribution to this area was the study by Gorra and Rampoldi (1987) on the influences of suggestive questions on testifier's answers: not surprisingly, results showed that the more suggestive the questions, the more distorted the testifier's answers, and that the effect of suggestion was a direct function of the time passed from the specific event under study. The recent contribution by De Cataldo Neuburger (1995), devoted to the psychology of penal trials, is limited to an overview of foreign literature and on that basis it gives a series of guidelines useful for those who have to take evidence (to listen to testimonies); likewise, the works by Gulotta (1990) and Farinoni (1996) are real mines of information, data and guidelines for actors in a penal trial, but they do not represent actual pieces of research. Among other useful studies is the contribution by Gulotta et al., (1996) on suggestibility and credibility assessment of children's testimonies of incest or sexual abuse.

Decision making processes

The third field to be mentioned here is that of the psychology of judiciary decision-making processes, a field studied mainly from a cognitive point of view. There is the contribution by Magrin (1995) who, through an overview of the different approaches to the field distinguishes, with reference to the psychology of USA juries' decisions, *algebraic*, which postulate an ideal, fully rational decision-maker, from *euristic* perspectives, which in turn presume the presence of concrete conceptualization and simplification strategies as an aid to the difficult decisionary task (Magrin, 1995; Pennington and Hastie, 1993).

An Italian example of this approach is represented by the work by Castellani (1992), who examines the cognitive structures of magistrates as a function of the degree of their professional experience: comparison between fifteen experienced (at least five years of service) with a sample of fifteen just hired young magistrates shows that the more experienced ones are more capable of mediating between opposing sides of jurisprudence, and flexible in taking opposing perspectives of colleagues or other qualified personnel, as well as being able to build up alternative 'possible stories' to compare with the one which is coming out of the specific case under examination. According to Castellani (1992) Italian magistrates operate through other ways, for instance making connections between specific evidence from a case and the narratological data, which in turn influences the construction of alternative stories, one of which is then chosen and becomes the official story on which the sentence is based.

It is worth stressing that the above cognitive approaches are very close to the new 'narratological' perspectives developed in the last few years (Bruner, 1992; Spence, 1987), which have shown that the construction of a 'story' is a very strong form of comprehension, as well as of conformity towards what appears to be strange, bizarre or alien to an individual or a social group. In this context, judicial decision-making processes can be seen as a powerful tool of normalization of a social situation against conflict, owing to a deviant or criminal phenomenon, through the construction, indeed, of a story which singles out a culprit and punishes him/her. From this point of view the criminal justice system could be interpreted as a social institution aimed at the management of subjects who have committed intolerable crimes, with the production of an official story which explains the reason why they behaved as they did, and condones their subsequent punishment, either from a symbolic or from an actual perspective.

A very useful contribution in this area is that by Cabras (1996b), through the content analysis of some newspaper articles about a false 'monster,' the case of Stefano Spilotros, a young man who falsely accused himself of being responsible for the murders of two children committed by another man. Cabras (1996b) shows the great difference between images of the man in newspapers respectively written in the place where the man lives, in the place where the crimes had been committed, and finally in a neutral place: this demonstrates that the community's image of the author of heinous crimes is strongly influenced by media's distortions. It is supposed that sensational cases give an opportunity for common discussion, an arena where particular social attitudes towards certain kinds of deviance can be developed; and in turn, such social attitudes can heavily influence the judicial decision making processes. Ongoing research into the authors of heinous crimes (multiple lust murders) shows indeed the interplay in the narrative construction of the cases of two 'monsters' between the first-grade trial and the mass media, whilst the appeal sentence gives, in both cases, a less emotional evaluation, an evaluation closer to the real psychiatric conditions of the defendants (Verde, 1996).

Last but not least we come to the important area where problems and difficulties linked with clinical interventions in 'compulsory situations' arise: this is a very broad context, which embraces a series of professional activities in the area of psychology/psychiatry, often performed very informally, even outside the strict formalities of 'due process of law.' All these interventions (concerning both adults and juveniles) have something in common: there is no direct mandate by the client to the professional, but the phantasm of an external, institutional organization which gives mandate to the technician to perform his/her intervention, whatever it is, arises. The result is a rather strange, often conflictual situation, where the psychologist/psychiatrist and his/her involuntary client confront. These are problems which have been discussed for some time, and which have given rise to opposing orientations: on one hand, the position of refusal of a professional intervention in which treatment and control (double agentry) are mixed together, with the high risk of distortion of the intervention itself (Traverso and Verde, 1981b; Bandini and Gatti, 1987b); on the other hand, the position which seeks intervention 'at any cost' (De Leo, 1987), using the tools of systemic psychology and of psychology of social action. Actually, the two diverging positions gave rise to a heated debate, not without accents of polemical arrows. Ours was a position which tended to guarantee an autonomy to the psychologist (or criminologist) which allowed him/her not to lose the internal setting of his/her intervention (Verde and Velle, 1995), even in institutional situations in which the main goal is not (or might not be) the support of the interests of the object of the consultation. The question is: can we give this aim up? Quadrio and Castigliani (1995) say no.

In a recent contribution, De Leo (1995b) seems to indicate clearly the most important needs, limitations and framework for professionals operating in the criminal justice system; however important ethical problems remain unsolved, and the primacy of a 'therapeutic model,' as opposed to the 'consultation model,' still seems to be questioned and is not yet well established or agreed upon. If things seem to be better off in the broader area of juveniles, in that of adults the situation is more problematic and the role of the psychologist operating, for instance, in prison risks becoming residual, often confined to a merely bureaucratic function.

REFERENCES

Altavilla, E. (1953). *La dinamica del delitto.* Vol. 1–2, UTET, Torino.

Balier, C. (1988). *Psychanalyse des comportements violents.* PUF, Paris, 1988.

Bandini, T., & Gatti, U. (1979). Limiti e contraddizioni dell'opera del criminologo clinico nell'attuale sistema penitenziario italiano. *Rassegna penitenziaria e criminologica, 12*, 165.

Bandini, T., & Gatti, U. (1987a). *Delinquenza giovanile.* Giuffré, Milano.

Bandini, T., & Gatti, U. (1987b). La minore età. In: G. Gulotta (Ed.), *Trattato di psicologia giudiziaria nel sistema penale.* Giuffré, Milano.

Bandini, T., Gatti, U., Marugo, M.I., & Verde, A. (1991). *Criminologia. Il contributo della ricerca alla conoscenza del crimine e della reazione sociale.* Giuffré, Milano.

Battacchi, M.W. (1995). I servizi psicologici nel campo delle devianze: un nodo di contraddizioni. In: A. Quadrio & G. De Leo (Eds.), *Manuale di psicologia giuridica.* LED—Edizioni Universitarie di Lettere Economia Diritto, Milano.

Blumstein, A. (1988). Science and technology in support of criminal justice. In: M. LeBlanc, P. Tremblay & A. Blumstein (Eds.) *Nouvelles Technologies et Justice Penale.* Les Cahiers de Recherches Criminologiques, Centre International de Criminologie Comparée, Université de Montréal, 9.

Bruner, J. (1992). *La ricerca del significato. Per una psicologia culturale.* Bollati Boringhieri, Torino.

Cabras, C. (Ed.) (1996a). *Psicologia della prova.* Giuffré, Milano.

Cabras, C. (1996b). Un mostro di carta. In: C. Cabras (Ed.), *Psicologia della prova.* Giuffré, Milano.

Canepa, G. (1974). *Personalità e delinquenza.* Giuffrè, Milano.

Canter, D. (1989). Offender Profiles. *The Psychologist, 2,* 12.

Canter, D., & Heritage, R. (1990). A multivariate model of sexual offence behavior: developments in offender profiling. *J. For. Psychiatry, 1,* 185.

Castellani, P. (1992). *Il giudice esperto.* Il Mulino, Bologna.

Ceretti, A. (1992). *L'orizzonte artificiale. Problemi epistemologici della criminologia.* CEDAM, Padova.

Ceretti, A. (1995). Dal sacrificio al giudizio: da Girard a Chapman. In: A. Francia (Ed.), *Il capro espiatorio.* Franco Angeli, Milano.

Cocchini, A., & Nicolì, M. (1993). Organizzazione e funzionamento di una Procura della Repubblica presso il Tribunale per i minorenni. *Quaderni del Centro Studi e Ricerche sull'Ordinamento Giudiziario dell'Università di Bologna, 3,* 13.

Cocchini, A., & Nicolì, M. (1994). Innovazione tecnologica e strategie di gruppo in una Procura della Repubblica presso il Tribunale per i minorenni. *Contributi di ricerca in psicologia e pedagogia, 3.*

De Cataldo Neuburger, L. (1995). Processo penale e psicologia. In: A. Quadrio & G. De Leo (Eds.), *Manuale di psicologia giuridica*. LED—Edizioni Universitarie di Lettere Economia Diritto, Milano.

De Cunzo, D. (1996). Epistemologia della prova: modelli teorici a confronto nel nuovo processo penale. In: C. Cabras (Ed.), *Psicologia della prova*. Giuffré, Milano.

De Leo, G. (1981). *La giustizia dei minori*. Einaudi, Torino.

De Leo, G. (1985). Responsabilità: definizioni e applicazioni nel campo della giustizia minorile. In: G. Ponti (Ed.), *Giovani, responsabilità e giustizia*. Giuffré, Milano.

De Leo, G. (1987). Verso una nuova razionalità nell'intervento educativo istituzionale. Relazione al Convegno *Jornadas sobre Educaciòn y Contròl*, Barcellona (Spagna).

De Leo, G. (1989). Categorie psico-sociali e interazioni operative nel nuovo processo penale minorile. In: F. Palomba (Ed.) *Il sistema del nuovo processo penale minorile*. Giuffré, Milano.

De Leo, G. (1995a). Oggetto, competenze e funzioni della psicologia giuridica. In A. Quadrio & G. De Leo (Eds.), *Manuale di psicologia giuridica*. LED—Edizioni Universitarie di Lettere Economia Diritto, Milano.

De Leo, G. (1995b). La psicologia clinica in campo giudiziario e penitenziario: problemi e metodi. In: A. Quadrio & G. De Leo (Eds.), *Manuale di psicologia giuridica*. LED—Edizioni Universitarie di Lettere Economia Diritto, Milano.

De Leo, G. (1996). Psicologia giuridica e prova processuale. In C. Cabras (Ed.), *Psicologia della prova*. Giuffré, Milano.

De Sanctis, S. (1929). Le Service Social dans les hopitaux psychiatriques, dans les tribunaux et dans les prisons en Italie. *Atti della Première Conference Internationale du Service Social, Parigi, 1929. Contributi Psicologici dell'Istituto di Psicologia Sperimentale della R. Università di Roma*, vol. VI, 1929–1933, 1–6.

Di Federico, G., Lanzara, G.F., & Mestitz A. (Eds.) (1993). *Verbalizzazione degli atti processuali, tecnologie video e gestione dell'innovazione nell'amministrazione della giustizia*. Consiglio Nazionale delle Ricerche, Roma.

Di Tullio, B. (1975). *Principi di criminologia generale e clinica con note di psicopatologia sociale*. V ed., Lombardo Editore, Roma.

Farinoni, P. (1996). Una ricerca sulla cross-examination. In: C. Cabras (Ed.), *Psicologia della prova*. Giuffré, Milano.

Ferracuti, F. (Ed.) (1988). *Trattato di criminologia, medicina criminologica e psichiatria forense*. Giuffrè, Milano.

Fornari, U., & Birkhoff, J. (1996). *Serial Killer. Tre "mostri" infelici del passato a confronto*. Centro Scientifico Editore, Torino.

Foucault, M. (1981). L'évolution de la notion d''individu dangereux' dans la psychiatrie légale. *Déviance et Sociétè, 5*, 403–422.

Girard, R. (1982). *Il capro espiatorio*. Adelphi, Milano.

Gorra, E., & Rampoldi, I. (1987). Come nell'interrogatorio la domanda può influenzare la risposta. In: G. Gulotta (Ed.), *Trattato di psicologia giudiziaria nel sistema penale*. Giuffré, Milano.

Gulotta, G. (1987a). Psicologia e processo: lineamenti generali. In: G. Gulotta (Ed.), *Trattato di psicologia giudiziaria nel sistema penale*. Giuffré, Milano.

Gulotta, G. (1987b). Psicologia della testimonianza. In: G. Gulotta (Ed.), *Trattato di psicologia giudiziaria nel sistema penale*. Giuffré, Milano.

Gulotta, G. (Ed.) (1990). *Strumenti concettuali per agire nel nuovo processo penale*. Giuffré, Milano.

Gulotta, G., De Cataldo, L., Pino, S., & Magri, P. (Eds.) (1996). Il bambino come prova negli abusi sessuali. In C. Cabras (Ed.). *Psicologia della prova*. Giuffré, Milano.

Lanza, L. (1982). La risposta giudiziaria dei Tribunali per i minorenni alla devianza penale minorile. In: G. Barbarito et al. (Eds.). *La risposta giudiziaria alla criminalità minorile*. Unicopli, Milano.

Magrin, M.E. (1995). Psicologia della decisione giudiziaria. In: A. Quadrio & G. De Leo (Eds.). *Manuale di psicologia giuridica*. LED—Edizioni Universitarie di Lettere Economia Diritto, Milano.

Marx, G.T. (1988). The Maximum Security Society. In: M. LeBlanc, P. Tremblay & A. Blumstein (Eds.), *Nouvelles Technologies et Justice Penale*. Les Cahiers de Recherches Criminologiques, Centre International de Criminologie Comparée, Université de Montréal, 9.

Mazzei, D. (1995). Interazioni fra funzioni di aiuto e controllo nella giustizia minorile. In: A. Quadrio & G. De Leo (Eds.). *Manuale di psicologia giuridica*. LED—Edizioni Universitarie di Lettere Economia Diritto, Milano.

Mestitz, A. (1992). La giustizia minorile nel settore civile: due casi a confronto. *Rassegna Italiana di Criminologia, 3*, 315.

Mestitz, A. (1995). Il funzionamento e l'organizzazione del 'sistema giustizia'. In: A. Quadrio A. & G. De Leo (Eds.), *Manuale di psicologia giuridica*. LED—Edizioni Universitarie di Lettere Economia Diritto, Milano.

Mira y Lopez, E. (1932). *Manual de psicologia juridica*. Salvat, Barcellona, trad. it., *Manuale di psicologia giuridica*, Giunti, Firenze, 1966.

Patrizi, P. (1995). Psicologia e processo penale minorile. In: A. Quadrio & G. De Leo (Eds.), *Manuale di psicologia giuridica*. LED—Edizioni Universitarie di Lettere Economia Diritto, Milano.

Patrizi, P. (1996). Il processo come metodo. In: C. Cabras (Ed.). *Psicologia della prova*. Giuffré, Milano.

Pennington, N., & Hastie, R. (1993). Reasoning in explanation-based decision making. *Cognition,* 49.

Ponti, G., & Fornari, U. (1995). *Il fascino del male. Crimini e responsabilità nelle storie di vita di tre 'serial killer'*. Raffaello Cortina Editore, Milano.

Ponti, G., & Merzagora, I. (1993). *Psichiatria e giustizia. Riflessioni sull'imputabilità dei malati di mente*. Raffaello Cortina Editore, Milano.

Quadrio, A., & De Leo, G. (1995). (Eds.). *Manuale di psicologia giuridica*. LED—Edizioni Universitarie di Lettere Economia Diritto, Milano.

Quadrio, A., & Castiglioni, M. (1995). Interazioni concettuali fra psicologia e diritto. In A. Quadrio & G. De Leo (Eds.). *Manuale di psicologia giuridica*. LED—Edizioni Universitarie di Lettere Economia Diritto, Milano.

Quadrio, A., & De Leo, G. (Eds.) (1995). *Manuale di psicologia giuridica*. LED—Edizioni Universitarie di Lettere Economia Diritto, Milano.

Ressler, R., Burgess, A.W., & Douglas, J.E. (1988). *Sexual Homicide: Patterns and Motives*. Lexington Books, Toronto.

Sabatè, M. (1979). *Comportamento, diritto e società*. Giuffré, Milano.

Spence, D.P. (1987). *Verità narrativa e verità storica*. Martinelli, Firenze.

Serra, C. (1987). Lo psicologo e il carcere. In: G. Gulotta (Ed.), *Trattato di psicologia giudiziaria nel sistema penale*. Giuffré, Milano.

Serra, C. (1995). Lo psicologo nel processo di trattamento penitenziario nel settore adulti. In A. Quadrio & G. De Leo (Eds.), *Manuale di psicologia giuridica*. LED—Edizioni Universitarie di Lettere Economia Diritto, Milano.

Traverso, G.B:, & Ciappi, S. (1995). New technologies in the criminal justice system with particular reference to the field of forensic psychiatry. *Rivista Italiana di Medicina Legale, XVII*, 1133–1154.

Traverso, G.B., & Ciappi, S. (1997). Disegno di legge di riforma del Codice Penale: note critiche a margine della nuova disciplina sull'imputabilità. *Rivista Italiana di Medicina Legale, XIX, 3*, 667–673.

Traverso, G.B., & Manna, P. (1988). La risposta istituzionale ai minori autori di reato: i risultati di una ricerca sul territorio di competenza della Corte di Appello di Genova. *Rassegna di Criminologia, XIX*, 277–308.

Traverso, G.B., & Manna, P. (1992): Law and Psychology in Italy. In: F. Lösel, D. Bender & T. Bliesener (Eds.), *Psychology and Law. International Perspectives* (pp.535–545). Walter de Gruyter, Berlin.

Traverso, G.B., & Verde, A. (1981a). *Criminologia critica*. CEDAM, Padova.

Traverso, G.B., & Verde, A. (1981b). Pericolosità e trattamento in criminologia. Note in margine alle VIII Giornate Internazionali di Criminologia Clinica Comparata. *La questione criminale, 7*, 503.

Verde, A. (1990). La risposta pubblica alla devianza minorile fra presa in carico e attribuzione di colpa. *Marginalità e società, 13, 58.*

Verde, A. (1996). La costruzione narrativa della realtà criminale: un'analisi criminologica delle pratiche narrative connesse ai contesti punitivi, Relazione conclusiva del Progetto di ricerca C.N.R. n. 93.04812.CT09, Università di Genova, Istituto di Criminologia e Psichiatria Forense.

Verde, A., & Velle, G. (1995). Il capro espiatorio e la nuova criminologia clinica. In: A. Francia (Ed.), *Il capro espiatorio. Discipline a confronto.* Franco Angeli, Milano.

PART 1
CAUSES AND PREVENTION OF OFFENDING

Chapter 1

THE NEED FOR A COORDINATED PROGRAM OF CROSS NATIONAL COMPARATIVE LONGITUDINAL RESEARCH

David P. Farrington

KEY ISSUES IN CRIMINOLOGY

The key issues that I will address fall into three categories. First, there are questions of descriptive epidemiology, such as: how do criminal careers develop over time? Second, there are causal questions, such as: what are the most important causes or risk factors for offending? Third, there are intervention questions, such as: what are the best interventions to prevent or reduce offending? In each of these categories, I will first discuss key questions that need to be addressed. Then I will discuss what we know, what we need to know, and how we can find this out. Finally, I will recommend an ambitious coordinated program of cross-national comparative longitudinal research.

CRIMINAL CAREERS

Key questions about criminal careers include the following:

- What proportion of the population commits offenses at different ages? What is the prevalence of offending?

This and other questions can also be asked about different populations (e.g. males versus females) and different types of offenses.

- What are the characteristics of offenders compared with non-offenders at different ages?
- When does offending start? What is the age of onset?
- When does offending stop? What is the age of desistance?
- How long do criminal careers last? What is their duration?
- How frequently do people commit offenses during their criminal careers?
- How far is there escalation or de-escalation in the seriousness of offending during criminal careers?
- How far is there specialization or versatility in offending?
- How far is there continuity or stability in offending over time?

- How far are there different behavioral manifestations of the same underlying construct (e.g. an antisocial personality) at different ages?
- How far are criminal careers types of more general antisocial careers?
- How far are there developmental sequences, pathways or progressions from one type of offending to another, or from childhood antisocial behavior to offending?
- How far can we predict the later criminal career from the criminal career so far?
- How are different criminal career features (e.g. age of onset, duration, frequency of offending) inter-related?

Conclusions about criminal careers depend on methods of measurement (e.g. official records or self-reports) and types of offenses. One of the early surprising findings was the high prevalence of offending. For example, in the Cambridge Study in Delinquent Development, which is a prospective longitudinal survey of 400 London males, 40% were convicted up to age 40 (Farrington, 1995b; Farrington et al., 1998). According to their self-reports, 96% had committed an offense that could have led to conviction up to age 32. However, even according to self-reports, only a minority had committed more serious offenses such as burglary (14%) and motor vehicle theft (15%; Farrington, 1989).

According to official records, offending often begins by age fourteen, has a peak prevalence in the teenage years (age 15–19) and then declines after age twenty (Farrington, 1986). In the Cambridge Study, the peak age of increase in the prevalence of offending by Study males was about fourteen, while the peak age of decrease was about twenty-three. However, some criminal careers can persist over many years and others do not begin until late in life. For example, a quarter of convicted fathers in the Cambridge Study were not convicted until after age 35, and the average duration of their criminal careers was 16 years (for fathers committing more than one offense; see Farrington et al., 1998).

A small fraction of the population (the "chronic offenders") account for a substantial fraction of all offenses. In the Cambridge Study, about 6% of the males accounted for about half of all the convictions up to age 40 (Farrington et al., 1998). Also, about 6% of the families accounted for half of all the convictions of all family members (Farrington et al., 1996). Most offenses under age seventeen were committed with others, but co-offending decreased steadily with age (Reiss & Farrington, 1991).

There is relative stability in offending, since the worst offenders at one age tend also to be the worst offenders at other ages. In the Cambridge

Study, three-quarters of those convicted as juveniles at age 10–16 were also convicted at age 17–24, compared with only 16% of the remainder (Farrington, 1992). There was also significant continuity in self-reported offending (Farrington, 1989). However, there were changes in absolute levels of offending over time. For example, the prevalence of marijuana use decreased significantly between ages 18 and 32 (from 29% to 19%), but there was a significant correlation between use at age 18 and use at age 32 (Farrington, 1990).

Offending is predominantly versatile rather than specialized, particularly at younger ages. In the Cambridge Study, the violent offenders committed an average of 1.7 violent offenses each up to age 32, but an average of 5.3 non-violent offences each (Farrington, 1991b). Violent offenses seemed to occur almost at random in criminal careers. Also, there is versatility in antisocial behavior generally, suggesting that offending is one element of a syndrome of antisocial behavior that arises in childhood and persists into adulthood (Farrington, 1991a). Offenders tend to be multiple problem youths.

Many other important facts are known about criminal careers, but I do not have space to review them here (see Farrington, 1997c). Instead, I will move on to what we need to know about criminal careers. Most previous criminal career research has been based on official records of arrests or convictions. More efforts are needed to investigate criminal career questions using repeated self-reports in prospective longitudinal surveys. Ideally, self-report information is needed about the relative timing of offenses. Self-reports would make it possible to study the probability of a (self-reported) offense leading to a conviction, and the characteristics of people with a high likelihood of committing undetected offenses (compared to others who have a high likelihood of being caught). Self-reports would also make it more possible to study criminal career issues for specific types of offenses.

Most prior criminal career research treats offenders as homogeneous, but different types of people may have different types of careers. For example, Moffitt (1993) distinguished between "adolescence-limited" and "life-course-persistent" offenders. Research is needed on what are the most useful typologies of offenders, and on their different developmental pathways to criminal careers. Also, more research is needed on female criminal careers; existing studies focus primarily on males.

An important research priority is to investigate stepping stones on developmental pathways leading to serious or chronic offending, to try to determine optimal opportunities for intervention (when there is some predictability but not too much stabilization). More research is also needed on predicting future criminal careers. It is also important to study failures in prediction, for example why some juvenile offenders do not become adult offenders (Farrington & Hawkins, 1991). This type of research can help to identify protective factors that might form the basis of interventions.

In the past, there has been little contact between developmental and situational researchers (Farrington, 1995a). More criminal career research is needed regarding situational factors and circumstances influencing criminal acts, so that it is possible to specify not only how and why criminal potential develops over time but also how and why the potential becomes the actuality of criminal acts. Similarly, more criminal career research is needed that incorporates biological factors (Farrington, 1997d) and community influences (Farrington, 1993a). Another important research priority is quantifying the total burden on society of chronic offenders, specifying their problems in different areas of life (e.g. education, employment, sexual, mental and physical health). This information is especially needed in assessing the costs and benefits of prevention and intervention programs.

CAUSES AND RISK FACTORS

Key questions about causes and risk factors include the following:

- What are the main causes of offending? Why do people commit offenses at different ages?
- What are the main risk factors for offending at different ages?

It is easier to establish risk factors (factors that predict an increased probability of offending) than causes. It is not easy to determine which risk factors have causal effects. Many researchers are doubtful about the value of asking people direct questions about why they committed offenses (Farrington, 1993b).

- What is the relative importance of different risk factors? How far do risk factors have independent, interactive or sequential effects on offending? For example, do communities influence families, and families influence children, so that communities have only indirect effects on offending?
- What are the main protective factors for offending at different ages?
- How well, and how early, can offending be predicted?

- What are the main causes or risk factors for different criminal career features such as onset, persistence, escalation, de-escalation and desistance?

Since they occur at different ages, the causes of some features are likely to be different from the causes of others.

- What are the effects of life events (such as getting married, getting divorced, leaving home, parental death, parental divorce) on the course of development of offending? Are there critical periods when effects of specific life events are greatest?
- What are the most useful theories for explaining onset, persistence, escalation, de-escalation, desistance, and the time course of criminal careers generally?

A great deal is known about the main risk factors or predictors of offending, from prospective longitudinal surveys in different countries (Farrington, 1996a, 1997c). Because of my interest in linking knowledge about risk factors and interventions, I will focus on risk factors that can be changed, rather than fixed risk factors such as gender. I will also focus on risk factors that might be explanatory or causal, rather than risk factors that might be merely symptoms of an underlying antisocial personality (e.g., bullying, heavy drinking, drug use).

Among the most important risk factors are:

- Hyperactivity-impulsiveness-attention deficit
- Low intelligence or attainment
- Convicted parents or siblings
- Poor parental supervision, harsh or erratic discipline
- Parental conflict, separation or divorce
- Low family income, poor housing
- Large family size
- Delinquent friends
- High delinquency rate school
- High crime neighbourhood

While these risk factors are well-established, there is little hard evidence about which of them are truly causal. The most compelling evidence of causality could be obtained in prevention or intervention experiments, but most such experiments are designed to test a technology rather than a theory. Interventions are often heterogeneous, including for example individual skills training, parent training and teacher training (Hawkins et al., 1991), because multi-modal interventions are more likely to be successful (Wasserman & Miller, 1998). However, unimodal interventions focussing on a single factor, such as poor parental supervision, could be useful in establishing causality.

After experiments, the next most convincing method of establishing causes is through quasi-experimental, within-individual analyses in which each individual is followed up before and after life events (Farrington, 1988). Because the same individuals are studied, many extraneous variables are held constant. In the Cambridge Study, the effects of unemployment on offending were established by comparing a person's offending during unemployment periods with the same person's offending during employment periods (Farrington et al., 1986b).

Crimes of dishonesty were more frequent during periods of unemployment. The effects of getting married and getting divorced were established by comparing a person's offending before and after these life events (Farrington & West, 1995). Offending decreased after getting married and increased after getting divorced. More analyses of this type are needed.

While a great deal is known about risk factors for offending in general, little is known about risk factors for different criminal career features such as onset, persistence, escalation, de-escalation and desistance. In the Cambridge Study, a convicted parent was a strong predictor of convictions in general but predicted later rather than early onset; and a delinquent sibling was a strong predictor of persistence in the adult years as opposed to desistance (Farrington & Hawkins, 1991).

Also, little is known about risk factors for different types of offenders such as chronic or persistent offenders. More is known about differences between offenders and non-offenders than about differences between persistent and occasional offenders. In the Cambridge Study, a convicted parent was the strongest predictor of occasional young offenders compared to non-offenders, but low family income was the strongest predictor of persistent compared to occasional young offenders (Farrington, 1999). The extent to which future chronic offenders can be predicted at the time of their first conviction is a question with important practical implications for policy-makers and practitioners; Blumstein et al. (1985) predicted 25 males to be chronic offenders, of whom 14 actually became chronics (out of 23 chronics altogether).

Also, little is known about protective factors, or about independent, interactive or sequential effects of risk and protective factors. Knowledge about protective factors could also be practically useful, since targeting protective factors could help to prevent onset, and foster early desistance. Wide-ranging theories are needed that explain how individual, family, peer, school and community factors influence the development of long-term criminal potential, how life events and short-term factors (e.g., quarrelling with a spouse, getting drunk) influence short-term criminal potential, and how criminal potential interacts with situational factors to produce criminal acts (e.g., Farrington, 1998).

An important issue for theory and practice is how far risk factors are general as opposed to specific for different types of offending and antisocial outcomes. It often seems that multiple overlapping risk factors predict multiple comorbid outcomes, largely because of the influence of multiple problem people in multiple problem families. While it is clear that the likelihood of offending increases with the number of risk factors (Farrington, 1997a), it is unclear how far the specific risk factors matter or are interchangeable. More research is needed to disentangle the specific and general effects of risk factors.

PREVENTION AND INTERVENTION ISSUES

Crime prevention methods can be classified into four categories (Tonry & Farrington, 1995):

- Developmental (designed to inhibit the development of criminal potential in individuals, focussing on risk and protective factors)
- Community (designed to change community institutions such as families, peers and organizations)
- Situational (designed to reduce criminal opportunities and increase the risk of offending)
- Criminal justice (deterrence, incapacitation and rehabilitation).

Key questions about prevention and intervention include the following:

- What are the most effective and cost-effective methods of preventing the onset of offending?
- What are the most effective and cost-effective methods of preventing persistence or escalation after onset?
- What are the most effective and cost-effective methods of fostering de-escalation or desistance from offending?
- What are the effects on criminal careers of criminal justice system rehabilitation methods, such as interpersonal skills training or anger

control techniques, as opposed to more traditional individual deterrence or incapacitative methods?

There are many demonstrations of the effectiveness of developmental prevention methods in well-designed experiments (Farrington, 1996a, 1996b). The most effective techniques include the following:

- Intensive home visiting of women during their pregnancy and the infancy of their children, to give advice about child care, infant development, nutrition and avoiding substance abuse (Olds et al., 1997).
- Pre-school intellectual enrichment programs designed to increase children's thinking and reasoning abilities (Schweinhart et al., 1993).
- Parent management training designed to encourage close monitoring of child behaviour and consistent and contingent rewards and punishments (Patterson et al., 1992).
- Interpersonal skills training to encourage children to think before they act and to consider the effect of their behaviour on others (Ross, 1995).
- Peer influence resistance training, to encourage children to resist peer pressures to commit deviant acts (Tobler, 1986).

These prevention methods can be implemented within a risk-focused community prevention program such as *Communities That Care* (Hawkins & Catalano, 1992). In this, risk and protective factors in the community are measured, and proven prevention techniques are implemented to tackle the most important risk factors.

Some rehabilitative treatment methods for delinquents have also proved to be effective. A large-scale meta-analysis of 200 experimental and quasi-experimental studies concluded that the most effective techniques were interpersonal skills training and cognitive-behavioural methods (Lipsey & Wilson, 1998). Hence, with regard to the reduction of offending by developmental prevention techniques, it is "never too early, never too late" (Loeber & Farrington, 1998).

Unfortunately, most of the existing experiments on prevention or treatment are based on small samples and have short follow-up periods, so the persistence of effects is unclear. Experiments with larger samples and longer follow-up periods are needed. Also most of the existing treatment experiments use only official record measures of recidivism. Follow-up interviews are needed to investigate effects on self-reported offending and on life success in a variety of areas (employment, education, relationship, substance abuse, etc.).

Little is known about optimal intervention strategies. In particular, it is unclear whether it is better to target the whole population using public health methods such as *Communities That Care* or whether it is better to target children at risk or known offenders. Also, little is known about the optimal intervention points in developmental pathways leading to offending or in criminal careers. Research is also needed on how to ascertain the best types of interventions for different types of persons and in different contexts (national, community, subculture, etc.).

There is a great need for more information about the cost-effectiveness of interventions. In evaluating developmental prevention techniques, it is important to measure a wide variety of outcomes as well as offending (unemployment, school failure, dependence on welfare benefits, teenage pregnancy, divorce/separation, substance abuse, etc.).

All benefits of an effective program need to be taken into account in weighing costs against benefits. The costs of crime are so enormous (Miller et al., 1996) that even a small reduction in offending could lead to an impressive benefit cost ratio, such as the 7:1 ratio of the Perry preschool project (Schweinhart et al., 1993). Situational prevention projects can also be highly cost-effective (Forrester et al., 1990).

THE NEED FOR LONGITUDINAL RESEARCH

In order to answer questions about the development of criminal careers and about risk factors for different criminal career features, prospective longitudinal surveys are needed in which people are followed up from childhood to adulthood using personal interviews (Loeber & Farrington, 1997). Ideally, longitudinal studies of offending should have:

- Repeated assessments at frequent intervals (e.g., every year)
- Reliable and valid measures
- Multiple data sources and informants (e.g., children, parents, teachers, peers, records)
- Numerous measured variables from different domains (e.g., biological, psychological, family, peer, school, neighborhood, socioeconomic)
- A long duration, to measure long developmental pathways and within-individual change
- Samples of at least several hundreds

- High risk samples drawn from cities, to maximize the yield of chronic and serious offenders.

For example, in the Pittsburgh Youth Study (Loeber et al., 1998), three samples, each of 500 inner city boys, were followed up, with assessments every 6 months from the boy, mother and teacher. The oldest (age 13) and youngest (age 7) samples have currently been followed up for 10 years, and attrition rates have been low. Numerous different risk factors and outcomes (offending, substance abuse, sexual behavior, and mental health problems) have been measured.

Such prospective longitudinal surveys have many advantages over cross-sectional surveys, including:

- Retrospective bias is avoided, since risk factors are measured before outcomes are known
- Causal order can be established unambiguously
- True predictions can be made
- Offenders and non-offenders emerge naturally, thus avoiding problems of drawing appropriate control groups, as in case-control studies
- Within-individual analyses can be carried out, thereby controlling more effectively for extraneous variables.

THE NEED FOR EXPERIMENTAL RESEARCH

In order to answer questions about the effectiveness of prevention and treatment methods, randomized experiments are needed. Such experiments could also help to establish whether risk factors had causal effects, to the extent that the intervention targeted a single risk factor. Ideally, experiments should have large samples, long follow-up periods and follow-up interviews. For example, in the Montreal longitudinal-experimental study (Tremblay et al., 1995) about 250 disruptive (aggressive/hyperactive) boys were identified at age six. Between ages seven and nine, the experimental group received individual skills training and parent training, and experimental and control boys were then followed up with yearly assessments (which showed that the experimental boys were less antisocial).

The main advantage of a randomized experiment is that it ensures that those who receive an intervention are closely comparable to the control group on all possible extravenous variables (within the limits of statistical fluctuation). A randomized experiment is better than a matching design because it is only possible to match on a limited number of variables (sometimes combined into a prediction score). However, in evaluating community interventions, a matching design is necessary, because it is impossible in practice to assign a large number of communities randomly to experimental and control conditions. Ideally, before and after measures should be compared in experimental and control communities (Farrington, 1997b).

MORE COMPLEX DESIGNS

A major problem with long-term prospective longitudinal surveys is that results may be long delayed. By the time crucial outcome results are obtained, instruments, methods, theories and policy concerns may appear to be outdated. There is also the problem that researchers age at the same rate as the subjects and are mortal. If a principal investigator begins a birth cohort study at age 45, it will probably be necessary to arrange for the direction of the study to be transferred to a younger investigator sooner or later. It is also difficult to secure a long-term guarantee of funding. The accelerated longitudinal design overcomes some of these problems. For example, four cohorts could be followed up simultaneously: the youngest from birth to age 6, the next from age 6 to age 12, the next from age 12 to age 18, and the oldest from age 18 to age 24 (Farrington et al., 1986a). In principle, this design would enable knowledge about development from birth to age 24 to be obtained in only 6 years. A final outcome measure in one cohort could be an initial measure in the next, such as conduct disorder at age 6 and early delinquency at age 12.

This design has some potential disadvantages, however. In particular, it is unclear how best to link up the cohorts, and it is not possible to study very long within-individual sequences. Nevertheless, it is potentially very promising and should be used more. For example, the original design of the Pittsburgh Youth Study called for three cohorts of boys to be followed up, from age 7 to age 10, age 10 to age 13, and age 13 to age 16 (Loeber et al., 1998). As mentioned, the follow-up periods of the oldest and youngest cohorts have now been extended to a total of 10 years. There are also advantages in combining longitudinal and experimental methods, by including interventions in longitudinal studies (Loeber & Farrington, 1997). The longitudinal-experimental design uses the same subjects to study risk factors and developmental pathways as well as the effects of interventions. The longitudinal data before the intervention helps to understand pre-existing trends and interactions between types of persons and types of treatments. The longitudinal data after the intervention helps to establish its long-term impact. Of course, there are also potential disadvantages with this design; for example, the experiment may interfere with the longitudinal study, and it may be necessary to restrict analyses of naturalistic development only to the control group.

The accelerated longitudinal and experimental designs could be combined by implementing different interventions in different cohorts. For example, in the four-cohort design of Farrington et al. (1986a), each intervention could be implemented half-way through the six-year follow-up period. A preschool intervention could be implemented at age 3, parent training at age 9, educational skills training at age 15, and employment skills training at age 21.

CROSS-NATIONAL COMPARATIVE LONGITUDINAL STUDIES

Surprisingly, there are few examples of coordinated cross-national comparative longitudinal surveys in the literature. There are good examples of coordinated comparative longitudinal surveys in different cities in the United States. For example, in the Program of Research on the Causes and Correlates of Delinquency, coordinated longitudinal studies have been carried out in Denver, Pittsburgh and Rochester (Thornberry et al., 1995). Big efforts were made to use common measures in these surveys, although their designs were different. Many key findings about risk factors and development were replicated in all three sites.

Project Metropolitan was originally planned in 1960 as a cross-national comparative longitudinal survey, to be conducted simultaneously in Norway, Denmark, Sweden and Finland (Janson, 1981). However, the project only got off the ground in Sweden and Denmark, and the Copenhagen project has yielded rather few publications (Hogh & Wolf, 1983); Project Metropolitan in Stockholm is best known internationally, and delinquency results can be found in Wikström (1990). The time is surely ripe now to mount a major comparative longitudinal study simultaneously in several European countries.

An advantage of cross-national comparative studies is that they would help to establish how far criminal careers, risk factors and intervention effects are the same or different in participating European countries. To the extent that results are similar, they might strengthen our confidence in universal findings and theories. To the extent that results are different, the challenge would be to explain the differences, perhaps by reference to features of national contexts.

PREVIOUS CROSS-NATIONAL COMPARATIVE STUDIES

The International Crime Victims Surveys constitute perhaps the best known series of cross-national comparative surveys in criminology (see e.g. Mayhew & Van Dijk, 1997). Similar questions about victimization were asked by telephone in 1989, 1992 and 1996 in a number of different countries in Europe and elsewhere. Another major effort was the International Self-Reported Delinquency Survey (Junger-Tas et al., 1994). Similar self-report questions were asked in 1992–93 in several different countries. The success of these initiatives suggests that an international comparative longitudinal survey would be feasible.

The classic book on cross-national longitudinal studies in criminology was edited by Weitekamp and Kerner (1994), based on a NATO conference on the same topic. Unfortunately, while the chapters in this book are excellent summaries of longitudinal studies in different countries, they rather serve to highlight the lack of coordinated cross-national longitudinal surveys. The only cross-national comparative chapter is by Farrington and Wikström (1994), comparing criminal careers in the Cambridge Study and in Project Metropolitan in Stockholm. While many aspects of these careers were similar, the peak in the age-crime curve largely reflected a peak in prevalence in London and a peak in frequency in Stockholm. Very few other cross-national comparisons of longitudinal results have been carried out, although Pulkkinen (1988) systematically compared her criminal career findings in Finland with those obtained in the Cambridge Study, again reporting many similarities.

One of the few systematic comparisons of risk factors in longitudinal surveys was completed by Farrington and Loeber (1999), comparing results in the Cambridge Study and in the middle cohort of the Pittsburgh Youth Study. In both cases, risk factors measured at age 10 were compared with court delinquency between ages 10 and 16, for inner-city boys. Generally, the replicability was remarkable. Most significant risk factors in one survey were comparably strong risk factors in the other. There were only two major exceptions: low social class was more important in Pittsburgh (possibly because the measure included parental education), and harsh maternal discipline was more important in London (possibly because the measure included a cold, rejecting maternal attitude).

CONCLUSIONS

In order to advance knowledge about the development of criminal careers, about the causes of offending, and about the prevention and treatment of offenders, longitudinal and experimental studies are needed. There are advantages in combining a multiple-cohort accelerated longitudinal design with experimental interventions in different cohorts.

The time is ripe to mount a coordinated program of cross-national comparative longitudinal studies. Perhaps the European Association of Psychology and Law could play a major role in organizing such a program, which could lead to great advances in knowledge. This would be a very ambitious project; as it may be the equivalent of the American space shuttle, perhaps we should call it the crime shuttle and try to get it off the ground. It would be most appropriate to mark the Millennium with a real Millennium project in Europe!

REFERENCES

Blumstein, A., Farrington, D. P., & Moitra, S. (1985). Delinquency careers: Innocents, desisters and persisters. In: M. Tonry & N. Morris (Eds.), *Crime and Justice* vol. 6 (pp. 187–219). Chicago: University of Chicago Press.

Farrington, D. P. (1986). Age and crime. In: M. Tonry & N. Morris (Eds.), *Crime and Justice*, vol. 7 (pp. 189–250). Chicago: University of Chicago Press.

Farrington, D. P. (1988). Studying changes within individuals: The causes of offending. In: M. Rutter (Ed.), *Studies of Psychosocial Risk* (pp. 158–183). Cambridge: Cambridge University Press.

Farrington, D. P. (1989). Self-reported and official offending from adolescence to adulthood. In: M. W. Klein (Ed.), *Cross-National Research in Self-Reported Crime and Delinquency* (pp. 399–423). Dordrecht, Netherlands: Kluwer.

Farrington, D. P. (1990). Age, period, cohort, and offending. In: D. M. Gottfredson & R. V. Clarke (Eds.), *Policy and Theory in Criminal Justice: Contributions in Honour of Leslie T. Wilkins* (pp. 51–75). Aldershot: Avebury.

Farrington, D. P. (1991a). Antisocial personality from childhood to adulthood. *The Psychologist, 4*, 389–394.

Farrington, D. P. (1991b). Childhood aggression and adult violence: Early precursors and later life outcomes. In: D. J. Pepler & K. H. Rubin (Eds.), *The development and treatment of childhood aggression* (pp. 5–29). Hillsdale, N.J.: Erlbaum.

Farrington, D. P. (1992). Criminal career research in the United Kingdom. *British Journal of Criminology, 32*, 521–536.

Farrington, D. P. (1993a). Have any individual, family or neighbourhood influences on offending been demonstrated conclusively? In: D. P. Farrington, R. J. Sampson & P-O. H. Wikström (Eds.), *Integrating Individual and Ecological Aspects of Crime* (pp. 7–37). Stockholm: National Council for Crime Prevention.

Farrington, D. P. (1993b). Motivations for conduct disorder and delinquency. *Development and Psychopathology, 5*, 225–241.

Farrington, D. P. (1995a). Key issues in the integration of motivational and opportunity-reducing crime prevention strategies. In: P-O. H. Wikström, R. V. Clarke & J. McCord (Eds.), *Integrating Crime Prevention Strategies: Propensity and Opportunity* (pp. 333–357). Stockholm: National Council for Crime Prevention.

Farrington, D. P. (1995b). The development of offending and antisocial behaviour from childhood: Key findings from the Cambridge Study in Delinquent Development. *Journal of Child Psychology and Psychiatry, 36*, 929–964.

Farrington, D. P. (1996a). The explanation and prevention of youthful offending. In: J. D. Hawkins (Ed.), *Delinquency and Crime: Current Theories* (pp. 68–148). Cambridge: Cambridge University Press.

Farrington, D. P. (1996b). *Understanding and Preventing Youth Crime*. York: Joseph Rowntree Foundation.

Farrington, D. P. (1997a). Early prediction of violent and non-violent youthful offending. *European Journal on Criminal Policy and Research*, 5, 51–66.

Farrington, D. P. (1997b). Evaluating a community crime prevention programme. *Evaluation*, 3, 157–173.

Farrington, D. P. (1997c). Human development and criminal careers. In: M. Maguire, R. Morgan & R. Reiner (Eds.), *The Oxford Handbook of Criminology* (2nd ed., pp. 361–408). Oxford: Clarendon Press.

Farrington, D. P. (1997d). Key issues in studying the biosocial bases of violence. In: A. Raine, P. A. Brennan, D. P. Farrington & S. A. Mednick (Eds.), *Biosocial Bases of Violence* (pp. 293–300). New York: Plenum.

Farrington, D. P. (1999). Predicting persistent young offenders. In: G. L. McDowell & J. S. Smith (Eds.), *Juvenile Delinquency in the United States and the United Kingdom* (pp. 3–21). London: Macmillan.

Farrington, D. P. (1998). Predictors, causes and correlates of male youth violence. In: M. Tonry & M. Moore (Eds.), *Youth Violence (Crime and Justice, vol. 24)* (pp. 421–475) Chicago: University of Chicago Press.

Farrington, D. P., Barnes, G., & Lambert, S. (1996). The concentration of offending in families. *Legal and Criminological Psychology*, 1, 47–63.

Farrington, D. P., Gallagher, B., Morley, L., St. Ledger, R. J., & West, D. J. (1986b). Unemployment, school leaving and crime. *British Journal of Criminology*, 26, 335–356.

Farrington, D. P., & Hawkins, J. D. (1991). Predicting participation, early onset, and later persistence in officially recorded offending. *Criminal Behaviour and Mental Health*, 1, 1–33.

Farrington, D. P., Lambert, S., & West, D. J. (1998). Criminal careers of two generations of family members in the Cambridge Study in Delinquent Development. *Studies on Crime and Crime Prevention*, 7, 85–106.

Farrington, D. P., & Loeber, R. (1999). Transatlantic replicability of risk factors in the development of delinquency. In: P. Cohen, C. Slomkowski, & L. N. Robins (Eds.), *Historical and Geographical Influences on Psychopathology* (pp. 299–329). Mahwah, N.J.: Erlbaum.

Farrington, D. P., Ohlin, L. E., & Wilson J. Q. (1986a). *Understanding and controlling crime*. New York: Springer-Verlag.

Farrington, D. P., & West, D. J. (1995). Effects of marriage, separation and children on offending by adult males. In: J. Hagan (Ed.), *Current Perspectives on Aging and the Life Cycle* Vol. 4: *Delinquency and Disrepute in the Life Course* (pp. 249–281). Greenwich, Connecticut: JAI Press.

Farrington, D. P., & Wikström P-O. H. (1994). Criminal careers in London and Stockholm: A cross-national comparative study. In: E. G. M. Weitekamp & H-J. Kerner (Eds.), *Cross-National Longitudinal Research on Human Development and Criminal Behaviour* (pp. 65–89). Dordrecht, Netherlands: Kluwer.

Forrester, D., Frenz, S., O'Connell, M., & Pease, K. (1990). *The Kirkholt Burglary Prevention Project: Phase 2*. London: Home Office.

Hawkins, J. D., & Catalano, R. F. (1992). *Communities that Care*. San Francisco: Jossey-Bass.

Hawkins, J. D., von Cleve, E., & Catalano, R. F. (1991). Reducing early childhood aggression: Results of a primary prevention programme. *Journal of the American Academy of Child and Adolescent Psychiatry*, 30, 208–217.

Hogh, E., & Wolf, P. (1983). Violent crime in a birth cohort: Copenhagen 1953–1977. In: K. T. van Dusen & S. A. Mednick (Eds.), *Prospective Studies in Crime and Delinquency* (pp. 249–267). Boston: Kluwer-Nijhoff.

Janson, C-G. (1981). Project Metropolitan: A longitudinal study of a Stockholm cohort (Sweden). In S. A. Mednick & A. E. Baert (Eds.), *Prospective Longitudinal Research: An Empirical Basis for the Primary Prevention of Psychosocial Disorders* (pp. 93–99). Oxford: Oxford University Press.

Junger-Tas, J., Terlouw, G-J., & Klein, M. W. (1994, Eds.). *Delinquent Behaviour among Young People in the Western World*. Amsterdam: Kugler.

Lipsey, M. W., & Wilson, D. B. (1998). Effective intervention for serious juvenile offenders: A synthesis of research. In: R. Loeber & D. P. Farrington (Eds.), *Serious and Violent Juvenile Offenders: Risk Factors and Successful Interventions* (pp. 313–345). Thousand Oaks, California: Sage.

Loeber, R., & Farrington, D. P. (1997). Strategies and yields of longitudinal studies on antisocial behaviour. In: D. M. Stoff, J. Breiling & J. D. Maser (Eds.), *Handbook of Antisocial Behaviour* (pp. 125–139). New York: Wiley.

Loeber, R., & Farrington, D. P. (1998). Never too early, never too late: Risk factors and successful interventions for serious and violent juvenile offenders. *Studies on Crime and Crime Prevention*, 7, 7–30.

Loeber, R., Farrington, D.P., Stouthamer-Loeber, M., & van Kammen, W. B. (1998). *Antisocial Behaviour and Mental Health Problems: Explanatory Factors in Childhood and Adolescence.* Mahwah, N.J.: Erlbaum.

Mayhew, P., & van Dijk, J. J. M. (1997). *Criminal Victimization in Eleven Industrialized Countries.* The Hague, Netherlands: Ministry of Justice.

Miller, T. R., Cohen, M. A., & Wiersema, B. (1996). *Victim Costs and Consequences: A New Look.* Washington, D.C.: U.S. National Institute of Justice.

Moffitt, T. E. (1993). Adolescence-limited and life-course-persistent antisocial behaviour: A developmental taxonomy. *Psychological Review, 100*, 674–701.

Olds, D. L., Eckenrode, J., Henderson, C. R., Kitzman, H., Powers, J., Cole, R., Sidora, K., Morris, P., Pettitt, L. M., & Luckey, D. (1997). Long-term effects of home visitation on maternal life course and child abuse and neglect: Fifteen-year follow-up of a randomized trial. *Journal of the American Medical Association, 278*, 637–643.

Patterson, G. R., Reid, J. B., & Dishion, T. J. (1992). *Antisocial Boys.* Eugene, Oregon: Castalia.

Pulkkinen, L. (1988). Delinquent development: Theoretical and empirical considerations. In: M. Rutter (Ed.), *Studies of Psychosocial Risk* (pp. 184–199). Cambridge: Cambridge University Press.

Reiss, A. J., & Farrington, D. P. (1991). Advancing knowledge about co-offending: Results from a prospective longitudinal survey of London males. *Journal of Criminal Law and Criminology, 82*, 360–395.

Ross, R. R. (1995). The reasoning and rehabilitation programme for high-risk probationers and prisoners. In: R. R. Ross, D. H. Antonowicz & G. K. Dhaliwal (Eds.), *Going Straight: Effective Delinquency Prevention and Offender Rehabilitation* (pp. 195–222). Ottawa: Air Training and Publications.

Schweinhart, L. J., Barnes, H. V., & Weikart, D. P. (1993). *Significant Benefits.* Ypsilanti, Michigan: High/Scope.

Thornberry, T. P., Huizinga, D., & Loeber, R. (1995). The prevention of serious delinquency and violence: Implications from the Programme of Research on the Causes and Correlates of Delinquency. In: J. C. Howell, B. Krisberg, J. D. Hawkins & J. J. Wilson (Eds.), *Sourcebook on Serious, Violent and Chronic Juvenile Offenders* (pp. 213–237). Thousand Oaks, California: Sage.

Tobler, N. S. (1986). Meta-analysis of 143 drug treatment programmes: Quantitative outcome results of programme participants compared to a control or comparison group. *Journal of Drug Issues, 16*, 537–567.

Tonry, M., & Farrington, D. P. (1995). Strategic approaches to crime prevention. In: M. Tonry & D. P. Farrington (Eds.), *Building a Safer Society: Strategic Approaches to Crime Prevention* (pp. 1–20). (*Crime and Justice,* vol. 19) Chicago: University of Chicago Press.

Tremblay, R. E., Pagani-Kurtz, L., Vitaro, F., Masse, L. C., & Pihl, R. O. (1995). A bimodal preventive intervention for disruptive kindergarten boys: Its impact through mid-adolescence. *Journal of Consulting and Clinical Psychology, 63*, 560–568.

Wasserman, G. A., & Miller, L. S. (1998). The prevention of serious and violent juvenile offending. In: R. Loeber & D. P. Farrington (Eds.), *Serious and Violent Juvenile Offenders: Risk Factors and Successful Interventions* (pp. 197–247). Thousand Oaks, California: Sage.

Weitekamp, E. G. M., & Kerner, H-J. (1994, Eds.). *Cross-National Longitudinal Research on Human Development and Criminal Behaviour.* Dordrecht, Netherlands: Kluwer.

Wikström, P-O. H. (1990). Age and crime in a Stockholm cohort. *Journal of Quantitative Criminology, 6*, 61–84.

Note: Parts of this chapter were previously published in: Farrington, D. P. (1999) A criminology research agenda for the next millenium. International Journal of Offender Therapy and Comparative Criminology, 43, 154–167 (Copyright Sage publications, inc).

Chapter 2

EARLY PREVENTION OF DELINQUENCY

Anna C. Baldry and Frans W. Winkel

Offenses committed by juveniles are no longer an exception but seem to be the rule. The source of information on the proportion of crimes committed by juveniles in the US, the National Crime Victimization Survey (NCVS), that captures information on crimes committed against persons age 12 or older, shows that in 1991 juveniles were responsible for 19% of all violent crimes (i.e. rape, personal robbery, aggravated and simple assault). (National Center for Juvenile Justice, 1995). The proportion of violent crimes committed by juveniles is disproportionately high compared with their share of the US population, and the number of these crimes is growing. If violent juvenile crime increases in the future as it has in the past ten years, experts estimate that by year 2010 the number of juvenile arrests for a violent crime will be more than double, and the number of juvenile arrests for murder will increase by nearly 150%. Moreover, 17% of all serious crimes in 1991 were committed by juveniles only, either alone (11%) or in juvenile groups (6%). Another 8% of serious violent crimes were committed by a group of offenders that included at least one juvenile and one adult. In 25% of all serious violent crimes a juvenile offender was involved; and of these crimes, more than half involved a group of offenders.

In self-report studies only 2–4% of the juveniles claim never having committed an offense (Handboek Gedrasgstherapie, 1988). Around 20% of adolescent boys have committed a relatively serious crime (shoplifting worth over 30 US dollars, vandalism etc.). About 5% of the juveniles are responsible for 50% of the crimes committed by juveniles (Farrington, 1983). Stephenson (1992) recently reported:

> in the United Kingdom, nearly 31 per cent of men born in 1953 had been convicted for a 'standard offense' by the age of 27, and the figure for those born in later years is likely to be substantially higher ... (pp. 41–42).

The figures are similar in other European countries.

One has to realize that most crimes aren't discovered or reported (Farrington, 1984).

A great deal of crime can be attributed to juveniles (Office of Juvenile Justice and Delinquency Prevention, 1995). In Italy from 1987 to 1992, the number of crimes reported, committed by juveniles, doubled (from 21,264 to 44,788), and the trend does not seem to be decreasing (ISTAT, 1993).

Serious forms of criminal behavior occur more often at a younger age. Following the media one doesn't have to search long: for example in May 1996 in the UK a 13 year old boy was convicted of murdering a female pedestrian by dropping a brick from an apartment building; in Belgium a train driver was killed by a concrete block thrown by two boys aged 13 and 17; in Italy, during July and August a group of boys aged 16 and 20 had fun at throwing stones from a flyover over 13 buses and lorries that passed by. Fortunately a tragedy was avoided but all vehicles sustained serious damage to their front windows and all drivers were extremely frightened. In North Holland a group of boys, some of them aged 13 and 14, were recently arrested for attempted rape.

In light of these figures it is unsuprising to find referrals to 'early intervention' issues in psychology and law literature (Farrington, 1987; LeBlanc & Loeber, 1993; Lyon, 1996; Menard & Huizinga, 1994; Tremblay, 1995; Zigler, Taussig & Black, 1992). A possible intervention strategy is to address the preventive measure to the influence of the 'stepping-stones' process of gateway-behaviors in relatively young children. The underlying assumption is that the 'discouraging' of that kind of behavior at a young age can contribute to the non-occurrence of criminal behavior at a later age (Hewitt, Eaves, Neal, & Meyer, 1988). Testing such an assumption requires longitudinal developmental psychological research (Le Blanc & Loeber, 1993; Pepler & Rubin, 1991).

Until now this assumption had just a 'face-validity'. Zigler et al. (1992, p. 1003) note in this regard:

> Data on the pre-delinquency programs reviewed here show that, for the short term, at least, they appear to be more effective than those initiated after delinquent habits have emerged. There is also growing evidence that problem behavior in small children predicts with some confidence later delinquency. For example, Farrington (1987) cited several studies showing that teacher ratings of problem behavior in kindergarten or first grade were strongly related to number

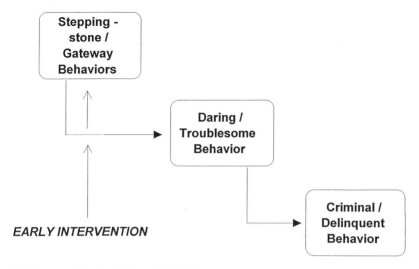

FIGURE 1: MODEL OF EARLY INTERVENTION

of police contacts and serious and chronic offenses in the mid- and late- teens. Loeber (1991) noted that disruptive and antisocial behavior patterns have increasing stability with age, suggesting that such behaviors become less malleable as children grow older.

In addition, a large number of criminal studies show that time after time early delinquent behavior is one of the most important predictors for later delinquency (Elliot, Huizinga & Ageton, 1985; Elliot, Huizinga & Menard, 1989; Le Blanc & Loeber, 1993).[1]

Empirically, there is little insight into the question how an effective early intervention can be designed and from what that efficiency can be measured. A possible effective ingredient could be stimulating the skills of placing oneself in the perspective of the other. These skills can be fortified by making clear to children that most things in life have several sides: in social interactions there is 'your own' perspective or the other's perspective (i.e. victim implicit narrative). The importance of such a skill can be sustained empirically.

Kohlberg (1984) distinguishes various moral development stages. He compared a group of delinquent juveniles with a matched non-delinquent one. His results suggest a retarded moral development (Gibbs, Basinger & Fuller, 1992). In most cases the delinquent group is at a pre-conventional level, the second group at a conventional level. An important aspect of the transition from pre- to conventional phases is the ability to place oneself in the position of another:

> While non delinquents tended to consider the effects of one's actions on others, delinquents'concerns centered on concrete and immediate self-interest (Guerra, Nucci & Huesmann, 1994, p. 21).

Social psychological research on aggressive behavior also documents a strong relationship between aggression and the incapacity to place oneself in the position of others (Ellis, 1982; Luengo, Otero, Carrillo-de-la-Pena & Miron, 1994; Miller & Eisenberg, 1988; Richardson, Hammock, Smith, Gardner & Signo, 1994). Several studies suggest that these kinds of skills can be influenced through specific training programs; focused training with the use of role-play resulted for Chandler (1973) in improved perspective taking skills (training-effect) and in a decrease of delinquent behavior of young people (generalization of carry-over-effect). Chalmers and Townsend (1990) found a similar training-effect on delinquent girls. Several studies on alternative sanctions based on the principle of exposure to victim's reactions and emotions, suggest a favorable effect on judging criminal behavior and on the recidive figure of delinquent juveniles (Groenhuijsen & Winkel, 1994; Winkel, 1993, 1997).

The literature in the social science field on instrumental and reactive aggression is quite broad and offers a variety of views based on (experimental) social psychology (see Bandura, 1973; Baron & Richardson, 1994; Berkowitz, 1993; Cornish & Clark, 1986; Dodge & Coie, 1987; Dodge & Crick, 1990; Dollard, Doob, Miller, Mowrer & Sears, 1939; Huesmann, 1994; Olweus, 1979; Spinetti & Rigler, 1972; Stephenson, 1992; Tuck & Riley, 1986; Widom, 1989, Winkel, 1996), on differential and developmental psychology (see Caprara, Perugini & Barbaranelli, 1994; Chalmers & Townsend, 1990; Ellis, 1987; Farley & Farley, 1972; Levine & Singer, 1988; Luengo, Otero, Carillo-de-la-Pena & Miron, 1994; Miller & Eisenberg, 1988; Winkel, 1993), and in the field of criminology (see Agnew, 1991; Akers, 1977; Akers, Krohn, Lanza-Kaduce & Radosevich, 1979; Rivera & Widom, 1990; Sutherland & Cressey, 1960; Thornberry, 1987; Thornberry, Lizotte, Krohn, Farnworth & Joon Lang, 1994; Warr & Stafford, 1991). Figure 2 gives a global summary of these approaches and offers an overview of the important determinants of reactive and instrumental aggression:

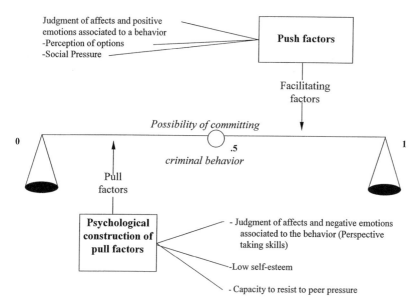

FIGURE 2:. MODEL OF FACTORS OF AGGRESSION: REACTIVE (REACTIVE DELINQUENT BEHAVIOR) AND INSTRUMENTAL (INSTRUMENTAL CRIMINAL BEHAVIOR)

Figure 2 suggests that the non-occurrence and occurrence of criminal behavior is the result of the relative weight of the push and pull factors. An intervention can be called successful if the balance falls in favor of the push factors.

The program (described above) can be called successful, in terms of figure 2 if:

1) enhanced perspective taking results in increasing negative affect, and decreasing positive emotions connected with this behavior (hypothesis 1);
2) this results in an increased awareness of the damage caused to victims as a consequence of such behavior (hypothesis 2).

The present research investigated how far the drawn effect (described here under 2) also exists for behavior not directly addressed in the program (carry-over-effect). And finally we investigated if the found learn-effects occurred at a general level or are found only in certain types of subjects, for example children with a low moral disengagement level as identified by Bandura (Bandura, Barbaranelli, Caprara & Pastorelli, 1996), or the highly emphatic ones (Bryant, 1982).

METHOD

Participants

A total of 62 middle school pupils participated in the experiment. Their mean age was 11.4 years old, (SD = .7). Forty-seven % was male, 53% female. Seventy-one % belonged to the middle social class, 19% to the lower social class, and the remaining 10% to the higher social class.

Procedure

The study was conducted in four parallel classes of the same grade of a middle school. Each class was divided into three small groups; each subject was randomly assigned to one of the experimental conditions.

Participants were exposed to a behavioral episode on video presented by a narrator under three experimental conditions. The behavioral episode involved a group of three 10-year-old boys throwing pine cones from a flyover at cars passing by. To make the video more lively, the narrated story was interrupted by images illustrating the episode. The behavioral episode and images were taken from the brochure 'Per ongeluk, expres, vanzelf' ('By accident, on purpose, by itself'). This brochure has been designed under the request of the Dutch Department of Justice in collaboration with the National victim assistance association, (Balm & Van Hest, 1991) for bullying preventive strategies in schools and among young people in general.

After watching the video, subjects had to fill in a questionnaire. The questionnaire consisted of three parts: the first one measured the dependent variables, the second one the background variables (Moral Disengagement and Empathy) and the third showed a pictorial image consisting of another behavioral episode utilized in a Dutch program to prevent bullying in schools (Van der Cingel, 1994). The picture showed two children teasing and making faces at a third boy. Subjects were then asked to rate the effect of this behavior on the boy.

Independent variables

The independent variables were incorporated in the video. The baseline condition consisted of the behavioral episode of the three boys throwing pine-cones from a flyover at cars passing by. This behavioral episode was introduced under 3 different experimental conditions:

I) a victim—implicit narrative, where the behavioral episode mainly evolves from the actors' point of view;

II) multiple perspectives instruction where viewers are told, *inter alia*, that objects usually have an inside and an outside, or more socially, there is 'your own' perspective and the other's perspective (+ condition I), and

III) a victim-explicit narrative, in which the victim's perspective is more vividly incorporated (+ condition II).

The behavioral episode consisting of condition I, contains the following fragments:

I like to visit my grandmother. My grandmother is quite special. She never complains and when you stay with her you are allowed to do whatever you want. It is even more special to visit her when the twins are also there. Pim and Tom are my cousins. They were born on the same day but have nothing in common. With Pim and Tom adventure is always guaranteed. That happens naturally. Last Sunday, for example.

My grandmother lives in a house next to a forest. You only have to cross the bridge over the highway and then you are there. So we went playing in the forest. Because there had been a storm, the ground was full of pine cones. Tom had an idea. Tom always has good ideas. We would collect pine cones for my grandmother. Pine cones for the open fire. They burn nice and smell good. She would be glad about it.

Because we couldn't carry all these pine cones, we used Tom's jacket as a bag. When the jacket was full, we tied it tightly. We carefully carried the big pack back to my grandmother. On the bridge it went wrong. I tripped and all the pine cones rolled on the ground. A few rolled underneath the flyover and fell on the road. We put the pine cones back into the jacket.

Then Pim got an idea. Pim always has good ideas. We would wave at the cars. In case they would wave back, you won a point. Just a few cars waved back. Then Tom thought that we should punish the cars which didn't wave back. We threw a pine cone to each car which didn't wave. Most of the times we threw them next to the cars. It is quite difficult to wave, to wait until they wave back and if not throw the pine cones. So we omitted the waving and we started only throwing pine cones.

When you hit the car, it sounded like '*Toink*'. Some cars got two or three pine cones on their roof. A red car arrived. It drove extremely fast. Pim, Tom and I all hit it. 'Toink! Toiink! Toiiink!' Three points! Then Pim shouted at once: 'Take care! Get out of here!' Past the flyover the red car braked and left the road. It drove towards the exit leading to the bridge! We ran to the forest. I hid myself behind a tree. Tom and Pim stood behind another one. We kept ourselves quiet. I would have liked to be with them behind their tree. But that one was too small and I didn't dare move.

The red car stopped on the bridge. A man got out. Tom's jacket was still lying on the bridge. The man looked at it and then he walked with big steps towards the edge of the forest. He shouted: 'I can see you. Come out!

'We didn't do anything. The man didn't enter the forest. He shouted: 'Be sure that I will inform the police! 'He walked back, got into his car and drove away.

We stood still for a long time. Then Pim and Tom ran towards my tree. Pim yelled: 'Get out of here! In a few minutes the police will arrive! 'His voice sounded hoarse. Tom looked pale. I told them that the best thing to do was return to my grandmother's house. There they wouldn't be able to find us.

We went back to my grandmother, without pine cones. We had coke and pie and we looked out of the window towards the flyover to see whether the police had arrived. Pim whispered that we could be chased because that man had our profiles. I told him that he had hardly seen us. Tom thought that man had indeed seen his jacket. It would be better if he didn't wear it for the next few weeks. We started playing chess and soon it became dark. The police still hadn't arrived. It was extremely scary. I told you before that you always get involved in adventures with the twins!

Because we were so good, we were allowed to stay longer. We went on playing until nine o'clock, first chess and then dominos. The police didn't arrive. When we left, we all got five dollars each from my grandmother. I already told you that my grandmother is quite special!

In the second condition the fragment was preceded by a multiple perspectives instruction. Fragments of the instruction follow:

All things and events in life have two sides, like the story I am going to tell you. The one side and the other side. A lot of things have two sides. (Examples are given). Everything has a main side and a secondary side, the most important side and a less important side. Which side is the important one, depends on who is looking at it. Most people think that their own side is the main side. Some people do not even know that there is also another side. Imagine, you are arguing with Paul. Then you surely think that you are right and that Paul is not. That is your main side. If you want to see the other side of something, then you have to look further than your nose...

The third condition continued with the victim-explicit narrative. Fragments follow:

My husband really loves his car. Maybe that sounds strange. But it is true. He washes and brushes it each Saturday. It is a red Mazda 323. A new one. Before we had this one, we always had a second-hand one. When my husband retired, we bought this one. 'My last one should be a new one ', my husband said. Now there is a dent and a scrape on the roof. Of course it can be repaired, hammered and painted. You will see nothing of it anymore. But for him the new thing has gone. 'Fucking children', he yelled when he came home on Sunday ... On his way back home there were children standing on the flyover. They were throwing something towards the cars.'It sounded like they were big stones', my husband said; 'like they were going right through the roof'. But they were pine cones. He discovered that when he drove onto the bridge to tell them the truth. Of course they were gone. These children are not crazy. But they are stupid anyway.

It all ended in a good way. But the front window could have been hit. Window broken ... And that with such a speed ... I shouldn't like to think about what could have happened in that case. Now there is only a dent and a scratch. You will see nothing of it anymore. But anyway, the new thing has gone for him, you know...

Background variables were measured with Bandura's Moral Disengagement Scale (Bandura, Barbaranelli, Caprara & Pastorelli, 1996; Caprara, Pastorelli & Bandura, 1993). The overall analyses of the scale, consisting of 32 items, was not reliable enough, (α = .63). We therefore removed those items with an i.t.c. r < .10, resulting in a 22-item Scale (α = .75). Subjects were split on the basis of the mean value, M = 2.74, SD = .41, indicating low or high moral disengagement. To measure empathy, we made use of Bryant's Index of Empathy for Children and Adolescents (Bryant, 1982). Subjects were divided on the basis of the mean point indicating high or low emotional empathy towards peers, M = 3.66, SD = .68. (Sample items of the Scale: 'It makes me sad to see a girl who can't find anyone to play with.' 'I really like to watch people open presents, even when I do not get a present myself', α = .71).

Dependent variables
To measure Affective Responses associated with the behavioral episode, two scales were used: a scale for positive affects (the adjectives used are: exciting, funny, boring, nice, brave, thrilling; α = . 81; Watson, Clark & Tellegen, 1988; Winkel, 1996), and a scale for negative affects (adjectives used are stupid and dangerous, α = .55). Sample items are: 'Do you think that what the boys did was funny?' , 'Do you think that what the boys did was stupid?' . Awareness of victimizing consequences also consisted of two scales: *Distress awareness* (measured with the following affects: distress and upset, α = .74), and *Fear awareness* (measured with the following affects: fearful, scared, jittery, a = .67). Sample items are: 'Do you think that the man driving the car was distressed?' 'Do you think that the man driving the car was scared?'

The same two scales were used for testing the carryover effect: for *Distress Awareness*, aα = .69, for *Fear Awareness*, α = .55). Sample items are: 'Do you think that the boy in the picture feels upset?' 'Do you think that boy in the picture is scared?' Answers were in terms of a 5-point rating scale ranging from 1 = not at all to 5 = a lot.

RESULTS

Data were first analyzed on the basis of a unifactorial design representing the three different experimental conditions (victim—implicit narrative vs. multiple—perspectives instruction vs. victim—explicit narrative). (See table 1). Dependent variables were *positive* and *negative affective responses* associated with the behavioral episode, *awareness* of the victim's *fear* and *distress* related to both the behavioral episodes. The general pattern emerging in the means is in line with the hypotheses. At a multivariate level, a main effect emerged approaching significance, $F(10, 108) = 1.80, p = .06$.

Univariate analyses revealed significant effects on positive affective responses, $F(2, 59) = 3.17, p < .05$, on *Distress awareness* of the victim, $F(2, 59) = 3.51, p < 0.5$, and *Fear awareness* of the victim as part of the carryover effect, $F(2, 59) = 3.69, p < .05$. Finally, post-hoc analyses (see table 1) suggest that the most effective intervention to reduce positive affective responses and to enhance awareness of victimizing consequences of such behavior, is to include a victim explicit narrative. Moreover, including a multiple perspectives instruction will also result in increasing awareness of the victimizing consequences.

To explore possible interactions, a 3 (Behavioral episode: victim—implicit narrative vs. multiple—perspectives instruction vs. victim—explicit narrative) × 2 (Moral disengagement: low vs. high) design and a 3 (Behavioral episode: victim—implicit narrative vs. multiple—perspectives instruction vs. victim—explicit narrative) × 2 (Empathy towards others: low vs. high) designs were utilized. At a multivariate level no interaction nor a Disengagement or Empathy main effect emerged.[2] However, univariate analyses, which of course should be treated with caution, revealed a significant main effect indicating that high morally disengaged subjects reported more positive affect, ($M = 2.52, SD = 1.03$ vs. $M = 2.08, SD = .72, F(1,55) = 5.41, p <.01$), and an interaction effect, $F(2,55) = 3.18, p < .05$, indicating that the program is working especially for high morally disengaged subjects. These subjects, which in terms of Bandura's assumptions have a high risk of behaving in an undesiderable way, associate more positive emotions with the behavior. The interaction which is drawn graphically in figure 3 suggests that especially the victim-explicit condition for morally disengaged children results in a reduced positive affect.

DISCUSSION

A victim explicit narrative in combination with a multiple perspective instruction can contribute to influencing the relative balance between

Table 1: Means and standard deviations of affective reactions and awareness of victimization in the three experimental conditions.

Dependent variables	Behavioral Episode		
	victim implicit narrative (I)	multiple perspective instructions + I (II)	Victim explicit narrative + II (III)
Affective responses			
Positive*			
M			
SD	2.44^{a,b}	2.58^a	1.95^b
	.98	.89	.75
Negative			
M	4.17	4.09	4.24
SD	.86	.99	1.07
Victimization awareness			
Distress*			
M			
SD	3.19^a	3.01^a	3.94^b
	1.11	1.36	.96
Fear			
M	2.89	3.00	3.27
SD	1.05	.88	.84
Victimization awareness (carryover effect)			
Distress			
M			
SD			
	3.50	3.81	4.04
	1.21	.95	.95
Fear*			
M	3.29^a	3.61^{a,b}	3.97^b
SD	.89	.93	.53

Note: Higher scores represent more emotions and more awareness
Different superscripts indicate significant (LSD) differences at $p < .05$
*F positive emotions (2,59) = 3.17, $p < .05$
*F distress awareness (2,59) = 3.51, $p < .05$
*F fear awareness (2,59) = 3.69, $p < .05$

push and pull factors in a favorable direction. By clearly showing the damage caused to the victim and the negative side of behavior, the associated positive affect reduces and the victim awareness increases. These effects don't seem to be restricted to the behavior described in the program, but can be generalized to other possible dangerous behavior. Interestingly, these effects aren't also restricted to a certain category of children: they can be found with high and low morally disengaged children. The applicability of 'showing the victim' by effectively designing an early intervention has been powerfully and empirically supported. The power of the statistical testing was due to the small number of participants in the study. This was to be expected a priori due to the substantial content overlap between the experimental conditions. This

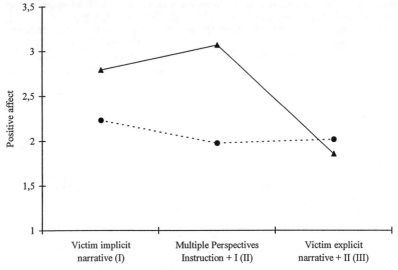

--•-- low moral disengagement --▲-- high m.d.

FIGURE 3: MEANS ON POSITIVE AFFECTIVE RESPONSES ASSOCIATED WITH THE BEHAVIORAL EPISODE: GROUP BY MORAL DISENGAGEMENT (LOW–HIGH)

research illustrates specifically the occurrence of effects on a cognitive-affective level. The underlying hypothesis is that these effects are important for the non- or occurrence of effects on 'gateway-behavior,' or even on later delinquent behavior. The testing of this hypothesis requires, as mentioned earlier, separate empirical follow-up research, in which longitudinal designs are used. In this research no behavioral-effects are mentioned, this will be surely criticized in the 'field of justice.' We don't share this opinion. Viewing the intensity and amount of this evaluated program, it seems to be naive to look for clear behavioral effects. Even stronger, the activating of clear behavioral effects, requires a much broader type and amount of intervention (Winkel, 1997). The reported results suggest that designing such interventions can produce beneficial effects in relation to 'showing the victim.'

NOTES

1 From the psychological point of view in criminal aetology 'behavioral history' is part of the so called 'big four': 'procriminal sentiments/ attitudes', 'delinquent associates' and 'personality'.
2 This could be due to the relatively small standard deviations of both scales used, (for Moral Disengagement Scale $M = 2.74$, $SD = .41$; for Empathy Scale $M = 3.66$, $SD = .68$).

REFERENCES

Agnew, R. (1991). The interactive effects of peer variables on delinquency. *Criminology, 29,* 47–72.
Akers, R.L. (1977). *Deviant Behavior: A Social-Learning Perspective.* Belmont, Ca.: Wadsworth.

Akers, R.L., Krohn, M.D., Lanza-Kaduce, L., & Radosevich, M.J. (1979). Social learning and deviant behavior: a specific test of a general theory. *American Sociological Review, 4,* 636–655.

Balm, M.-J., & Van Hest, J. (1991). '*Per ongeluk, expres, vanzelf: Waargebeurde verhalen over dingen die eigenlijk niet kunnen'. ('By accident, on purpose, by itself')* Leiden: Zorn Uitgeverij.

Bandura, A. (1973). Englewood Cliffs, N.J.: Pr.. *Aggression: A Social-learning Analysis* entice-Hall.

Bandura, A., Barbaranelli, C., Caprara, G.V., & Pastorelli, C. (1996). Mechanisms of Moral Disengagement in the Exercise of Moral Agency. *Journal of Personality and Social Psychology* (in press).

Baron, R.A., & Richardson, D.R. (1994). *Human Aggression* (2nd Edition). New York: Plenum.

Berkowitz, L. (1993). *Aggression. Its Causes, Consequences, and Control.* New York: McGraw-Hill.

Bryant, B.K. (1982). An Index of Empathy for Children and Adolescents. *Child Development, 53,* 413–425.

Caprara, G.V., Perugini, M., & Barbaranelli, C. (1994). Studies of Individual Differences in Aggression. In: M. Potegal & J.F. Knutson, (Eds.). *The Dynamics of Agression* (pp. 123–154). Hillsdale, N.J.: Lawrence Erlbaum.

Chalmers, J.B., & Townsend, M.A.R. (1990). The Effects of Training in Social Perspective Taking on Socially Maladjusted Girls. *Child Development, 61,* 178–190.

Chandler, M.J. (1973). Egocentrism and Antisocial Behavior: The Assessment and Training of Social Perspective Taking Skills. *Developmental Psychology, 9,* 326–332.

Cornish, D.B., & Clarke, R.V. (1986). (Eds.). *The Reasoning Criminal.* New York: Springer.

Dodge, K.A., & Coie, J.D. (1987). Social Information Processing Factors in reactive and proactive aggression in children and peer groups. *Journal of Personality and Social Psychology, 53,* 1146–1158.

Dodge, K.A., & Crick, N.R. (1990). Social information-processing bases of aggressive behavior in children. *Personality and Social Psychology Bulletin, 16(1),* 8–22.

Dollard, J., Doob, L.W., Miller, N.E., Mowrer, O.H., & Sears, R.R. (1939). *Frustration and Aggression.* New Haven: Yale University Press.

Elliot, D.S., Huizinga, D., & Ageton, S.S. (1985). *Explaining Delinquency and Drug Use.* Beverly Hills, Ca: Sage.

Elliot, D.S., Huizinga, D., & Menard, S. (1989). *Multiple Problem Youth: delinquency, substance use, and mental health problems.* New York: Springer.

Ellis, L. (1987). Relationships of criminality and Psychopathy with 8 other apparent behavioral manifestations of sub-optimal arousal. *Personality and Individual Differences, 8,* 905–925.

Ellis, L. (1982). Empathy: A Factor in Antisocial Behavior. *Journal of Abnormal Child Psychology, 10,*123–134.

Farley, F.H., & Farley, S.V. (1972). Stimulus-seeking motivation and delinquent behavior among institutionalized delinquent girls. *Journal of Consulting and Clinical Psychology, 39,* 94–97.

Farrington, D.P. (1983). Offending from 10 to 25 years of age. In: K van Dusen & S.A. Mednick (Eds.), *Prospective Studies of Crime and Delinquency.* Boston: Kluwer-Nijhoff.

Farrington, D.P. (1984). Delinquent and Criminal Behavior. In: A. Gale & A.J. Chapman. (Eds.), *Psychology and Social Problems* (pp. 55–79). Chichester: John Wiley.

Farrington, D.P. (1987). Early Precursors of Frequent Offending. In: Wilson, J.Q., &

Fattah, E. A. (1991). *Understanding Criminal Victimization.* Ontario: Prentice Hall.

Loury, G.C. (Eds.). *From Children to Citizens: vol 3, Families, Schools and Delinquency Prevention* (pp. 27–50). New York: Springer.

Groenhuijsen, M., & Winkel, F.W. (1994). The focusing on victims program as a new substitute penal sanction for youthful offenders: a criminal justice and a social-psychological analysis. In: G.F. Kirchhoff, E. Kosovski & H.J. Schneider, H. (Eds.), *International Debates of Victimology* (pp. 306–329). Monchengladbach: WSVN-Publishers.

Guerra, N.G., Nucci, L., & Huesmann, L.R. (1994). Moral Cognition and Childhood Aggression. In: L.R. Huesmann (Ed.), *Aggressive Behavior: Current Perspectives* (pp. 13–35). New York, N.Y.: Plenum.

Gibbs, J.C., Basinger, K.S., & Fuller, D. (1992). *Moral Maturity: Measuring the Development of Sociomoral Reflection.* Hillsdale, N.J.: Erlbaum.

Handboek Gedragstherapie (1988). *Aflevering 19*. Deventer: Kluwer.

Hewitt, J.K., Eaves, L.J., Neale, M.C., & Meyer, J.M. (1988). Resolving causes of developmental continuity or tracking: 1. Longitudinal Twin studies during growth. *Behavior Genetics, 18*, 133–151.

Huesmann, L.R. (1994). (Ed.). *Aggressive Behavior: Current Perspectives*. New York: Plenum.

Huesmann, L.R., Eron, L.D., Klein, R., Brice, P., & Fischer, P. (1983). Mitigating the imitation of aggressive behavior by changing children's attitudes about media violence. *Journal of Personality and Social Psychology, 44*, 899–910.

Kohlberg, L. (1984). *The Psychology of Moral Development: Essays on moral development*. San Francisco: Harper and Row.

Le Blanc, M., & Loeber, R. (1993). Precursors, auses, and the evelopment of riminal ffending. In: D.F. Hay & A. Angold (Eds.). *Precursors and Causes in Development and Psychopathology* (pp. 233–265). New York: Wiley.

Levine, J.D., & Singer, S.I. (1988). Delinquency, substance abuse, and risk taking in middle-class adolescents. *Behavioral Sciences and the Law, 46, 3*, 385–400.

Luengo, M.A., Otero, J.M., Carrillo-De-La-Pena, M.T., & Miron, L. (1994). Dimensions of antisocial behavior in juvenile delinquency: a Study of personality variables. *Psychology, Crime, and Law, 1*, 22–37.

Lyon, J. (1996). Introduction: Adolescents who offend. *Journal of Adolescence, 19*, 1–5.

Menard, S., & Huizinga, D. (1994). Changes in conventional attitudes and delinquent behavior in adolescence. *Youth and Society, 26*, 23–53.

Miller, P.A., & Eisenberg, N. (1988). The relation of empathy to aggressive and externalising antisocial behavior. *Psychological Bulletin, 103(3)*, 324–344.

National Center for Juvenile Justice (1995). *Juvenile offenders and victims: A focus on violence*. Pittsburgh, PA: NCJJ.

Olweus, D. (1979). Stability of aggressive reaction patterns in males: a review. *Psychological Bulletin, 86(4)*, 852–875.

Pepler, D.J., & Rubin, K.H. (1991). (Eds.) *The Development and treatment of childhood aggression*. Hillsdale, N.J.: Lawrence Erlbaum.

Richardson, D.R., Hammock, G.S., Smith, S.M., Gardner, W., & Signo, M. (1994). Empathy as a cognitive inhibitor of Interpersonal Aggression. *Aggressive Behavior, 20*, 275–289.

Rivera, B., & Widom, C.S. (1990). Childhood victimization and violent offending. *Violence and Victims, 5, 1*, 19–36.

Spinetti, J.J., & Rigler, D. (1972). The Child-Abusing parent: A psychological review. *Psychological Bulletin, 77(4)*, 29–304.

Stephenson, G.M. (1992). *The psychology of criminal justice*. Oxford, UK: Blackwell.

Sutherland, E.H., & Cressey, D.R. (1960). *Principles of criminology* (6th Edition). Chicago: Lippincott.

Thornberry, T.P. (1987). Toward an interactional theory of delinquency. *Criminology, 25*, 863–891.

Thornberry, T.P., Lizotte, A.J., Krohn, M.D., Farnworth, M., & Joon Lang, S. (1994). Delinquent peers, beliefs, and delinquent behavior: A longitudinal test of interactional theory. *Criminology, 32(1)*, 47–85.

Toch, H. (1969). *Violent Men*. Middlesex: Penguin.

Tremblay, R. (1995). Early Intervention Programs. Keynote-Address. 5th Symposium on Psychology and Law under the auspices of EAPL. Budapest: Hungary.

Tuck, M., & Riley, D. (1986). The theory of reasoned action: a decision theory of crime. In: D.B. Cornish & R.V. Clarke (Eds.), *The Reasoning Criminal* (pp. 156–169). New York: Springer.

Warr, M., & Stafford, M. (1991). The influence of delinqent peers: What they think or what they do? *Criminology, 29*, 851–865.

Widom, C.S. (1989). Does violence beget violence? A critical examination of the literature. *Psychological Bulletin, 106*, 3–28.

Winkel, F.W. (1993). Opvattingen van Jeugdige Delinquenten over Crimineel Gedrag: 2 studies naar 'gunstige definities' en gerichtheid op criminaliteit. *Tijdschrift voor Ontwikkelingspsychologie, 20*, 151–170.

Winkel, F.W. (1996). Criminal Behavior and the Pre-Victimization Process: three studies on neutrali-sation, redefinition, and desensitisation. In: S. Redondo, V. Garrido, J. Perez & R. Barbarett, (Eds.), *Advances in Psychology and Law: International Contributions.* New York, N.Y.: De Gruyter.

Winkel, F.W. (1996a). A propositional theory of Reactive Violence: some implications for controlling aggression against personnel in the mass transit system. In: G.M. Stephenson, & N. Clark, (Eds.), *Investigative and Forensic Decisionmaking.* Leicester: BPS.

Zigler, E., Taussig, C., & Black, K. (1992). Early Childhood Intervention: A promising preventative for juvenile delinquency, *American Psychologist, 47,* 997–1006.

Chapter 3

EMPATHY AND OFFENDER BEHAVIOR: THE MOTIVATIONAL CONTEXT

Adelma M. Hills

INTRODUCTION

Empathy is widely considered to be a factor in altruistic or prosocial behavior. There is, in fact, a considerable amount of research literature to support the view that empathy has this motivational function (see Batson, Turk, Shaw & Klein, 1995). Experiencing empathy for another motivates us to want to help them when they are in distress, and acts to deter behaviors that are likely to cause distress in others. As such, a lack of empathy has been postulated as part of the explanation for various forms of antisocial behavior including sexual offending, aggression and delinquency in juveniles, which should in theory be deterred by empathy (see Luengo, Otero, Carrillo-de-la-Peña & Mirón, 1994; Marshall, O'Sullivan & Fernandez, 1996). Furthermore, such is the importance attached to empathy that empathy training is included in most treatment programs for sex offenders.

THE NATURE OF EMPATHY

Empathy is a notoriously problematic concept however, and a summary of the major concerns is warranted. To begin with there is controversy over the definition of empathy, particularly about whether it is affective or cognitive in nature, and also whether it is a unidimensional or multidimensional construct. Associated with empathy is a shared emotional experience and a cognitive perspective-taking component, as well as other affective responses that include feelings of personal distress, and feelings of sympathy and compassion. Notably, the emphasis has been on negative emotions (pain and distress in others) and some theorists even appear to limit the definition of empathy to negative emotions. However, most acknowledge that we can empathize with the positive experiences of others as well, although positive empathic experience has received very little attention in the literature. It is likely that positive empathic experiences contribute to an emotional bonding with others (Staub, 1987).

The nature of empathic emotion is also debated. Is it the same emotion as that of the target, or an emotional experience that while not necessarily identical is consistent with the target's situation? A definition advanced by Martin Hoffman is arguably one of the most precise and the most useful. He defined empathy as an 'affective response more appropriate to someone else's situation than to one's own' (Hoffman, 1987, p. 48). Clearly, in this definition empathy is a congruent emotion that may or may not exactly match that of the target.

In Hoffman's conceptualization factors such as cognitive perspective-taking mediate the emotional experience and contribute to the empathic process, but they are not the empathy itself. The emotional experience constitutes the empathy, and it is the emotion that is the motivational force for subsequent behavior. Arguably, a process approach to empathy is more useful than the notion of a multidimensional construct, for the latter blurs the distinction and possible causal links between components. An unfolding process approach to empathy has also been proposed by Marshall in his work with sex offenders. His model involves four stages:

> 1) recognition of the emotional state of the observed person; 2) viewing the world from the observed person's perspective; 3) experiencing the same (or nearly the same) emotional state as the target person; and 4) deciding to respond, or not, in a way that terminates the cause of the other's distress or that consoles the other person. (Marshall et al., 1996, pp. 95–96).

Only by careful examination of the empathic process is it possible to fully appreciate the role of empathy in an individual's behavior. Two complications serve to illustrate this point. Both Hoffman and Marshall conceptualize empathy as an emotional experience congruent with that experienced by the target. This definition requires that the observer accurately apprehends the situation and emotional state of the target. It is in this context that Staub (1987) has raised the problem of false empathy. Here, the observer intends to empathize with the target, but fails to accurately perceive the target's experience, and so experiences an incongruent emotion that is not empathic even though the observer believes it is. This 'empathic' emotion is congruent with the *perceived* situation of the target, but not the actual situation. False empathy is always a very real danger, because in taking the perspective of another we tend to imagine, based on our own experience, how 'we' would think and feel in the same circumstances, which may not be what the other is thinking and feeling at all. Accurate empathy (see also Marangoni, Garcia, Ickes & Teng, 1995) requires a keen understanding of the way the target experiences the world.

A second complication arises from the proposition that both cruelty and empathy have similar origins (see Rapoport, 1974). Cruelty is exemplified in the situation where one accurately takes the perspective of the other, accurately recognizes the distressed emotional state of the other, appreciates what that state is like, but fails to empathize, and instead experiences satisfaction or pleasure from the other's suffering, and even acts to intensify or cause suffering. It is not enough, therefore, to simply distinguish between empathy and lack of empathy. Rather, it is important to distinguish between the various manifestations of lack of empathy, as distinct from false empathy and accurate empathy, for these distinctions have profound implications for the motivation and subsequent behavior of the observer. The differences are largely a function of where 'deficits' occur in the empathic process.

Another debate concerns whether empathy is dispositional or situation specific. Moreover, most measures of empathy presuppose empathy to be a trait. However, it would seem more appropriate to view empathy as both dispositional and situational. There is evidence that individuals differ in their tendency to experience empathy across different situations, and that empathy can be situation specific within individuals. At the same time characteristics of different situations render empathy more or less likely across individuals (see Davis, 1994). It behooves researchers therefore, to carefully consider which aspect they are interested in and to use appropriate measures. Global dispositional measures, although they are most often used, may well be of little value when more situation specific measures are required.

There is extensive literature relevant to these issues (see Davis, 1994). The purpose here is not to engage in further review of this literature, but rather to focus upon hitherto neglected aspects that have become apparent in several areas of empathy research. These aspects concern the motivational context in which empathy occurs.

THE MOTIVATIONAL CONTEXT OF EMPATHY: IDENTIFICATION, SELF-INTEREST, AND VALUE RELEVANCE

Work with sex offenders, for example, proceeds from the notion that deficits in empathy have both ability and motivational components. However, training programs tend to emphasize the skills involved in empathy such as emotional recognition, perspective taking, and emotional experience and expression (e.g., Marshall et al., 1996). While these are clearly important there are dangers in assuming that skills training is all that is needed, for empathy needs to be understood in the motivational context in which it occurs. To this end, it is argued that three motivational bases need to be examined: identification, self-interest, and value relevance. Diverse literature converges on the importance of these three aspects, especially recent theories on the motivational bases of attitudes and behavior (Hills, 1991, 1993), and the origins of attitude importance (Boninger, Krosnick & Berent, 1995).

Identification

It is reasonable to assume that empathy has evolved to serve a social purpose, to facilitate mutual support amongst in-group as opposed to out-group members. As such, there is a recognized bias in empathic responding. It is more strongly elicited by people who are familiar and similar to ourselves than by those who are different. Empathy even extends to non-humans when there is some basis for feeling a bond with them. Research on attitudes toward the treatment of animals (Hills, 1991, 1993, 1995) has suggested that empathy may only occur in the presence of identification with another. Identification is defined as a feeling of union between the self and the other, a feeling of 'oneness' or 'we-ness' that derives from perceived similarity or interdependence (Dovidio, 1984; Hornstein, 1976). It leads us to confer intrinsic value on the other, that is, to value the other for its own sake, not for any instrumental significance to us as a source of tangible harms and benefits. Naess (1984), in another context, that of attitudes toward the natural world, has further conceptualized identification as a process whereby the interests of the other are reacted to as if they were our own. Where there exists the opposite of identification, that is, feelings of alienation (based on perceived dissimilarity or threat), a profound barrier is created that can place the other beyond the scope of empathy. Alienation, it seems, can remove the need for concern about the other's well-being.

Recent experimental studies by Batson et al. (1995) have produced results consistent with these theoretical positions. In addition to a motivation function, Batson et al. have proposed that empathy serves an information function in that it 'carries information about the degree to which one values the other person's welfare and wants to have his or her need relieved' (p. 300). This idea of empathy as information is in accord with functional theories of emotion (e.g., Buck, 1985) that view emotion as a mechanism for providing information about motivation, that is, about the things we value and care about. Batson et al. (1995) showed by manipulating the perceived similarity between a participant and target that the welfare of a similar target was valued more than the welfare of a dissimilar target. The effects of similarity on empathy and helping supported the proposition that empathy and prosocial behavior occur when another person is perceived to be in need, and that person's welfare is valued for its own sake (as a function of similarity).

While there is evidence that perceived similarity leads to a valuing of another's welfare, and therein to the experience of empathy for them, another important factor is that of threat or conflict. Research evidence in support of this has come through another concept related to identification, that of moral exclusion (Opotow, 1990). Moral exclusion concerns one's scope of justice and occurs when individuals or groups are perceived to be outside one's moral community, and beyond the scope of prohibitions against harmful treatment, and considerations of fairness and justice. Experiments conducted by Opotow (1993), again addressing animals and the scope of justice, supported the commonly accepted proposition that moral exclusion increases as a function of conflict. However, Opotow also found a similarity by conflict interaction, which suggested that being perceived as similar leads to moral inclusion, but only in the absence of conflict. Under conditions of high conflict perceived similarity resulted in greater moral exclusion, a possible explanation being that similar competitors are seen as more likely than dissimilar competitors to be competing for the same things as oneself, therefore, they pose a potentially greater threat to one's own survival. Further evidence for the interactive nature of conflict and similarity was provided in an earlier study by Judd (1978), who found that the presence of conflict can influence actual judgments of similarity, so that 'enemies' come to be characterized in terms of their dissimilarities. Thus, feelings of alienation rather than identification predominate for enemies, with the result that empathy toward them becomes 'deactivated'.

Self interest

A fundamental consideration that cannot be overlooked where empathy is concerned is that it takes place in a motivational context where invariably there are self-interested or instrumental motives present; where one has needs, wants, and desires of one's own, in addition to whatever valuing of the other may exist. Indeed, as previously discussed, where there is conflict or a threat to one's own well-being this can bring about a devaluing of the other, leading to feelings of alienation and the suppression of empathy. Conflict and threat give primacy to self-interest, and weaken identification and empathy.

Even in the absence of overt conflict or threat, instrumental motives are implicated to some extent in most if not all situations. Moreover, there is evidence to suggest that people are aware empathy motivates helping behavior, and that they actively avoid attending to empathy inducing cues when there are costs to helping, or when empathy is likely to interfere with instrumental goals. In a study by Shaw, Batson, and Todd (1994) participants (university students) chose to listen to an empathy inducing appeal to help a homeless man much more often under conditions of low cost than of high cost. Low cost involved sending letters to potential financial sponsors of the homeless man, while high cost involved meeting the person and spending time with him.

Value relevance

A third factor that ought not be overlooked is the value relevance of empathy. There is an extensive literature to suggest that values and beliefs central to one's worldview motivate attitudes and behavior (see Boninger et al., 1995; Hills, 1991, 1993), however, their role in the empathic process has received almost no attention and has yet to be clearly established. Although speculative, it is possible to envisage a number of ways in which values might impinge on empathy. For example, people whose values emphasize individualism, dominance, and materialism or self gratification are unlikely to be very attentive to the welfare of others, and so might be restricted in their experience of identification and empathy. Similarly, a liberal versus conservative value orientation is likely to influence the extent to which people are able and willing to empathize with the disadvantaged in society. Furthermore, the values and beliefs men hold about the status and role of women in society are likely to have an impact on their motivation and ability to empathize with women, and vice versa. Finally, just as threat reduces perceived similarity, so shared values are an important source of the perceived similarity that gives rise to identification and empathy (see Perrott & Taylor, 1994).

A MODEL OF ABILITY AND MOTIVATIONAL FACTORS IN EMPATHY

The conclusion to be drawn from this analysis is that a complete understanding of empathy requires an assessment of the motivational factors operating in the situation, as well as attention to the empathic processes of emotional recognition and perspective taking. A model of the role of ability and motivational factors in empathy is proposed in Figure 1. As illustrated in the model, empathic ability is determined by emotional recognition and cognitive perspective taking. The model allows for a

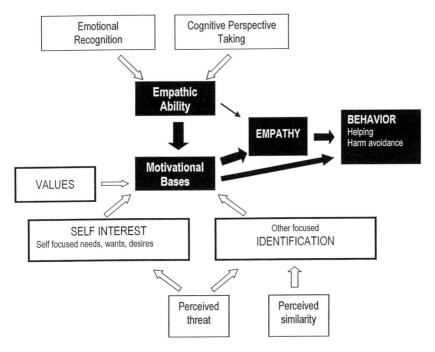

FIGURE 1: MODEL OF ABILITY AND MOTIVATIONAL FACTORS IN EMPATHY

direct path between empathic ability and empathy in accord with Hoffman's (1987) view of empathy as an innate response capable of involuntary arousal as a function of emotional recognition. For the most part, however, the effect of empathic ability on the experience of empathy is expected to be indirect, mediated by motivational factors that foster or inhibit empathic emotion. The effect of motivational factors on empathy-related behavior is mediated by empathy in the model, although a direct effect of motivational factors on behavior is also postulated. This allows, for instance, for self-interested elements of motivation to determine behavior even if contradictory empathic responses are present. Where this results in harm being done to others, such situations are likely to lead to feelings of guilt and attempts to rationalize the behavior. A direct effect of other motivational factors also accommodates the fourth step in Marshall's model, "deciding to respond, or not, in a way that terminates the cause of the other's distress or consoles the other person" (Marshall et al., 1996, p. 96). Even in the presence of empathy, other motivations may prevent the follow through to helping behavior.

Motivational bases in the model are a function of identification, self interest and values, with identification (and its opposite, alienation) largely dependent on perceived similarity. It is important to note that it is *perceived* similarity that determines identification. Hornstein (1976) has argued that perceptions of similarity and difference can be made on the basis of specific (and sometimes superficial) distinctions and are not necessarily dependent on *objective* similarities and differences. The basis of perceived similarity should always be a matter of empirical investigation. Finally, threat is also hypothesised to affect identification, in addition to having direct relevance to self interest.

The model attempts to delineate the strongest connections among the concepts. However, there are clearly problematic aspects. For example, there may well be a recursive process that can operate between empathy and identification. A direct empathic response following the recognition of emotional cues could be expected to contribute to the perceived similarity between the self and the other, thereby producing a sense of identification. Consistent with this proposition Batson et al. (1995) found support for the hypothesis that a direct manipulation of empathy would lead to increased valuing of a target person's welfare. For the most part, however, it is argued that the strongest influence is in the direction of identification/alienation facilitating or inhibiting empathy.

The model should possibly include another component between empathy and behavior, that is, those emotional states of sympathy and personal distress that can attend upon empathy (see Davis, 1994). Empathy for another in distress tends to be transformed into feelings of compassion, concern, or sympathy for the victim that motivate helping behavior. At the same time, a state of personal distress can arise in response to seeing another in extreme distress. Personal distress has been described as the self-interested aspect of empathy, for it involves a focus on one's own aversive feelings of distress, anxiety, and discomfort, and may prompt avoidance rather than helping, because the primary motivation is to relieve one's own aversive state. Arguably, there is still a need to clarify the role of these other emotional experiences in the empathic process.

IMPLICATIONS FOR CRIMINAL BEHAVIOR

Sex offenders

While acknowledging the importance of treatment programs aimed at enhancing empathic ability in sex offenders, it is clear that motivational factors ought not be overlooked. In view of the theoretical importance of identification, an important question is the extent to which offenders perceive themselves as fundamentally different from their victims. Thus, where sex offenders are concerned rather more attention needs to be focussed on establishing how offenders see their victims, that is, as persons very similar to or very different from themselves. Even more important, then, is establishing the basis of perceived differences with a view to providing information and experiences to counteract the perception. It may not be sufficient to simply encourage perspective taking ability (i.e., seeing the situation from the perspective of the victim), unless at the same time it is possible to generate a sense of the victim being someone like the self, so that the offender cares about the victim's welfare.

Hanson (in press; see also Hanson & Scott, 1995) has taken a similar theoretical position in arguing that empathic and sympathetic responses are threatened by indifferent or adversarial relationships between offender and victim. In his view, caring is the third component of empathy after perspective taking and empathic emotion. As such, therapeutic interventions are required that encourage offenders to care about their victims and to value their welfare. Whether it is possible to devise such interventions is another question. Hanson has also drawn attention to the complications that arise when male offenders perceive women as enemies, for example, because of a history of feeling humiliated by them. Hanson rightly observes that in such cases empathic ability training can be counterproductive, because the offender wants his victim to suffer. As in the case of cruelty, the more able the offender is to apprehend suffering the more he may enjoy causing it.

A second focus must be on understanding the instrumental motivations that sustain offending behavior, and how these interact with empathy. The importance of self-interested motives suggests that empathy skills training should proceed in the context of simultaneous attention to the instrumental outcomes of the offending behavior for the offender. Even if empathy training enhances empathic ability, and a sense of identification is engendered, the person still has the option of actively avoiding empathy inducing cues whenever instrumental motives predominate. Greater awareness of the empathic process could even facilitate such avoidance. It is naïve to believe, therefore, that an increased capacity for victim empathy following therapeutic interventions will necessarily prevent or reduce offending behavior.

The importance of understanding instrumental motives is further apparent in the situation where motives of sexual gratification, for instance, prevail even though conflicting empathic emotions are also present. Hanson (in press) has noted that under these circumstances an increased ability to empathize could again be counterproductive, as it may increase feelings of guilt and shame. An individuals' efforts to cope with shame in particular can be characterised by withdrawal, hostility, defensive rationalisations, and victim blaming, rather than sympathy and helping.

Juvenile offenders

Another area that could well stand to benefit from an understanding of the role of empathy is that of juvenile delinquency and offending. The problem of juvenile crime is a major community concern in Australia at the present time, particularly with respect to young Aboriginal offenders (Chappell & Wilson, 1994). Many young Aboriginal people appear to have a profound sense of alienation from the non-Aboriginal population that can be expected to preclude an experience of empathy for their victims. It is also likely that the reverse applies: the sense of alienation that many in the non-Aboriginal population have for Aboriginal people precludes them experiencing empathy in response to the situation faced by many young Aboriginals. In this area, therefore, there is merit in trying to identify the precise sources of a sense of alienation—on both sides—with a view to targeting them in offender rehabilitation and community education programs. Incidentally, while the problem may be exacerbated with Aboriginal juveniles, similar issues arise with juvenile offenders per se, that is, in terms of how they perceive, and are perceived by people in the mainstream community.

The role of conflict or threat is important in this context not only from the point of view of young Aboriginals who might see themselves in conflict with non-Aboriginal society, but also from the point of view of other Australians who might perceive young Aboriginal people as posing a threat to them. The apparent lack of empathy shown by Aboriginal juveniles for members of mainstream society (e.g., the police, innocent victims killed in stolen car chases, and victims of violent assault) almost certainly contributes to a sense of alienation from them on the part of other Australians. This alienation may transcend that experienced toward other juvenile offenders whose motives are seen more in terms of self interest. Once entrenched, feelings of alienation can inhibit empathic responses on both sides, leading to escalating conflict, aggression, and intolerance.

It is in this area too that the importance of values arises. If Aboriginal and non-Aboriginal Australians have, or perceive themselves as having, fundamentally different values this itself can be a basis of perceived dissimilarity, feelings of alienation, and a reciprocal lack of empathy. Moreover, the same argument can be applied to juvenile offenders per se, especially if they see themselves as members of a juvenile in-group that is detached from the mainstream adult out-group. Research is needed to identify the value systems that exist, and to address seriously the question of whether one group really is incomprehensible to the other, or whether there are any bases of commonality that allow for channels of communication to be opened and utilized.

There are two other potentially important research questions that follow from the in-group, out-group dichotomy. The first is whether juvenile offenders have a generalized empathy deficit, or whether they are capable of empathizing normally with members of their in-group. A related question—if it is indeed the case that juvenile delinquents do not care about their victim's welfare—is who or what, if anything, do they care about? Some understanding of the answer to these questions must have implications for the way we attempt to deal with the problem of juvenile crime and delinquency.

CONCLUSION

The purpose of this paper has been to review some of the issues surrounding empathy and to draw attention to the motivational context in which it occurs, since this has tended to be neglected in both the literature and in applied areas such as empathy training for sex offenders. Arguably, there is a need for greater awareness of the nature of empathy and the complexities of the empathic process, with this need being manifest in three areas:

a) the conceptual and theoretical understanding of empathy;
b) research into the empathic process, with special attention to issues of how empathy is measured in specific situations;
c) the application of empathy to practical problems, including its use in intervention programs.

The model of ability and motivational factors in empathy that has been proposed is offered both as a theoretical foundation from which to systematically examine empathy and related constructs, and as a framework to guide therapeutic interventions. This more expansive conceptualization of empathy raises issues for consideration in established areas such as empathy training for sex offenders, and provides new perspectives on interventions with other offender populations, especially juvenile offenders.

REFERENCES

Batson, C.D., Turk, C.L., Shaw, L.L., & Klein, T.R. (1995). Information function of empathic emotion: Learning that we value the other's welfare. *Journal of Personality and Social Psychology, 68*, 200–313.

Buck, R. (1985). Prime theory: An integrated view of motivation and emotion. *Psychological Review, 92*, 389–413.

Boninger, D.S., Krosnick, J.A., & Berent, M.K. (1995). Origins of attitude importance: Self-interest, social identification, and value relevance. *Journal of Personality and Social Psychology, 68*, 61–80.

Chappell, D., & Wilson, P. (1994). *The Australian Criminal Justice System: The mid 1990s*. Sydney: Butterworths.

Davis, M.H. (1994). *Empathy: A social psychological approach*. Dubuque, IA: Wm. C. Brown.

Dovidio, J.F. (1984). Helping behavior and altruism: An empirical and conceptual overview. In: L. Berkowitz (Ed.), *Advances in experimental social psychology* (pp. 361–427). Vol. 17. New York: Academic Press.

Hanson, R.K. (in press). Assessing sexual offenders' capacity for empathy. Psychology, *Crime and Law*.

Hills, A.M. (1991). *The motivational bases of attitudes toward animals, and their relationship to attitude structure and dynamics*. Unpublished doctoral dissertation, Curtin University of Technology, Bentley, Western Australia.

Hills, A.M. (1993). The motivational bases of attitudes toward animals. *Society and Animals, 1*, 111–128.

Hills, A.M. (1995). Empathy and belief in the mental experience of animals. *Anthrozoös, 8*, 132–142.

Hoffman, M.L. (1987). The contribution of empathy to justice and moral judgement. In: N. Eisenberg & J. Strayer (Eds.), *Empathy and its development* (pp. 47–80). Cambridge: Cambridge University Press.

Hornstein, H.A. (1976). *Cruelty and kindness: A new look at aggression and altruism*. Englewood Cliffs, New Jersey: Prentice Hall.

Judd, C.M. (1978). Cognitive effects of attitude and conflict resolution. *Journal of Conflict Resolution, 22*, 483–498.

Luengo, M.A., Otero, J.M., Carrillo-de-la-Peña, M.T., & Mirón, L. (1994). Dimensions of antisocial behavior in juvenile delinquents: A study of personality variables. *Psychology, Crime and Law, 1*, 27–37.

Marangoni, C., Garcia, S., Ickes, W., & Teng, G. (1995). Empathic accuracy in a clinically relevant setting. *Journal of Personality and Social Psychology, 68*, 854–869.

Marshall, W.L., O'Sullivan, C., & Fernandez, Y.M. (1996). The enhancement of victim empathy among incarcerated child molesters. *Legal and Criminological Psychology, 1*, 95–102.

Naess, A. (1984). Identification as a source of deep ecological attitudes. In: M. Tobias (Ed.), *Deep ecology* (pp. 256–270). San Diego, CA: Avant Books.

Opotow, S. (1990). Moral exclusion and injustice: An introduction. *Journal of Social Issues, 46*, 1–20.

Opotow, S. (1993). Animals and the scope of justice. *Journal of Social Issues, 49*, 71–85.

Perrott, S.B., & Taylor, D.M. (1994). Ethnocentrism and authoritarianism in the police: Challenging stereotypes and reconceptualizing ingroup identification. *Journal of Applied Social Psychology,* *24,* 1640–1664

Rapoport, A. (1974). Conflict in man-made environments. Baltimore: Penguin.

Shaw, L.L., Batson, C.D., & Todd, R.M. (1994). Empathy avoidance: Forestalling feeling for another in order to escape the motivational consequences. *Journal of Personality and Social Psychology,* *67,* 879–887.

Staub, E. (1987). Commentary on Part I. In: N. Eisenberg & J. Strayer (Eds.), *Empathy and its development* (pp. 103–115). Cambridge: Cambridge University Press.

Chapter 4

SOCIAL INFORMATION PROCESSING IN BULLIES, VICTIMS, AND COMPETENT ADOLESCENTS[1]

Thomas Bliesener and Friedrich Lösel

INTRODUCTION

Juvenile violence is a major social problem in many countries (e.g., Loeber & Farrington, 1998; Pfeiffer, 1997). This also holds for bullying and other forms of aggressive behavior at school (e.g., Olweus, 1994; Smith et al., 1998). In Germany, for example, various longitudinal surveys indicate a moderate increase in violence and delinquency among students (Lösel, Bliesener & Averbeck, 1998; Mansel & Hurrelmann, 1998; Tillman, 1997). Although it is unclear how far increases may be due to a heightened awareness of violence as well as to specific assessment methods (Lösel, 1995), many teachers, school administrators, parents, and students report negative experiences in this field (e.g., Funk, 1995; O'Moore & Hillery, 1989; Schwind, 1995; Slee, 1993; Smith & Erth, 1994; Whitney & Smith, 1993). Single cases of severe injuries or suicides among persistently victimized students are only the peak of everyday aggression among youngsters.

Due to the public concern with this problem, research on violence at school has expanded substantially. Of particular interest is the exhibition of persistent aggression against other students who have less power and frequently become victimized. This bullying goes beyond forms of rough-and-tumble play and is related to the field of serious and violent offending. Studies have examined the behavioral, personality, family, and other characteristics of typical bullies (e.g., Besag, 1989; Callaghan & Joseph, 1995; Farrington, 1992; Haapasalo & Tremblay, 1994; Killias & Rabasa, 1997; Loeber & Hay, 1997; Lösel, Averbeck & Bliesener, 1997; Olweus, 1994; Rigby & Cox, 1996; Slee, 1995a). For example, they are a little stronger, more dominant, impulsive, and less empathic than other students. They more often come from difficult families with an aggressive and inconsistent style of education. Their aggressive behavior is relatively stable over time. It is also not limited to the school context but relates to general delinquency and crime.

Although there are various correlates of victimization too, the picture seems to be less clear here. This may be due to heterogeneity within the group of victims (e.g., juveniles who are or who are not aggressive themselves). Persistently victimized students tend to be younger than their attackers and to have a weaker physical constitution (Lagerspetz, Björkqvist, Bert & King, 1982; Lowenstein, 1977; Killias & Rabasa, 1997; Olweus, 1979, 1984, 1994). Findings on the otherness of victims are inconsistent: Whereas Lagerspetz et al. (1982) reported a higher rate of physical problems such as obesity, speech impairments, and the like in a group of victimized Norwegian students, Olweus (1979) found no differences in comparison to nonvictimized students. A clearer picture has been generated by studies on social and personality characteristics of victims (Bowers, Smith & Binney, 1994; Deluty, 1981; Lösel, Bliesener & Averbeck, 1997; Perry, Kusel & Perry, 1988). For example, victimized students tend to be socially less will-integrated, more anxious, less self-confident, and more submissive in conflict situations than their nonvictimized peers.

This kind of research shifts the focus to the interactive conditions involved in acts of violence between bullies and victims (see Bandura, 1997; Boulton, 1993; Dodge, 1986; Krappmann & Oswald, 1995; Lösel, 1995; Pepler & Craig, 1995). The difficulties of students in social behavior have been traced back particularly to cognitive factors. Crick and Dodge (1994; Dodge & Crick, 1990) have integrated numerous findings into a theoretical model of social information processing. They argue that an individual has to:

a) perceive and encode the situational and social cues;
b) produce a mental representation and interpretation of the situation;
c) set own goals for the interaction;
d) develop possible responses to the situation;
e) evaluate these possible reactions; and finally,
f) carry out a response that seems to be adequate and efficacious.

Aggressive behavior may result from deficits and distortions at all of these levels of information processing and action generation.

For example, it has been confirmed repeatedly that aggressive children and adolescents exhibit specific problems. When interpreting situations they frequently prove to be less able to adopt a social perspective. That is, they have deficits in recognizing the intentions and motives of their social partners (intention-cue detection: Dodge, Murphy & Buchsbaum, 1984; Dodge, Price, Bacharowski & Newman, 1990). Studies have also reported that aggressive children and adolescents exhibit a specific distortion in their interpretations of the intentions of a social partner in ambiguous situations known as the hostile attributional bias (Coie, Dodge, Terry & Wright, 1991; Dodge & Tomlin, 1987; Guerra & Slaby, 1990; Nasby, Hayden & DePaulo, 1979; Slaby & Guerra, 1988). During the goal-setting phase, aggressive children and adolescents often generate less competent solutions (Renshaw & Asher, 1983), although they have just as many response alternatives at their disposal as their nonaggressive peers (Asarnow & Callan, 1985). However, the response alternatives they develop exhibit less variety (Rubin, Bream & Krasnor, 1991) and are more impulsive and physically or verbally aggressive (Klicpera & Gasteiger-Klicpera, 1996). When selecting and evaluating responses, antisocial juveniles' anticipations of their consequences are more short-term and less differentiated (Crick & Dodge, 1989; Gottfredson & Hirschi, 1990; Lösel, 1975). This is also supported by empirical studies revealing that aggressive adolescents anticipate more positive consequences of aggressive responses (Bernfeld & Peters, 1986; Deluty, 1983, 1985; Perry & Rasmussen, 1986). Likewise, they also rate the efficacy of their aggressive reactions more positively (Garber, Quiggle, Pank & Dodge, 1991; Perry et al., 1986).

Compared with conspicuously aggressive or normal students, victimized students build up fewer response alternatives for tackling conflict situations, tend to expect adults to intervene in the conflict situation, and report markedly lower expectations regarding the efficacy of self-confident and assertive behavior (Asher, Renshaw & Geraci, 1980; Crick & Ladd, 1991; Rubin, 1982; Wustmans & Becker, 1997).

These and other results have demonstrated that sociocognitive factors play an important role in explaining juvenile violence (see Crick & Dodge, 1994). Programs on social information processing also seem to be rather promising in the field of prevention and intervention (see Lösel, 1996; Tremblay & Craig, 1995). However, the cognitive approach should not be viewed in isolation, but within the context of other influences (e.g., family processes, informal social control, developmental psychopathology). More research is needed that demonstrates generalizable results over different cultures, institutional contexts, age groups, degrees of violence, varied methods, and so forth. The main focus is still on the information processing of aggressors and their deficits. Less is known about related cognitive processes of victims or about competencies for nonviolent conflict resolution. Against this background, we included the sociocognitive approach as one level of explanation in a comprehensive study of aggression among students in Germany (Bliesener & Lösel,

2000). The present paper reports some descriptive results on violence at school and compares characteristics of information-processing in different groups. These groups are:

a) bullies;
b) victims;
c) students who are both frequently aggressive and victimized ('bully/victims');
d) nondeviant ('normal') students; and
e) particularly socially competent students.

Findings presented here are taken from the first part of our study, a screening in schools.

METHOD

Sample

A total of 1,163 male and female students attending 52 seventh- and eighth-grade classes at 11 secondary schools in the Bavarian cities of Nuremberg and Erlangen completed written questionnaires in their classes. Their mean age was 14.0 years (SD = .89). The percentage of non-German students was 25.6. The sample can be considered to be broadly representative of the student population of the two cities, the main types of school (Hauptschule, Realschule and Gymnasium), and the 7th and 8th grades.

Instruments

We assessed experience of violence from the bully, victim, and observer perspective with a specially adapted short form of the 'Bully/Victim Questionnaire' of Olweus (1989). We asked how far adolescents directly or indirectly either pestered other or were pestered themselves at school or on the way to and from school. According to factor analyses, the 51 items can be grouped into three scales (Bliesener & Lösel, 2000): *Physical Aggression* (hitting, kicking, locking someone in [e.g., not letting a fellow student leave the classroom], damaging the property of others either individually or in group, carrying weapons, threatening with weapons); *Verbal Aggression/Tolerance of Violence* (verbal provocation, teasing, pleasure in oppressing others, positive attitude to violence); and *Victimization* (passive exposure to physical and verbal violence, rejection and exclusion from cliques of fellow students). Whereas the first two factors correlated (.77), both were independent from the third factor.

We surveyed individual levels of mediatory and *competent behavior* in interpersonal conflicts with the scale on conflict management taken from the Interpersonal Competence Questionnnaire developed by Buhrmester, Furman, Wittenberg & Reis (1988).

In addition to the self-reports on social behavior, we also developed a procedure for teachers in which they had to use a Q-sort technique to allocate each student in the class on 7-point scales (see Lösel, 1975). These scales covered the following five dimensions of social behavior: *social competence, aggressiveness, popularity, impulsivity,* and *dominance.*

Alongside the measures of aggression and other forms of social behavior, we applied a series of standardized instruments assessing potential causes and correlates. These included, for example, demographic characteristics, family climate, school climate, leisure time activities, coping styles, and emotional and behavioral problems. These findings are reported in Bliesener and Lösel (2000) and Lösel et al. (1995, 1997). For the topic of this report on *social information processing*, we used a specially developed seminstructured procedure. Three typical interpersonal conflict scenarios for adolescents were presented in the following form (to save space, we present only the boys' version here):

1. You are standing around in the schoolyard with several other students. Then Klaus comes up to you. You've never got on very well with Klaus. He jostles you and says, 'You're in for it today!'
2. Heike, a girl in your class, has invited you to her party next weekend. This afternoon, when school's over, Heike and Bernd come up to you. Heike says, 'I'm sorry, but you can't come to my party after all.' Bernd nods his head, and says with a smirk, 'Oh, what a pity!'
3. Last week, your class went on a school trip. Each of you bought a soft drink. Michael wanted a drink too, but he didn't have enough money. You gave him what he needed. Today, you are standing around with several other students, and you ask Michael for your money back. He says, 'There's no need to make such a fuss about a few pennies!'

After reading each scenario, the adolescents had to give unstructured answers to questions on how they perceived the situation, what their reaction would be, and what consequences it would have.

These unstructured answers were coded according to categories of social information processing. The category system referred to the following stages:

a) *Interpretation of the situation*, that is, attributions regarding the causes of conflict (biased perception of hostility from others, emphasis on one's own contribution to the conflict);
b) *Clarification of goals* for managing the conflict (egocentric goal assertion, giving up one's own goals, trying to understand the situation/deescalation);
c) *Response access or construction* (impulsive-uncontrolled reactions, situation-clarifying, competent reactions); and
d) *Response decision* (anticipation of positive and negative consequences).

The objectivity of this coding was satisfactory. Levels of agreement ranged from 75.0 to 89.1%.

Selection of subgroups

To examine how far specific aspects of social information processing relate to aggression, victimization, or competent resolution of conflict, the sample was split into subgroups. These subgroups were formed on the basis of the following five criteria:

a) self-reported active experience of aggression (sum index of the first two scales in the bullying questionnaire);
b) teacher ratings on aggressiveness;
c) self-reported social competence (on the conflict management scale);
d) teacher ratings on social competence; and
e) self-reported degree of victimization (third scale in the bullying questionnaire).

The *bully* group contained those students with high scores on Criteria 1 and 2 and only moderate to low scores on the other three criteria. Students with high scores on Criteria 1,2, and 5 were viewed as aggressive victims and labeled *bully/victims*, those with high scores on Criterion 5, as nonaggressive *victims*, and those with high scores on Criteria 3 and 4 were labeled *competent* students. In all groups, the cut-off for a high score was set at the upper one quarter (75th percentile) of the gender-specific score distribution. Finally, for purposes of comparison, a so-called *normal* group was selected with mid-range scores (25th–75th percentile) on all criteria. To obtain similar proportions of boys and girls in the groups,

32 girls were dropped at random from the normal group and 15 girls from the competent one.

Data on the prevalence of violence

As could be anticipated (Coie & Dodge, 1997), there were marked gender differences in the experience of violence in this age group. A total of 26.9% of boys reported that they had experienced violence in their school or class 'frequently,' 'very frequently,' or 'all the time' (alongside 33.1% 'occasionally,' 40.0% 'hardly ever' or 'never') compared with only 14.9% of girls (alongside 30.2% 'occasionally,' 54.3% 'hardly ever' or 'never'). When asked which aggressive actions they had exhibited themselves toward a fellow student during the last 6 months, both genders revealed a predominance of milder forms of aggression such as teasing and verbal attacks. Table 1 shows exemplary results for 5 items. Physical violence in the form of hitting and kicking took a close second place in the order of frequency among boys. Boys generally showed higher prevalence rates on all five forms of aggression studied. However, girls came close to the frequency of the boys in verbal aggression (see Arora & Thompson, 1987).

Passive experience of violence also revealed a higher prevalence for the milder forms of aggression as well as higher percentages for boys (see Table 2). The proportion of students engaging in hitting and kicking was higher than the corresponding proportion of victims, whereas proportions of victims were higher for vandalism directed toward fellow students.

Although girls reported lower victimization rates across all forms of aggression, they nonetheless exhibited a much higher fear of victimization. Indeed, 14.4% reported that they 'often,' 'very often,' or 'always' were afraid of violence in their school or class (alongside 16.5% 'occasionally,' 69.1% 'hardly ever' or 'never'), whereas only 5.6% of boys reported such high levels of fear (alongside 13.2% 'occasionally,' 81.2% 'hardly ever' or 'never').

Characteristics of the five groups

Table 3 reports various characteristics of the selected groups. The groups of persistent bullies and victims were similarly large. Each of them represented about 5% of the whole sample. Only approximately 2% of the students showed high scores in aggression as well as in victimization (bully/victims). Age revealed a tendency known from other studies for

Table 1: Frequencies of various forms of aggression at school for boys (above) and girls (below).

		Never	Once or twice	More than twice	Once a week	More than once a week
1.	How often have you hit or kicked	35.5	44.2	12.4	4.1	3.8
	another student yourself?	73.5	20.8	4.0	0.5	1.1
2.	How often have you threatened or	86.8	8.4	2.0	0.8	2.0
	locked in another student?	94.5	3.8	1.1	0.2	0.4
3.	How often have you teased another student	32.2	38.2	16.5	6.2	6.9
	or said horrible things to him or her?	43.7	39.5	11.7	1.6	3.5
4.	How often have you intentionally broken	86.9	8.7	1.8	0.8	1.8
	something belonging to another student?	94.5	4.6	0.7	0.0	0.2
5.	How often have you threatened another	93.5	3.8	1.5	0.7	0.7
	student with a weapon?	98.7	0.7	0.2	0.2	0.2

Table 2: Frequencies of victimization through various forms of aggression at school for boys (above) and girls (below).

		Never	Once or twice	More than once	Once a week	More than once a week
1.	How often have you been hit or kicked	52.0	34.6	9.2	2.1	2.1
	by other students?	77.6	18.2	2.7	0.4	1.1
2.	How often have you been threatened or	81.0	14.9	2.8	0.3	1.0
	locked in by other students?	88.5	9.3	1.1	0.4	0.7
3.	How often have you been teased by other	31.5	39.5	16.6	3.8	8.7
	students or have they said horrible things to you?	38.7	39.6	13.0	2.7	6.0
4.	How often have other students intentionally	77.3	16.3	4.1	1.1	1.1
	broken something belonging to you?	84.2	13.1	1.6	0.5	0.5
5.	How often have you been threatened with a	93.5	4.2	1.1	0.7	0.5
	weapon by other students?	99.3	0.4	0.0	0.2	0.2

bullies to belong to the older and victims to the younger students in the class (see Olweus, 1984). However, these differences were not significant in the present study. Nationality also revealed only a nonsignificant trend: German adolescents were slightly under-represented in the bully group and overrepresented among the victims.

In contrast to these variables, the subgroups did reveal significant differences in school grades. Whereas competent students always had the best grades, bullies showed deficits in major academic subjects like English language and mathematics. The students in the victim group also tended to have poor grades, and these were significantly worse than those of competent students. They also tended to be physically less fit: together with the bully/victim group, victims had the lowest grades in sports, whereas the bullies performed slightly better. In summary, the comparison of school

Table 3: Gender distribution, age, nationality, academic performance and teacher ratings of social behavior in the subgroups.

	Bullies	Victims	Bully/ Victims	Normals	Competents
	n = 61	n = 60	n = 25	n = 138	n = 61
Proportion of boys	68.9%	65.0%	64.0%	67.4%	67.2%
Mean age	14.3	13.9	13.9	14.1	13.9
Proportion of German-national students	68.9%	85.0%	80.0%	73.9%	80.3%
School grades[1]:					
– German	3.5_a	3.5_a	3.3_a	3.3_a	2.8_b
– English	3.8_a	3.5_{ab}	3.3_{ab}	3.2_b	2.7_c
– Mathematics	3.7_a	3.5_{ab}	3.7_{ab}	3.3_b	2.7_c
– Sports	2.0_{ac}	2.3_{bc}	2.4_c	1.9_a	1.8_a
Teacher ratings of social behavior:					
– Impulsivity	5.49_a	3.73_b	5.20_a	3.51_b	3.05_c
– Dominance	5.08_a	3.37_b	4.58_c	3.61_b	4.16_c
– Popularity	4.07_a	3.25_b	3.76_a	3.89_a	4.57_c

Note: Values marked with different indices differ significantly ($p \leq .05$; χ^2 test or Duncan test).
[1] German school grades range from 1 (very good) to 6 (failure)

grades produced a picture of deviant students who may have deficits in cognitive performance.

Significant group differences were also found in the teacher ratings of social behavior. As Table 3 shows, teachers clearly attributed problems of impulsivity and dominance to the bullies; however, they did not rate them as unpopular. Similar characteristics appeared for the bullies who had also been frequently victimized. In contrast, pure victims were rated as relatively non-dominant, unpopular, and less impulsive, but they did not differ significantly from the normal group in impulsivity and dominance. The competent students on the other hand were rated as least impulsive, most popular and moderately dominant compared to the other groups.

Group differences in social information processing
To find out how far our groups differed in social information processing, we analyzed the answers to the fictious conflict scenarios. Table 4 reports the means of various cognitive variables in the three scenarios. Unexpectedly, there were no significant differences between groups in hostility bias. Neither bullies nor victims exhibited a higher level than the normal or competent groups. There were slight differences regarding emphasis on one's own contribution to the causes of the conflict: bullies, as anticipated, produced lower scores. However, a particularly strong emphasis on one's own contribution, as observed in traumatized victims of

Table 4: Subgroup comparison of characteristics of social information processing.

	Bullies	Victims	Bully/ Victims	Normals	Competents
Interpretation of situation:					
- Hostility bias	2.15	2.03	1.68	2.14	2.36
- Emphasis on own contribution	2.31$_a$	2.20$_a$	2.96$_b$	2.27$_a$	2.52
Clarification of goals:					
- Egocentrism/Intention to do harm	1.59$_a$	1.12$_b$	1.40	1.11$_b$	1.33
- Understanding of situation/Deescalation	.72$_a$	1.18$_b$	.72	1.06$_b$	1.15$_b$
- Abandoning own goals	.10	.12	.08	.09	.16
Response access of construction:					
- Impulsive reactions	2.75$_a$	.72$_b$	2.20$_a$	.85$_b$	.56$_b$
- Clarification, information-seeking	.90$_a$	1.82$_{bc}$	1.12$_a$	1.65$_b$	2.05$_c$
- Number of response alternatives	4.85	5.42	5.04	4.53$_a$	5.66$_b$
Response decision:					
- Anticipation of positive consequences	.51$_a$	.80	.40	.54$_a$	.90$_b$
- Anticipation of negative consequences	1.69	1.67	1.92	1.70	1.74
Positive consequences of impulsive reactions[1]	13.26$_a$	2.98$_c$	8.92$_b$	3.91$_c$	2.39$_c$

Note: Value marked with different indices differ significantly (p ≤ .05; Duncan test).
[1] See text for explanation of interaction term.

violence (Falsetti & Resick, 1995; Mittendoff, 1995), could not be ascertained in our victim group. In contrast, it was the aggressive victims who revealed significantly higher scores than bullies, victims, or normal students.

The reported goals of interaction revealed clear and significant differences between groups. As anticipated, the groups with a lot of experience as bullies exhibited a notably stronger tendency to assert their own goals without considering the interests of their conflict partners. This tendency was much less marked not only in victims but also in the normal group. The competent students took an intermediate position. The relation was almost completely inverted for individual goals directed toward an understanding of the situation, the motives of the conflict partner, as well as mediation and deescalation of the conflict. Bullies and bully/victims reported such interaction goals significantly less frequently than victims, whereas competent students reported them significantly more frequently. In contrast, there were no group differences regarding abandoning one's own goals. The expectation that victims would be more willing to abandon their goals rashly and adapt to the goals of their conflict partners could not be confirmed. However, it has to be considered here that goals in this category are hardly ever reported (see Table 4). So this finding could also be due to the low base rate and small variance.

The clearest differences of all between groups were found for spontaneous responses, particularly for impulsive, uncontrolled reactions. As anticipated, the two groups with predominantly aggressive behavior patterns were also those who reported far more rash reactions triggered by internal impulses in response to the conflict scenarios. The other three groups exhibited broadly comparable scores. The extent of competent, mediatory behavior in the form of inquiring and explaining took the opposite direction: there were markedly lower scores in the bully group and the bully/victim group compared with a broadly unanimous higher level in the other groups. The competent students had the anticipated maximum score. However, groups with problems in social behavior did not differ from the other two groups in the number of action alternatives they reported. Thus, this finding, which has been ascertained previously in aggressive adolescents (Asarnow & Callan, 1985), is confirmed for the victims of interpersonal violence as well.

Turning to the anticipation of consequences of one's own actions in the conflict situation, the competent students reported more positive consequences than the bullies, but also more than the normal group. In contrast, groups were homogeneous in terms of expecting negative consequences. We compiled an index for anticipated positive consequences combined with own impulsive reactions (interaction term of both variables). This revealed a clear difference between groups (see Table 4). A more detailed comparison between observed frequencies of combinations of these dichotomized variables and their expected frequencies confirmed the following assumptions: bullies frequently anticipated positive consequences of their own impulsive reactions, but tended to be skeptical about the consequences of nonimpulsive reactions. The majority of bully/victims reported impulsive reactions, but anticipated negative consequences. The situation was completely opposite in competent students: they hardly ever exhibited impulsive reactions, but had more favorable expectations regarding the consequences of their actions. However, the idea that victims more frequently anticipate negative consequences, regardless of how they act in the situation, could not be confirmed.

DISCUSSION

The prevalence data show that milder forms of aggression such as teasing or saying horrible things are dominant in both active aggression and in experiences of victimization. This agrees with findings from other German and international studies (see, e.g., Hoover, Oliver & Hazler, 1992; Niebel, Hanewinkel & Ferstl, 1993; O'Moore & Hillery, 1992; Schwind,

1995; Sharp, 1995; Todt & Busch, 1996). Nonetheless, approximately 65% of male adolescents report that they have hit or kicked others at least once or twice in the past 6 months, and almost 8% of them report that they engage in such behavior at least once a week. Whereas the former percentage is higher than that in several other studies from German-speaking countries (e.g., Killias, 1995; Meier, Melzer, Schubarth & Tillmann, 1995), our prevalence rates for persistent behavior are very consistent with other German findings (e.g., Hanewinkel & Knaack, 1997; Tillmann, 1997; Todt & Busch, 1996; for an overview, see Lösel & Bliesener, 1998). The differential prevalence rates in the field of occasional use of violence may be due, in part, to nuances in the formulation of items, the survey context, confidentiality, and so forth.

The prevalence data in our study are also very similar to those found internationally. Eleven percent of our students report being exposed to verbal bullying often (at least once a week) and 26.9% occasionally; whereas 6.5% admit exposure to physical bullying frequently and 16.3% occasionally (Lösel, Averbeck & Bliesener, 1997). In the Irish study, the prevalence for frequent serious bullying was 8% (O'Moore & Hillery, 1989). Perry, Kusel and Perry (1988) found that 10% of a sample of American students were victims of frequent, not just verbal, bullying; and 8.4% of the students in an Australian study (Slee, 1995b) reported that they were frequent victims of serious bullying. Roughly similar levels are also found in Norwegian and Swedish studies (Olweus, 1991; Roland, 1989). In contrast, higher prevalences have been reported in England (e.g., Lane, 1989; Smith, 1991; Stephenson & Smith, 1989). However, particularly when carrying out international comparisons, it is necessary to take account of differences in survey methods, definitions, and the specific connotations of the terms used. Even when surveys are based on identical instruments, comparability cannot always be taken for granted (van Dijk, Mayhew & Killias, 1990).

The exposure of boys is continuously higher, for both the active exercise of violence and the direct, passive experience of it. However, such gender differences are small or disappear for those forms of victimization that include indirect aggressions such as exclusion and denigration (Averbeck, Bliesener, Liehmann & Lösel, 1996). This indicates that it may be that girls are not generally less aggressive but use different ways to express their hostility to other students (Popp, 1997). Although girls report less active and passive aggression, they seem to be much more afraid of violence than boys. This is in line with gender-specific differences in fear of crime (see Bilsky, Pfeiffer & Wetzels, 1993; Kury, 1995). The stronger perception of threat may be due, on the one hand, to the imbalance in physical strength causing the girls' perception of violence to be shaped more by qualitative rather than quantitative aspects. On the other hand, physical aggressions are much taken for granted among boys in the line with their social roles (rough-and-tumble play, see Oswald, 1996; Pellegrini, 1989).

That age does not differentiate significantly between bullies and victims may be due, in part, to the relatively small group sizes and low range in our study.

It is interesting to see that the proportion of active aggression is higher in hitting and kicking than the corresponding proportions of victimization. This indicates aggression by groups and concentration on selected victims as described in the concept of bullying. In contrast, proportions of victimization are higher for vandalism against fellow students. In this case, an inverse victim-bully relation as found in hitting/kicking hardly seems plausible. Perhaps, different patterns of interpretation are involved in these two findings. According to self-perception theory (Bem, 1972), adolescents may tend to emphasize their own active involvement in the aftermath of a physical conflict, while tending to play down similar attacks on their own person. In cases of destruction of property, the action tends to be evaluated as nonintentional and inadvertent from the actor's perspective, whereas persons whose property has been damaged tend to interpret the action as intentional and thus view themselves as victims.

A more detailed inspection of the prevalence data of Tables 2 and 3 shows that response frequencies do not reveal a discrete drop in the quantifiers as would be expected by the inverted J curve that is typical for normative behavior. In our results, there is a slight increase in frequencies at the upper end (several times per week). This pattern has also been observed in research on delinquency (Moffitt, 1993). It points to a subgroup of persistently exposed students. These particularly marked cases of bullies and victims form a substantial part of our subgroups.

The subgroups of persistent bullies and victims indentified here each make up about 5% of the total sample. This is in line with the prevalence rates found in several international studies (e.g., Hanewinkel & Knaack, 1997; Olweus, 1994; O'Moore & Hillery, 1989). The characteristics of these groups are mostly consistent with the literature. This indicates that our classification of subsamples for comparing social information processing is adequate.

The bullies' achievement at school is relatively poor. This confirms general results on academic deficits of seriously antisocial juveniles (e.g., Farrington, 1992). However, the bullies do not differ from the normal and competent students in their sports grades. Here, the victims and bully/victims are significantly worse. Although we did not measure body build or strength in this part of the research project (see Bliesener & Lösel, 2000), these results on sports grades fit indirectly into correlations between physical constitution and violence (e.g., Killias & Rabasa, 1997; Olweus, 1994).

Bullies tend to be more frequently of non-German origin, whereas victims are slightly more often German. That this difference fails to attain statistical significance suggests that ethnic background may have only a minor influence on bullying in Germany (see, also, Fuchs, 1997). In contrast to various very aggressive acts of xenophobia (e.g., Willems & Eckert, 1995), our data indicate that non-German adolescents are not a particular risk group for everyday aggression at school. The minor role of ethnic variables may also be due to the fact that our foreign students come from ordinary German speaking classes and have often grown up in Germany.

From the perspective of their teachers, bullies are described as very impulsive and dominant. This supports findings concerning comorbidity of antisocial behavior and attention deficits as well as hyperactivity/impulsive disorders (Hinshaw, 1992; Moffitt, 1990). However, bullies are not seen as socially isolated or unpopular. This integration in (eventually deviant) social networks may even reinforce and stabilize their aggressive behavior (Bender & Lösel, 1997; Tremblay, Masse, Vitaro & Dobkin, 1997). In interpersonal conflict situations, bullies exhibit clear deficits in their ability to adopt the other person's perspective in either affective or social terms. They try to assert their own goals in an egocentric manner without asking about the concerns of their conflict partner or taking these into account. Although their action reportoire in such conflicts does not contain fewer alternatives than that of competent peers, it is marked by more impulsive or rash and less information-seeking, clarifying, or consensus-seeking reactions. They are also more convinced of the efficacy of their impulsive approach. All these results are in line with the hypotheses on social information processing in aggressive juveniles (Crick & Dodge, 1994). Contrary to expectations, we have been unable to ascertain any bias in this group toward perceiving and interpreting the other as hostile. This lack of a hostility bias in the perceptions of aggressive young persons differs from the findings of Coie et al. (1991) or Lochman and Dodge (1994). Methodological differences may be involved here: whereas studies in which the phenomenon could be confirmed worked mostly with videotaped or real-life conflict scenarios, students in our study have to rate fictitious scenarios presented in written form. This procedure demands a higher level of abstraction in participants and thus may have been less adequate for adolescents with deficits in their perception and processing of social situations.

The bully/victims, in other words, students who are frequently victimized but are also very aggressive themselves, exhibit characteristics of social information processing that are closer to those of bullies than pure victims. They also tend to be egocentric and less frequently strive for understanding of the situation and their conflict partner. Their reactions show a similar level of impulsivity to that of bullies, and they rarely exhibit deescalating behavior. The only clear discrepancy compared with bullies is in estimating the consequences of their actions: they report mostly impulsively aggressive reactions in conflict situations, while simultaneously tending to anticipate negative consequences for this behavior. In view of tendential differences in age and sports grades, it is possible that this is a group of aggressive students whose aggression is less successful because of their physical constitution. In addiction, they frequently experience victimization themselves as a consequence of their own provocative, impulsive behavior.

That there are more victimized students with low scores in active violence than members of the latter 'mixed' group is in line with data reported by Olweus (1993). The majority of our victims seem to be passive sufferers. Thus, our study fails to confirm the claim that victimization is mainly an outcome of own aggressive behavior in interactions (e.g., Killias & Rabas, 1997). This may be due to our strict selection of typical cases. As other results of our study have shown, the pure victims have mean scores in internalizing problems (e.g., anxiety, depression, withdrawal) that are similar to those found in clinical samples in youth psychiatry (Lösel et al., 1997). Despite widespread stereotypes, these victims are also not 'swots.' Their academic grades are even a little below average. From the teacher perspective, they are seen as being socially isolated and rather submissive in their behavior. They also tend to be a little younger. However, victims do not stand out in terms of their social information processing. They consistently exhibit very similar mean scores to those of the normal group. This, again, may relate to our selection of conflict scenarios and they way in which thay have been presented. Some other studies have used retrospective ratings on personally experienced conflict situations (e.g., Lagerspetz et al., 1982; Rubin, 1982). Victim-related cognitive schema and scripts may be more dominant in situations with a specific perpetrator (who plays the active part) but may be less activated by the fictitious situations given to our students. This interpretation is supported by results showing that victimization is less stable over time and less general across situations than bullying behavior (Bliesener & Lösel, 2000; Olweus, 1993).

Those students who describe themselves as being competent in social conflicts and are also rated as competent by their teachers, have the 'best' mean scores on nearly all variables. Although they are no older than the other students, they show better grades, are less impulsive, and also more popular. They do not adapt submissively but exhibit more dominance than normal students, and, of course, much more dominance than victims. In contrast to the most dominant bullies, however, they are less egocentric and engage in more information seeking and deescalation in social conflicts. They have access to a broader repertoire of response alternatives and do not tend toward impulsive reactions from which they expect no positive consequences. Although not all differences attain statistical significance, these results clearly indicate a theoretically sound symmetry between the information processing deficits of aggressive students and the respective competencies of socially well-adapted youngsters.

As paper-and-pencil measures and fictitious scenarios may have short-comings, we tested the hypotheses on social information-processing and other constructs in a second part of our project in more detail. Selected groups of the bullies, victims, normal and competent students were assessed in our laboratory one year after the study presented here. We observed triads of students in specially developed conflict games, role plays, and competitions. Alongside physiological parameters, cognitive achievement, and dispositional characteristics, we assessed specific aspects of interaction behavior by using trained observers. In addition, we conducted intensive interviews addressing the perception and evaluation of one's own and the others' actions. Results of this part of the study are presented in Bliesener and Lösel (2000). Overall, these more detailed analyses are in line with the present results and sometimes show differences that were less apparent here (e.g., hostility bias). Thus, our research confirms situation-related perceptions and thought patterns as relevant factors in the manifestation and escalation of violence among young persons. However, one should bear in mind that even in our cross-sectional design, some differences are nonsignificant and only small. This indicates that information processing should not be seen as the only field of explanation. Within a broader context, for example, temperament, neuropsychological, family, peer and socioeconomic factors as well as different pathways in the development of antisocial behavior must also be taken into account (e.g., Loeber, 1990; Moffitt, 1993). Nonetheless, addressing sociocognitive and cognitive-behavioral deficits seems to be a particularly promising way of intervening in juvenile aggression and delinquency (Lösel, 1996; Tremblay & Craig, 1995).

NOTES

1   This study was supported by a grant from the Federal Office of Criminal Investigation (*Bundeskriminalamt*). We also wish to thank Jonathan Harrow, Bielefeld Germany, for his help in translating the text.

REFERENCES

Arora, C.M.J., & Thompson, D.A. (1987). Defining bullying for a secondary school. *Education and Child Psychology, 4,* 110–120.

Asarnow, J.R., & Callan, J.W. (1985). Boys with peer adjustment problems: Social cognitive precesses. *Journal of Consulting and Clinical Psychology, 53,* 80–87.

Asher, S.R., Renshaw, P.D., & Geraci, R.L. (1980). Children's friendships and social competence. *International Journal of Psycholinguistics, 7,* 27–39.

Averbeck, M., Bliesener, T., Liehmann, A., & Lösel, F. (1996). Gewalt in der Schule: Zusammenhänge von Schulklima und Schulleistungen mit unterschiedlichen Typen der Konfliktlösung. In: E. Witruk & G. Friedrich (Eds.), *Pädagogische Psychologie im Streit um ein neues Selbstverständnis* (pp. 584–591). Landau: Empirische Pädagogik.

Bandura, A. (1997). *Self-efficacy.* New York: Freeman.

Bem, D. (1972). Self-perception theory. In: L. Berkowitz (Ed.), *Advances in experimental social psychology, vol. 6.* New York: Academic Press.

Bender, D., Lösel, F. (1997). Protective and risk effects of peer relations and social support on antisocial behaviour in adolescents from multi-problem milieus. *Journal of Adolescence, 20,* 661–678.

Bernfeld, G.A., & Peters, R.D. (1986). Social reasoning and social behavior in reflective and impulsive children. *Journal of Clinical Child Psychology, 15,* 221–227.

Besag, V. (1989). *Bullies and victims in school.* Milton Keynes: Open University Press.

Bilsky, W., Pfeiffer, C., & Wetzels, P. (1993). Feelings of personal safety, fear of crime and violence and the experience of victimization amongst elderly people: Research instrument and survey design. In: W. Bilsky, C. Pfeiffer, P. Wetzels (Eds.), *Fear of crime and criminal victimization* (pp. 245–267). Stuttgart: Enke.

Bliesener, T., & Lösel, F. 2000, in press *Aggression un Gewalt unte Jugendlichen* Neuwied: Luchterham.

Boulton, M.J. (1993). Children's abilities to distinguish between playful and aggressive fighting: A developmental perspective. *British Journal of Developmental Psychology, 11,* 249–263.

Bowers, L., Smith, P.K., & Binney, V. (1994). Perceived family relationships of bullies, victims and bully/victims in middle childhood. *Journal of Social and Personal Relationships,11,* 215–232.

Buhrmester, D., Furman, W., Wittenberg, M.T., & Reis, H.T. (1988). Five domains of interpersonal competence in peer relationships. *Journal of Personality and Social Psychology, 55,* 991–1008.

Callaghan, S., & Joseph, S. (1995). Self-concept and peer victimization among schoolchildren. *Personality and Individual Differences, 18,* 161–163.

Coie, J.D., & Dodge, K.A. (1997). Aggression and antisocial behavior. In: W. Damon & N. Eisenberg (Eds.), *Handbook of Child Psychology, 5th ed.* (pp. 779–862). Vol. 3. New York: Wiley.

Coie, J.D., Dodge, K.A. Terry, R., & Wright, V. (1991). The role of aggression in peer relations: An analysis of aggression episodes in boys' play groups. *Child Development, 62,* 812–826.

Crick, N.R., & Dodge, K.A. (1989). Children's perceptions of peer entry and conflict situations: Social strategies, goals, and outcome expectations. In: B. Schneider, J. Nadel, G. Attili & R. Weisberg (Eds.), *Social competence in developmental perspective* (pp. 396–399). New York: Plenum.

Crick, N.R. & Dodge, K.A. (1994). A review and reformulation of social information-processing mechanisms in children's social adjustment. *Psychological Bulletin, 115*, 74–101.

Crick, N.R., & Ladd, G. (1991). Children's perceptions of the consequences of aggressive behavior: Do the ends justify being mean? *Developmental Psychology, 26*, 612–620.

Deluty, R.H. (1981). Alternative-thinking ability of aggressive, assertive, and submissive children. *Cognitive Therapy and Research, 5*, 309–312.

Deluty, R.H. (1983). Children's evaluations of aggressive, assertive, and submissive responses. *Journal of Clinical Child Psychology, 12*, 124–129.

Deluty, R.H. (1985). Cognitive mediation of aggressive, assertive and submissive behavior in children. *International Journal of Behavioral Development, 8*, 355–369.

Dodge, K.A. (1986). A social information precessing model of social competence in children. In: M. Perlmutter (Ed.), *Minnesota Symposium on Child Psychology, 18* (pp. 77–125). Hillsdale, NJ: Erlbaum.

Dodge, K.A., & Crick, N.R. (1990). Social information-processing biases of aggressive behavior in children. *Personality and Social Psychology Bulletin, 16*, 8–22.

Dodge, K.A., Murphy, R.R., & Buchsbaum, K. (1984). The assessment of intention-cue detection skills in children: Implications for developmental psychopathology. *Child Development, 55*, 163–173.

Dodge, K.A., Price, J.M., Bachorowski, J.A., & Newman, J.P. (1990). Hostile attributional biases in severely aggressive adolescents. *Journal of Abnormal Psychology, 99*, 385–392.

Dodge, K.A., & Tomlin, A. (1987). Utilization of self-schemas as a mechanism of interpretational bias in aggressive children. *Social Cognition, 5*, 280–300.

Falsetti, S.A., & Resick, P.A. (1995). Causal attributions, depression, and post-traumatic stress disorder in victims of crime. *Journal of Applied Social Psychology, 25*, 1027–1042.

Farrington, D.P. (1992). Psychological contributions to the explanation, prevention, and treatment of offending. In: F. Lösel, D. Bender & T. Bliesener (Eds.), *Psychology and Law: International Perspectives* (pp. 35–51). Berlin: De Gruyter.

Fuchs, M. (1997). Ausländische Schüler und Gewalt an Schulen. Ergebnisse einer Lehrer—und Schülerbefragung. In: H.G. Holtappels, W. Heitmeyer, W. Melzer & K.J. Tillmann (Eds.), *Forschung über Gewalt and Schulen* (pp. 119–136). Weinheim: Juventa.

Funk, W. (1995). Gewalt and Schulen: Ergebnisse aus dem Nürnberger Schüler-Survey. In: S. Lamnek (Ed.), *Jugend und Gewalt. Devianz und Kriminalität in Ost und West* (pp. 119–138). Opladen: Leske & Budrich.

Garber, J., Quiggle, N.L., Panak, W., & Dodge, K.A. (1991). Aggression and depression in children: Comorbidity, specificity, and cognitive processing. In: D. Cicchetti & S. Toth (Eds.), *Rochester Symposium on Developmental Psychopathology: Internalizing and Externalizing Expressions of Dysfunction* (pp. 225–264). Vol. 2. Hillsdale, NJ: Erlbaum.

Gottfredson, M.R., & Hirschi, T. (1990). *A general theory of crime*. Stanford: Stanford University Press.

Guerra, N., & Slaby, R. (1990). Cognitive mediators of aggression in adolescent offenders: II. Intervention. *Developmental Psychology, 26*, 269–277.

Haapasalo, J., & Tremblay, R.E. (1994). Physically aggressive boys from age 6 to 12: Family background, parenting behavior, and prediction of delinquency. *Journal of Consulting and Clinical Psychology, 62*, 1044–1052.

Hanewinkel, R., & Knaack, R. (1997). Mobbing: Eine Fragebogenstudie zum Ausmaß von Aggression und Gewalt an Schulen. *Empirische Pädagogik, 11*, 403–422.

Hinshaw, S.P. (1992). Academic underachievement, attention deficits, and aggression: Comorbidity and implications for intervention. *Journal of Consulting and Clinical Psychology, 60*, 893–903.

Hoover, J.H., Oliver, R.L., & Hazler, R.J. (1992). Bullying: Perceptions of adolescent victims in the midwestern USA. *School Psychology International, 13*, 5–16.

Killias, M., (1995). Situative Bedingungen von Gewaltneigungen Jugendlicher. In: S. Lamnek (Ed.), *Jugend und Gewalt. Devianz und Kriminalität in Ost und West* (pp. 189–206). Opladen: Leske & Budrich.

Killias, M., & Rabasa, J. (1997). Weapons and athletic constitution as factors linked to violence among male juveniles. *British Journal of Criminology, 37,* 446–457.

Klicpera, C., & Gasteiger Klicpera, B. (1996). Die Situation von 'Tätern' und 'Opfern' aggressiver Handlungen in der Schule. *Praxis der Kinderpsychologie und Kinderpsychiatrie, 45,* 2–9.

Krappmann, L., & Oswald, H. (1995). *Alltag der Schulkinder. Beobachtungen von Interaktionen und Sozialbeziehungen.* Weiheim: Juventa.

Kury, H. (1995). Wie restitutiv eingestellt ist die Bevölkerung? Zum Einfluß der Frageformulierung auf die Ergebnisse von Opferstudien. *Monatsschrift für Kriminologie und Strafrechtsreform, 78,* 84–98.

Lagerspetz, K.M.J., Björkqvist, K., Berts, M., & King, E. (1982). Group aggression among school children in three schools. *Scandinavian Journal of Psychology, 23,* 45–52.

Lane, D.A. (1989). Violent histories: Bullying and criminality. In: D.P. Tartum & D.A. Lane (Eds.), *Bullying in Schools* (pp. 95–104). Stoke-on-Trent: Trentham Books.

Lochman, J.E., & Dodge, K.A. (1994). Social-cognitive processes of severly violent, moderately aggressive, and nonaggressive boys. *Journal of Consulting and Clinical Psychology, 62,* 366–374.

Loeber, R. (1990). Disruptive and antisocial behavior in childhood and adolescence: Development and risk factors. In: K. Hurrelmann & F. Lösel (Eds.), *Health hazards in adolescence* (pp. 233–257). Berlin: De Gruyter.

Loeber, R., & Farrington, D.P. (1998). *Serious and violent juvenile offenders: Risk factors and successful interventions.* Thousand Oaks, CA: Sage.

Loeber, R., & Hay, D.F. (1997). Key issues in the development of aggression and violence from childhood to early adulthood. *Annual Review of Psychology, 48,* 371–410.

Lowenstein, L.F. (1977). Who is the bully? *Home and School, 11,* 3–4.

Lösel, F. (1975). *Handlungskontrolle und Jugenddelinquenz.* Stuttgart: Enke.

Lösel, F. (1995). Entwicklung und Ursachen der Gewalt in unserer Gesellschaft. *Gruppendynamik, 26,* 5–22.

Lösel, F. (1996). Working with young offenders: The impact of meta-analyses. In: C.R. Hollin & K. Howells (Eds.), *Clinical approaches to working with young offenders* (pp. 57–82). Chichester: Wiley.

Lösel, F., Averbeck, M., & Bliesener, T. (1997). Gewalt zwischen Schülern der Sekundarstufe: Eine Untersuchung zur Prävalenz und Beziehung zu allgemeiner Aggressivität und Delinquenz. *Empirische Pädagogik, 11,* 327–349.

Lösel, F., & Bliesener, T. (1999). School bullying in Germany. In: P.K. Smith, Y. Morita, J. Junger-Tas, D. Olweus, R. Catalano & P. Slee (Eds.), *The nature of school bullying. A cross-national perspective* (pp. 224–249). London: Routledge.

Lösel, F., Bliesener, T., & Averbeck, M. (1995). *Gewalttätiges und gewaltfreies Konfliktlösungsverhalten in der frühen Jugend: Eine Bedingungs—und Prozessanalyse. 2. Zwischenbericht.* Institut für Psychologie und Sozialwissenschaftliches Forschungszentrum der Universität Erlangen-Nürnberg.

Lösel, F., Bliesener, T., & Averbeck, M. (1997). Erlebens- und Verhaltensprobleme von Tätern und Opfern. In: H.G. Holtappels, W. Heitmeyer, W. Melzer & K.J. Tillmann (Eds.), *Forschung über Gewalt an Schulen* (pp. 137–153). Weinheim: Juventa.

Lösel, F., Bliesener, T., & Averbeck, M. (1999). Hat die Delinquenz von Schülern zugenommen? Ein Vergleich im Dunkelfeld nach 22 Jahren. In: M. Schäfer & D. Frey (Eds.), *Aggression und Gewalt unter Kindern und Jugendlichen.* (pp. 65–89) Göttingen: Hogrefe.

Mansel, J., & Hurrelmann, K. (1998). Aggression und delinquentes Verhalten Jugendlicher im Zeitvergleich. *Kölner Zeitschrift für Soziologie und Sozialpsychologie, 50,* 78–109.

Meier, U., Melzer, W., Schubarth, W., & Tillmann, K.J. (1995). Schule, Jugend und Gewalt. *Zeitschrift für Sozialisationsforschung und Erziehungssoziologie, 15,* 168–182.

Mittendorff, C. (1995). Professionelle Betreuung von traumatisierten Opfern. In: Bundeskriminalamt (Ed.), *Das Opfer und die Kriminalitätsbekämpfung* (pp. 167–179). Wiesbaden: Bundeskriminalamt.

Moffitt, T.E. (1990). Juvenile delinquency and attention-deficit disorder: Developmental trajectories from age three to fifteen. *Child Development, 61,* 893–910.

Moffitt, T.E. (1993). Adolescence-limited and life-course-peristent antisocial behavior: A developmental taxonomy. *Psychological Review, 100,* 674–701.

Nasby, W., Hayden, B., DePaulo, B.M. (1979). Attributional bias among aggressive boys to interpret unambigious social stimuli as displays of hostility. *Journal of Abnormal Psychology, 89,* 459–468.

Niebel, G., Hanewinkel, R., & Ferstl, R. (1993). Gewalt und Aggression in schleswig-holsteinischen Schulen. *Zeitschrift für Pädagogik, 39,* 775–798.

Olweus, D. (1979). Stability of aggression. *Psychological Bulletin, 86,* 852–875.

Olweus, D. (1984). Aggressors and their victims: Bullying at school. In: N. Frude & H. Gault (Eds.), *Disruptive behavior in school* (pp. 57–76). New York: Wiley.

Olweus, D. (1989). *The Olweus Bully/Victim Questionnaire.* Mimeograph, Bergen.

Olweus, D. (1991). Bully/victim problems among schoolchildren: Basic facts and effects of a school-based intervention program. In: D.J. Pepler & K.H. Rubin (Eds.), *The development and treatment of childhood aggression* (pp. 411–448). Hilldale, NJ: Lawrence Erlbaum.

Olweus, D. (1993). Victimization by peers: Antecedents and long-term outcomes. In: K.H. Rubin & J.B. Asendorpf (Eds.), *Social withdrawal, inhibition, and shyness in childhood* (pp. 315–341). Hillsdale, NJ: Erlbaum.

Olweus, D. (1994). Bullying at school: Long-term outcomes for victims and an effective school-based intervention program. In: L.R. Huesmann (Ed.), *Aggressive behavior: Current perspectives* (pp. 97–130). New York: Plenum Press.

O'Moore, A.M., & Hillery, B. (1989). Bullying in Dublin schools. *Irish Journal of Psychology, 10,* 426–441.

Oswald, H. (1996). Zwischen 'Bullying' und 'Rough and Tumble Play'. Beitrag zum 40. Kongress der Deutschen Gesellschaft für Psychologie in München.

Pellegrini, A.D. (1989). What is a category? The case for rough-and-tumble play. *Ethology and Sociobiology, 10,* 331–341.

Pepler, D.J., & Craig, W.M. (1995). A peek behind the fence: Naturalistic observations of aggressive children with remote audiovisual recording. *Developmental Psychology, 31,* 548–553.

Perry, D.G., Kusel, S.L., & Perry, L.C. (1988). Victims of peer aggression. *Developmental Psychology, 24,* 807–814.

Perry, D.G., Perry, L.C., & Rasmussen, P. (1986). Cognitive social learning mediators of aggression. *Child Development, 57,* 700–711.

Pfeiffer, C. (1997). *Juvenile crime and juvenile violence in European countries.* Tagungsmaterialien der EU Conference on Crime Prevention: Towards an European Level, 11–14.5.1997, Norwijk, NL.

Pfeiffer, C., Brettfeld, K., Delzer, I., & Link, G. (1996). Steigt die Jugendkriminalität. In: C. Pfeiffer & H. Barth (Eds.), *Forschungsthema 'Kriminalität'. Interdisziplinäre Beiträge zur kriminologischen Forschung, Band 5* (pp. 19–53). Baden-Baden: Nomos.

Popp, U. (1997). Geschlechtersozialisation und Gewalt an Schulen. In: H.G. Holtappels, W. Heitmeyer, W. Melzer & K.J. Tillmann (Eds.), *Forschung über Gewalt an Schulen* (pp. 207–223). Weinheim: Juventa.

Renshaw, P.D., & Asher, S.R. (1983). Children's goals and strategies for social interaction. *Merrill-Palmer-Quarterly, 29,* 353–374.

Rigby, K., & Cox, I. (1996). The contribution of bullying at school and low self-esteem to acts of delinquency among Australian teenagers. *Personality and Individual Differences, 21,* 609–612.

Roland, E. (1989). Bullying: The Scandinavian research tradition. In: D.P. Tattum, & D.A. Lane (Eds.), *Bullying in schools* (pp. 58–71). London: Trentham Books.

Rubin, K.H. (1982). Social and social-cognitive developmental characteristics of young isolate, normal, and sociable children. In: K.H. Rubin & H.S. Ross (Rds.), *Peer relationships and social skills in childhood* (pp. 353–374). New York: Springer.

Rubin, K.H., Bream, L.A., & Krasnor, L.R. (1991). Social problem solving and aggression in childhood. In: D.J. Pepler & K.H. Rubin (Eds.), *The development and treatment of childhood aggression* (pp. 219–248). Hillsdale, NJ: Lawrence Erlbaum.

Schwind, H.D. (1995). Gewalt in der Schule—am Beispiel von Bochum. In: S. Lamnek (Ed.), *Jugend und Gewalt: Devianz und Kriminalität in Ost und West* (pp. 99–118). Opladen: Leske & Budrich.

Sharp, S. (1995). How much does bullying hurt? The effects of bullying on the personal wellbeing and educational progress of secondary aged students. *Educational and Child Psychology, 12,* 81–88.

Slaby, R.G., & Guerra, N.G. (1988). Cognitive mediators of aggression in adolescent offenders: 1. Assessment. *Developmental Psychology, 24,* 580–588.

Slee, P.T. (1993). Bullying: A preliminary investigation of its nature and the effects of social cognition. *Early Child Development and Care, 87,* 47–87.

Slee, P.T. (1995a). Peer victimization and its relationship to depression among Australian primary school students. *Personality and Individual Differences, 18,* 57–62.

Slee, P.T. (1995b). Bullying in the playground: The impact of inter-personal violence on Australian children's perceptions of their play environment. *Children's Environments, 12,* 320–327.

Smith, P.K. (1991). The silent nightmare: Bullying and victimization in school peer groups. *Psychologist, 4,* 243–248.

Smith, P.K., & Erth, S. (1994). *School bullying—Insights and perspectives.* London: Routledge.

Smith, P.K., Morita, Y., Junger-Tas, J., Olweus, D., Catalano, R., & Slee, P. (Eds.), (1999). *Nature of school bullying: A cross-national perspective.* London: Routledge.

Stephenson, P., & Smith, D. (1989). Bullying in the Junior School. In: D.P. Tattum & D.A. Lane (Eds.), *Bullying in schools* (pp. 45–57). Stoke-on-Trent: Trentham Books.

Tillmann, K.J. (1997). Gewalt an Schulen: Öffentliche Diskussion und erziehungswissenschaftliche Forschung. In: H.G. Holtappels, W. Heitmeyer, W. Melzer & K.J. Tillmann (Eds.), *Forschung über Gewalt an Schulen: Erscheinungsformen und Ursachen, Konzepte und Prävention* (pp. 11–25). Weinheim: Juventa.

Todt, E., & Busch, L. (1996). *Wissenschaftliche Begleitung des Modellversuchs 'Schule ohne Gewalt' im Lohn-Dill-Kreis. Bericht über drei Untersuchungen an Schülern und Schülerinnen der Jahrgangstufen 5 bis 9.* Fachbereich Psychologie der Justus-Liebig-Universität Gießen.

Tremblay, R.E., & Craig, W. (1995). Developmental crime prevention. In: M. Tonry & D.P. Farrington (Eds.), *Building a safer society: Strategic approaches to crime prevention* (pp. 151–236). Chicago: University Press.

Tremblay, R.E., Masse, L.C., Vitaro, F., & Dobkin, P.L. (1997). The impact of friends' deviant behaviour on early onset of delinquency: Longitudinal data from 6 to 13 years of age. *Development and Psychopathology, 7,* 649–667.

van Dijk, J.J.M., Mayhew, P., & Killias, M. (1990). *Experience of crime across the world. Key findings from the 1989 international crime survey.* Deventer: Kluwer.

Whitney, I., & Smith, P.K. (1993). A survey of the nature and extent of bullying in junior/middle and secondary schools. *Educational Research, 35,* 3–25.

Willems, H., & Eckert, R. (1995). Wandlungen politisch motivierter Gewalt in der Bundesrepublik. *Gruppendynamik, 26,* 89–123.

Wustmans, A., & Becker, P. (1997). Strategien von Schülerinnen und Schülern zum Umgang mit Gewalt in der Schule. *Empirische Pädagogik, 11,* 311–326.

PART 2
STUDIES OF CRIME AND OFFENDERS

Chapter 5

HOMICIDE AND ATTEMPTED HOMICIDE IN GENOA OVER A THIRTY YEAR PERIOD

Giovanni B. Traverso, Lara Bagnoli and Silvio Ciappi

INTRODUCTION

The characteristics associated with criminal homicide have captured the attention of social and behavioral scientists for many years. Needless to say, the number of studies on homicide is testimony to the fascination with which the most irreversible of crimes is viewed and interpreted.

Perhaps the most influential Italian study on homicide is Bandini, Gatti and Traverso's work (1983) on criminal homicide in Genoa, a piece of research in which for the first time the phenomenon was empirically analyzed and the general homicidal patterns evaluated according to the two major types of the crime: *murder* and *attempted murder*. Since then, the study of the social characteristics of offenders and victims in homicidial cases has led a number of criminologists to speculate on the origins and phenomenology of violent behavior both at national and regional levels (Chinnici & Santino, 1986; Lanza, 1994; Traverso et al., 1995; Merzagora, 1995; Traverso et al., 1997; Traverso and Ciappi, 1999).

It is worthwhile to stress that homicide studies in Italy have been encouraged not only for the specific criminological type of offense, but also for the regional widespread phenomenon. Italy has a mean annual homicide rate per 100,000 persons equal to 1.85, approximately one-tenth of the US mean annual rate. Particularly interesting is the evaluation of the regional patterns of homicide which shows that the South maintains the highest homicide rates, while the North and Mid regions have similar levels of violence. As a result, cities such as Palermo or Reggio Calabria show mean annual homicide rates comparable to the most violent European and North American metropolitan areas.

Two theoretical perspectives have been advanced to explain this long-standing Southern dominance in the level of killing: the first emphasizes the presence of a regional subculture of violence (i.e. organized crime) (Gastil, 1971); the second focuses on high levels of economic deprivation (Loftin & Hill, 1974; Parker, 1989).

The present study is part of a larger project that analyzes the phenomenology of voluntary homicide and attempted homicide cases (N = 403)

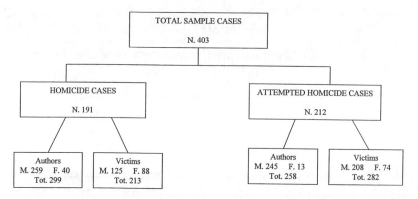

FIGURE 1: HOMICIDE AND ATTEMPTED HOMICIDE IN GENOA (1961–1990)

that occurred under the jurisdiction of the Criminal Court (Corte d'Assise d'Appello) of Genoa during the period 1961–1990 (Fig. n.1). More specifically, the present piece of research focuses on the 557 individually indicted for voluntary homicide and/or attempted homicide and judged by the above mentioned Criminal Court with the goal of analyzing the predictor variables of specific types of homicide.

SOCIAL CHARACTERISTICS OF DEFENDANTS AND VICTIMS AND OTHER CIRCUMSTANCES OF THE CRIME

The analysis that follows is based on social and demographic information concerning 557 homicide defendants and 495 victims. Table n.1 shows all the variables included in the study along with the results of the crosstabular analysis and its statistical significance.

The major findings of our study are the following:

1. *Sex*: males contribute disproportionately to the cases in our sample; as we can see, males rather than females are more likely to be both authors and victims of attempted homicide.
2. *Age*: with regard to the age variable, the data show that, on the whole, our sample is made up of fairly young people (the mean age of the authors is 34.4 years; the mean age of the victims is 38.0). There is a significant difference between the two types of homicide: younger offenders are significantly more likely to be represented in the attempted homicide group. Same results do not hold for the victim.
3. *Place of birth*: one of the most important variables taken into account by the international criminological literature on homicide is

Table 1: Factors associated with homicide

Authors	Type of homicide		
	Homicide %	Attempted %	p
Sex (Male)	86.6	95.0	.005
Age (<34)	56.5	67.4	.01
Birth (South)	31.7	53.7	.0001
Marital Status (Married and/or previously married)	44.6	39.6	n.s.
Education (Low)	64.0	73.9	.03
Job (Unemployed)	21.5	31.9	.01
Prior convictions (Yes)	41.2	58.8	.0001
Victims	%	%	p
Sex (Male)	58.7	74.0	.005
Age (<34)	41.2	47.5	n.s.
Birth (South)	31.9	45.7	.003
Marital Status (Married and/or previously married)	59.1	53.8	n.s.
Education (Low)	55.7	60.4	n.s.
Job (Unemployed)	13.4	14.8	n.s.
Relationship	%	%	p
Within the family	26.7	12.4	.0001
Crime	%	%	p
Weapon (Gun)	46.0	47.9	n.s.
Location (author's and/or victim's home)	47.2	25.1	.0001
Confession (Yes)	32.3	24.7	n.s.
Escape (Yes)	63.6	67.5	n.s.
Arrest (<24 h)	41.1	64.0	.0001

P's are referred to χ-square values.

the ethnic background of offenders and victims. Also in our sample, this variable has its own great importance: people born in Southern regions of the country are more likely to be represented in the attempted homicide group and this result holds true for both authors and victims.

4. *Marital status*: no significant difference can be found for this variable between the groups analyzed and this is true both for the authors and for the victims.

5. *Education*: in our sample, the majority of offenders and victims had only the elementary diploma, which means having successfully passed the fifth grade of school, or had an even lower level of education. Data suggest that defendants with lower levels of education are

more likely to be involved in attempted homicide cases. For the victims no significant difference between the groups was observed.

6. *Occupation*: as a whole, in our sample, defendants and victims are concentrated in the less prestigious occupational categories: 42.6% of the offenders and 49.5% of the victims were unemployed (some are retired, housekeepers, students). Comparison between the groups shows that unemployed defendants are more likely to be represented in the attempted homicide group. No statistical difference is found among the victims.

7. *Prior convictions*: about half of the defendants in the present study were found to have a prior criminal record. There are statistically significant differences between the two groups examined: career criminals are more likely to belong to the group of attempted homicide defendants.

8. *Relationship*: in our sample, 19.1% of the relationships between author and victim involves family members; about 40% of the homicide cases occurred among individuals with previous deep social interactions; in the remaining 39.2% of all the cases strangers confronted one another in the homicidal situation. Defendants who interacted in their crime with family members were more likely to belong to the group of homicide rather than to the group of attempted homicide. The difference is statistically significant.

9. *Weapons*: in about half of the cases, the death of the victim was by a gun shot wound. Knives or blunt instruments were used in 33.3% of the cases, while other modes of inflicting death occurred rarely. Defendants who did not use a gun, preferring other offending tools, were more likely to be represented in the attempted homicide group.

10. *Location*: about one half of homicide victims and about a quarter of attempted homicide victims are assailed in a private residence, either their home, or the author's home or their common home. Data suggest that there is a statistical difference between the two groups considered: when the offense occurs in a private residence it is more likely to belong to the homicidal group.

11. *Confession*: murderers are more likely to confess the crime, while others are found more often to deny their responsibility.

12. *Behavior after the crime*: in our analysis, a variable strictly linked with the specific type of crime is the behavior of the defendant immediately after the crime. Our data show that most of the attempted assailants (65.5%) run away rapidly from the scene of the offense. No statistical difference is found between the two groups considered.

13. *Arrest*: in our sample, in a high percentage of cases (72.2%), the perpetrators of the offenses are apprehended by the police within the temporal space of seven days. A statistical difference can be observed between the two groups examined: early arrests are more likely to occur in attempted homicide cases.

Summing up, these findings are reflective of earlier research on homicide. In fact, a comparison of both the national and international literature on the social characteristics of homicide defendants shows similar marginal distributions: males in their thirties, with an elementary school education or less, unemployed or employed as unskilled or semiskilled laborers, previously convicted constitute a relevant part of our sample, similar to the samples of homicides elsewhere studied.

Also our data about the relationships between offenders and victims, as well as the circumstances of the offense, seem to parallel those found in earlier studies, showing high percentages of defendants and victims closely related in terms of familiar and social ties, and a widespread use of firearms.

CONCLUSIONS

One major finding of our research is to show that homicide and attempted homicide—two phenomena that traditionally have not been differentiated on the assumption that in both events there is a clear intention to kill and that the victim survives independently from the the will of the offender—are very different social and cultural occurrences, perpetrated by authors with a social and economic background that is significantly different. In fact, attempted homicide, differently from homicide, is more likely to be perpetrated by young, immigrant males, with a prior history of arrests and convictions, who confront a victim outside the family, severely wounding him/her with a knife or a blunt instrument.

As a provisionary conclusion, we can argue that our data seem to support a socio-cultural theoretical model of explanation of violent behavior (Swigert & Farrell, 1976), a model in which social disorganization due to rapid social change, industrialization, urbanization and cultural diversity is seen as a major contributor to the problem of crime and violence in society.

REFERENCES

Bandini, T., Gatti, U., & Traverso, G.B. (1983). *Omicidio e controllo Sociale*. Franco Angeli, Milano.

Chinnici, G., & Santino, U. (1986). *L'omicidio a Palermo e provincia negli anni 1960–1966 e 1978–1984*. Collana di studi statistico-sociali e demografici, Università di Palermo.

Gastil Raymond, D. (1971), Homicide and a regional culture of violence. *American Sociological Review, 36*, 412–427.

Lanza, L. (1994). *Gli omicidi in famiglia*. Giuffrè, Milano.

Loftin, C., & Hill, R. (1974) Regional subculture and homicide: An examination of the Gastil-Hackney thesis. *American Sociological Review, 39*, 714–724.

Merzagora, I., Zoja, R., Gigli, F. (1995). *Vittime di omicidio. Fattori di predisposizione alla vittimizzazione, caratteristiche delle vittime, scenari di omicidio a Milano*. Giuffrè, Milano.

Parker, R.N. (1989). Poverty, subculture of violence and type of homicide. *Social Forces, 67*, 983–1007.

Swigert, V.L., & Farrell, R.A. (1976). *Murder, Inequality and the Law*. Heath and Co., Lexington.

Traverso, G.B., Ciappi, S., & Leone, G. (1995). Omicidio e tentato omicidio nella città di Firenze (1961–1985). *Rassegna Italiana di Criminologia, VI*, 2.

Traverso, G.B., Ciappi S., Marugo M.I., & Bagnoli L. (1997). Omicidio e tentato omicidio nella città di Genova: il trentennio 1961–1990. *Rassegna Italiana di Criminologia, VIII*, 2.

Traverso G.B., & Ciappi S. (1999). Fenomenologia dell'omicidio. In: G. Giusti (ed.), *Trattato di Medicina Legale e Scienze Affini*, Cedam, Padova, vol. IV.

Chapter 6

MATRICIDES AND PATRICIDES: COMPARISONS FROM A U.S. FORENSIC SAMPLE

John L. Young, Marc Hillbrand and Reuben T. Spitz

INTRODUCTION

A parricide is the killing of one or both parents by a son or daughter. In the U.S.A., whereas one in seven homicide victims is killed by a stranger (Heide, 1989), one in four is killed by a relative. Among intrafamilial homicides, about one in ten is a parricide (Heide, 1993a). Parricides account for about 2% of all homicides committed yearly in the U.S.A.(Heide, 1989). In the United Kingdom, parricides comprise 1 to 2% of all homicides (Green, 1981). In France, parricides constitute about 3% of all homicides (Devaux, Petit, Perol, 1974, cited in d'Orban & O'Connor, 1989).

Matricides and patricides differ in function of the age of the perpetrator. Combining worldwide data yields a 15:1 male-to-female ratio among youthful perpetrators of parricide (Hillbrand, Alexandre, Young & Spitz, in press). Among their victims, there were twice as many fathers as mothers. Among adult offenders the male-to-female ratio is 5 to 1. However, mothers outnumber fathers as victims of adult offenders by 2 to 1. Worldwide, males widely outnumber females as perpetrators of parricide (d'Orban & O'Connor, 1989) which parallels the overrepresentation of males as perpetrators of violence in general. Patricides appear to outnumber matricides in most countries from which data are available. Matricide may even be nonexistent in countries like Japan (Hirose, 1970, cited in d'Orban & O'Connor, 1989).

Patricidal offenders appear to differ from their matricidal counterparts, particularly with respect to crime dynamics. The purpose of this chapter is to summarize the available literature on parricides, with a particular emphasis on differences between patricides and matricides. We will then describe a study that we conducted comparing patricidal and matricidal offenders in a sample of institutionalized forensic patients.

In the U.S.A., perpetrators of parricide are typically middle-class males without a prior history of violence or delinquency (Heide, 1993a; Mones, 1991). Patricidal offenders typically are under the age of 30, whereas matricidal offenders tend to be between the ages of 20 and 50. Ninety-two percent of fathers and 86% of mothers are single victims of single offenders (Heide, 1993b, p. 63). Twenty-five percent of patricides are committed by adolescents under the age of 18, while the same figure for matricides is 15%. The rate of parricides by juveniles stayed constant from 1977 to 1986, while the rate of parricides by adults had increased.

In the U.S.A., Caucasians commit the vast majority of parricides. African Americans, though overrepresented among homicide perpetrators with an age-adjusted homicide rate six times greater than Caucasians (Holinger, 1987), are equally likely as Caucasians to commit domestic homicides (Centerwall, 1984), but are significantly underrepresented among parricide perpetrators. No convincing explanation for this startling fact has emerged.

Patricides are more likely to involve the use of a firearm, while matricides are more likely to involve a cutting instrument, blunt object, or bodily assault (Heide, 1993c). Juveniles use firearms more frequently than adult offenders in their crime. Adult as well as juvenile offenders are more likely to kill their fathers with a firearm than any other weapon.

Crime dynamics in parricide are quite different in parricides committed by juveniles and those committed by adults. Because of space limitations, we refer the reader to Hillbrand, Alexandre, Young & Spitz (in press) for a discussion of the factors associated with juvenile parricides. In summary, child abuse is a frequent precursor of parricide by youths, but severe mental illness and conduct disorder or antisocial personality disorder have also been shown to be precursors of parricide by youths. It remains unclear what differentiates the minority of abused children who go on to commit parricide from the majority that does not.

Whereas adolescents may kill their abusive parents because they believe that they cannot leave the family home, adults possess a greater array of choices and resources to allow them to leave an abusive environment (Heide, 1995a). Having been the victim of physical abuse by a parent is thus a less prominent motive for parricide in adults than in youths.

Worldwide, studies of parricides reveal that most adult parricidal offenders suffer from severe and prolonged mental illness, with clinical symptoms prominent years before the homicide in most cases. Alcohol and other substance use disorders are strikingly rare in this group. Most perpetrators are not involved in psychiatric treatment at the time of the crime. The offender-victim relationship prior to the crime often involves lack of financial independence, unemployment, and a dependent or even enmeshed relationship with the parent(s). Severe familial discord is frequent.

Common precursors of parricide include past aggressive behavior by the victim as well as the perpetrator. Prior physical abuse by the victim is considerably rarer among adult than youthful parricidal offenders, and may be more common among female than male offenders. Parasuicidal behavior by the perpetrator prior to the crime appears to be more frequent among females than males. Threats of harm and battery of the victim prior to the crime are common. Most parricidal offenders do not have prior convictions for violent crimes. Other precursors of parricides include delusions related to homosexuality (Cravens et al., 1985), actual incest (d'Orban & O'Connor, 1989), and homosexual incest panic (Green, 1981). Command hallucinations to harm the parent often precede the crime (Green, 1981).

Most parricides occur in the home of the victim with only the victim and the perpetrator present (Green, 1981). The most commonly used methods in the U.S.A. include blunt force, stabbing, firearms, and asphyxiation. In countries were firearms are much less readily available, blunt force, stabbing, and asphyxiation are the most commonly used methods. Weapons are used less frequently in parricides than in other homicides, suggesting that many of these crimes were committed 'on the spur of the moment' by whatever method was available (e.g., bare hands, household implements). Remarkably, following the crime, most perpetrators make no attempts to flee (McKnight et al., 1966; Green, 1981). The only striking difference between U.S., Canadian, British and Polish studies of parricide is the pattern of firearm use. This suggests that parricide is a phenomenon that is not considerably influenced by culture, at least in the Western world.

Of great interest to parricide scholars is the question of the motive of the crime. Green (1981) described a sample of parricides from the United Kingdom and reported that the apparent motives were persecutory paranoid (delusional beliefs about the parent and sometimes also other family members), altruistic (belief that the perpetrator was dying and that it would be unkind to leave their parent with no one to look after them), or other (attempts to break away from a domineering parent, jealousy, impulsivity and rage). These three types of apparent motives were seen primarily in schizophrenic, mood disordered, and personality disordered patients, respectively.

METHODS

We screened the records of all patients admitted to the State of Connecticut's single maximum security mental hospital over the course of its 30-year history, identifying those who had been referred after being charged with killing either parent. We excluded the two cases who had slain both parents as well as those whose victims were other than biological parents. Some of the cases were seen before trial; most were in treatment following acquittal on the grounds of insanity. In Connecticut, insanity is decided according to the American Law Institute standard, namely that at the time of the act the accused, due to a mental disease or defect (the legal language for mental illness in the U.S.) lacked substantial capacity either to appreciate the wrongfulness of his act or to conform his conduct to the requirements of the law. The defense bears the burden of proof by a preponderance of the evidence; both voluntary intoxication and antisocial behavior-based diagnoses are excluded.

The authors, aided by trained and supervised assistants, performed the screening of the records and the collection and coding of the data. Information gathered included demographic, clinical, and legal history along with details surrounding the fatal episode. Where feasible, the Chi-squared test was applied to evaluate for statistical significance based on a p-value of less than 0.05.

Results

A total of 25 parricide perpetrators were identified, all male. Ten had killed their mother, and 15 their father. (We excluded the two individuals who had killed both parents, since their small number precluded meaningful analysis.) There was one black perpetrator, a matricide, and the remaining 24 were white. Age at the time of the crime ranged from 17 to 40 with a mean of 26 years. There was a predominance of 11 (41%) unskilled workers, 9 (33%) chronically unemployed, and 5 (19%) students. At the time of their parricides nearly all, 22 (81%), were unemployed. Sixteen (64%) of the parricides were living with their victims at the time, and another 3 (12%) had moved in within one month of the event. In 8 cases (32%) the household consisted only of the perpetrator and the victim, and in another 13 (52%) it included the victim's spouse. All but two of the murders took place in or near the victim's home, predominantly in the living room or a bedroom. Half of the victims were skilled workers or professionals. Rates of mental illness and alcohol abuse were over one-third among first degree relatives in these families. However, only one victim was found to have a criminal history.

Schizophrenia was the perpetrators' predominant diagnosis, attributed to 21 (84%). Mood disorders were present in 3 (12%) of the cases, and personality disorders in 4 (16%). The group's intelligence was in the normal range with a normal distribution. The extent of alcohol and other substance abuse was somewhat difficult to gauge from our data, but was apparent at the time of the act in one-fourth of the cases. Most of the perpetrators, 19 (76%), were not in treatment at the time of the parricide, and there were 5 (20%) who had been recommended for admission to a hospital a week prior to their crimes. Nearly half, 11 (44%) were acutely psychotic when they killed their parent.

A history of some form of abuse by 10 (40%) of the victims was apparent. But only 2 (8%) had verbally provoked their perpetrators shortly before the act. Three (12%) of the perpetrators were classified as acting to escape enmeshment at the time.

In contrast to some of the existing literature, we found a paucity of prior threats related to our subjects' acts. Yet they were a strikingly violent group, with high rates of past violent behavior and prior felony convictions (which may or may not have involved violence). They also showed considerable violence after their index crimes, either before arrest or later in the legal process.

The major purpose of this report was to compare and contrast these results according to victim. These results are shown in Table 1.

Table 1: Results according to victim

Victim	Father	Mother
N	15	10
Median Age (yr)	27	23
Unemployed	6	3
Felony History	3	3
Prior Threats	1	2
Frankly Psychotic	9	2
Acutely Intoxicated	3	3
*Not Hospitalized	5	0
Violent History	7	5
Violent Afterward	5	6
*Living With Victim	7	9
Living or Bedroom	5	5
Escaping Enmeshment	1	2
Abuse by Victim	6	4
*Acquitted	14	6

$*p < 0.05$

In Table 2, we offer a comparison of the weapons used.

Table 2: Weapon used

Victim	Father	Mother
gun	5	2
knife	7	4
blunt object	1	1
hands	2	2

Data missing from 1 case

In addition to the data noted above, the outcomes of the legal proceedings are included. It is notable that those who killed their fathers were significantly more likely to be acquitted on the grounds of insanity.

DISCUSSION

For the greatest part, our results confirm what is in the literature. Since sample size in most studies is smaller than in ours, this confirmation has some value. A striking example is that of race. As mentioned, we found only one black individual and no hispanics. Information gathered early in our investigation confirms this. We scoured the facilities of the Department of Corrections for parricides, expecting to develop a comparison group for the study, but administrative considerations precluded any significant gathering of data. However, in the course of this effort it did become clear that there were no blacks or hispanics charged with or convicted of parricide to be found in any of the state's jails or prisons.

Despite the relatively large number in our sample, categories of interest in the analysis of differences between the matricides and patricides were often too numerous to permit reliable measures of statistical significance. In this light the three exceptions stand out, especially that none of the matricides had been recently recommended to a mental hospital. They lacked this obvious marker of an acute exacerbation of mental illness, and in keeping with this finding, secondly, they enjoyed significantly less success in gaining acquittal on the basis of insanity. Further, although statistical significance was not quite reached, their rate of being found frankly psychotic at the time of the killing was much lower than for the patricides. To the best of our knowledge these are new findings.

Thirdly, the individuals who killed their mothers were more likely to be living with their victims at the time. This result extends to male matricides one of the findings of d'Orban and O'Connor (1989) regarding some women who killed their mothers. In our efforts to record motives of our sample, we saw a tendency for an altruistic view on the part of some patients, that is a belief that somehow the victim would be better off dead.

Looking at the data on choice of weapon, we note a tendency, not reaching statistical significance, for firearms to predominate among the patricides. This is generally found in similar studies where it is attributed to the need for greater force to overcome a male than a female victim. The overall frequency of this weapon choice reflects the ready availability of guns in the U.S.

Finally, we are struck by the generally high levels of violence shown by our subjects. This was true before the index crime and continued afterward in many cases, somewhat more among the matricides. To some extent at least, the patricides proved a sicker group, more likely to win acquittal on the ground of insanity and to be classed as acutely psychotic at the time of their crime. Although their prior violence rate equaled that of the matricides, they were somewhat less violent afterward.

CONCLUSION

Although they constitute only a small proportion of homicides, parricides evoke more than a small proportion of the emotional suffering. They produce an important and avoidable negative impact on the world's public health. As we learn about them in more detail and greater depth we can work more effectively toward reducing their number. It would be particularly useful to learn more about how they relate to other homicides, both resembling them and differing significantly from them. Likewise, it would prove helpful to dissect out the similarities and differences between patricides and matricides. To this end, we expect that it would be useful to know which of the variables we have identified would prove significant with a still larger sample and which would not. We look forward to collaborations that will answer this important question, along with others raised in this chapter.

REFERENCES

Adams, K.A. (1974). The child who murders: A review of theory and research. *Criminal Justice and Behavior, 1,* 51–61.

Bender, L. (1959). Children and adolescents who have killed. *American Journal of Psychiatry, 116,* 510–513.

Bumby, K.M. (1994). Psycholegal considerations in abuse-motivated parricides: Children who kill their abusive parents. *The Journal of Psychiatry and Law, 22,* 51–90.

Busch, K.G., Zagar, R., Hughes, J.R., Arbit, J., & Bussell, R.E. (1990). Adolescents who kill. *Journal of Clinical Psychology, 46,* 472–485.

Campion, J., Cravens, J.M., Rotholc, A., Weinstein, H.C., Covan, F., & Murray, A. (1985). A study of 15 matricidal men. *American Journal of Psychiatry, 142,* 312–317.

Centerwall, B.S. (1984). Race, socio-economic status, and domestic homicide, Atlanta, 1971–1972. *American Journal of Public Health, 74,* 813–815.

Chamberlain, T.J. (1986). The dynamics of a parricide. *American Journal of Forensic Psychiatry, 7,* 11–23.

Corder, B.F., Ball, B.C., Haizlip, T.M., Rollins, R., & Beaumont, R. (1976). Adolescent parricide: A comparison with other adolescent murder. *American Journal of Psychiatry, 133,* 957–961.

Cravens, J.M., Campion, J., Rotholc, A., Covan, F., & Cravens, R.A. (1985). A study of 10 men charged with patricide. *American Journal of Psychiatry, 142,* 1089–1092.

Daniel, A.E., & Holcomb, W.R. (1985). A comparison of men charged with domestic and non-domestic homicide. *Bulletin of the American Academy of Psychiatry and Law, 13,* 233–241.

Deutsch, A. (1950). *Our rejected children.* Boston: Little, Brown.

Devaux, C., Petit, G., & Perol, Y. (1974). Sur le parricide en France. *Annales Medico-Psychologiques.*

D'Orban, P.T., & O'Connor, A. (1989). Women who kill their parents. *British Journal of Psychiatry, 154,* 27–33.

Duncan, J.W., & Duncan, G. M. (1971). Murder in the family: A study of some homicidal adolescents. *American Journal of Psychiatry, 127,* 1498–1502.

Dutton, D.G., & Yamini, S. (1995). Adolescent parricide: An integration of social cognitive theory and clinical views of projective-introjective cycling. *American Journal of Orthopsychiatry, 65,* 39–47.

Freud, S. (1949). Dostoyevsky and parricide. *International Journal of Psychoanalysis, 26,* 1–8.

Goetting, A. (1989). Patterns of homicide among children. *Criminal Justice and Behavior, 16,* 63–80.

Green, C.M. (1981). Matricide by sons. *Medicine, Science, and the Law, 21,* 207–214.

Heide, K.M. (1989). Parricide: Incidence and issues. *The Justice Professional, 4,* 18–41.

Heide, K.M. (1993b). Juvenile involvement in multiple offender and multiple victim parricides. *Journal of Police and Criminal Psychology, 9,* 53–64.

Heide, K.M. (1993a). Parents who get killed and the children who kill them. *Journal of Interpersonal Violence, 8,* 531–544.

Heide, K.M. (1993c). Weapons used by juveniles and adults to kill parents. *Behavioral Sciences and the Law, 11,* 397–405.

Heide, K.M. (1994). Evidence of child maltreatment among adolescent parricide offenders. *International Journal of Offender Therapy and Comparative Criminology, 38,* 151–162.

Heide, K.M. (1995b). Dangerously antisocial youths who kill their parents. *Journal of Police and Criminal Psychology, 10,* 10–14.

Heide, K.M. (1995a). *Why kids kill parents.* Thousand Oaks, CA: Sage publications.

Heide, K.M., & Solomon, E.P. (1991, November). *Responses to severe childhood maltreatment: Homicidal fantasies and other survival strategies.* Presented at the 43rd annual meeting of the American Society of Criminology, San Francisco, CA.

Hillbrand, M., Alexandre, J. W., Young, J.L., & Spitz, R.T. (In press). Parricides: Characteristics of offenders and victims, legal factors and treatment issues. *Aggression and Violent Behavior.*

Hirose, K. (1970). A psychiatric study cases of parricide. *Acta Criminologica Japonica, 36,* 29.

Holinger, P.C. (1987). *Violent deaths in the United States: An epidemiologic study of suicide, homicide, and accidents.* New York: Guilford Press.

Hull, J.D. (1987, October 19). Brutal treatment, vicious deeds. *Time,* 68.

James, J.R. (1994). Turning the tables: Redefining self-defense theory for children who kill abusive parents. *Law and Psychology Review, 18,* 393–407.

Krohn. J. (1986). Addressing the oedipal dilemma in Macbeth. *Psychoanalytic Review, 73,* 333–347.

Lewis, C.N., & Arsenian, J. (1977). Murder will out: A case of parricide in a painter and his painting. *The Journal of Nervous and Mental Disease, 164,* 273–279.

Lewis, D.O., Moy, E., Jackson, L.D., Aaronson, R., Restifo, N., Serra, S., & Simos, A. (1985). Biopsychosocial characteristics of children who later murder: A prospective study. *American Journal of Psychiatry, 142,* 1161–1167.

McCully, R.S. (1978). The laugh of Satan: A study of a familial murderer. *Journal of Personality Assessment, 42*, 81–91.

McGinnis, J. (1991). *Cruel doubt.* New York: Simon & Schuster.

McKnight, C.K., Mohr, J. W., Quinsey, R.E., & Erochko, J. (1966). Matricide and mental illness. *Canadian Psychiatric Association Journal, 11*, 99–106.

Meloff, W., & Silverman, R. A. (1992). Canadian kids who kill. *Canadian Journal of Criminology, 34*, 15–34.

Mones, P. (1991). *When a child kills: Abused children who kill their parents.* New York: Pocket Books.

Mouridsen, S.E., & Tolstrup, K. (1988). Children who kill: A case study of matricide. *Journal of Child Psychology and Psychiatry and Allied Disciplines, 29*, 511–515.

Myers, W.C. (1992). What treatments do we have for children and adolescents who kill? *Bulletin of the American Academy of Psychiatry and Law, 20*, 47–48.

Newhill, C.E. (1991). Parricide. *Journal of Family Violence, 6*, 375–394.

Patterson, G.R. (1992). Developmental changes in antisocial behavior. In: R. DeV. Peters, R.J. McMahon & V.L. Quinsey (Eds.), *Aggression and violence throughout the life span* (pp. 52–82). Newbury Park, CA: Sage.

Post, S. (1982). Adolescent parricide in abusive families. *Child Welfare, 61*, 445–455.

Rozycka, M., & Thille, Z. (1972). Murdering of parents. *Psychiatria Polska, 6*, 159–168.

Rudnytsky, P. (1988). The persistence of myth: Psychoanalytic and structuralist perspectives. *Psychoanalytic Review, 75*, 153–176.

Russell, D.H. (1965). A study of juvenile murderers. *Journal of Offender Therapy, 9*, 55–86.

Sadoff, R.L. (1971). Clinical observations on parricide. *Psychiatric Quarterly, 45*, 65–69.

Sargent, D. (1962). Children who kill-A family conspiracy? *Social Work, 7*, 35–42.

Scherl, D.J. (1966). A study of adolescent matricide. *Journal of the American Academy of Child Psychiatry, 5*, 569–593.

Shulman, H.M. (1957). A social science view of delinquency causation and control. In: F.J. Cohen (Ed.), *Youth and crime* (pp. 124–145). New York: International Universities Press.

Singhal, S., & Dutta, A. (1990). Who commits patricide? *Acta Psychiatrica Scandinavica,82*, 40–43.

State v. Janes, 822 P.2d 1238, Wash. App. (1992); *State v. Janes,* 850 P.2d 495, Wash. (1993).

Tanay, E. (1973). Adolescents who kill parents-reactive parricide. *Australian and New Zealand Journal of Psychiatry, 7*, 263–277.

Weisman, A.M., & Sharma, K.K. (1997). Forensic analysis and psycholegal implications of parricide and attempted parricide. *Journal of Forensic Sciences, 42*, 1105–1111.

Wertham, F. (1941). *Dark legend: A study in murder.* New York: Duell, Sloan and Pearce.

Chapter 7

OFFENDER PROFILING AND DEGREE OF VIOLENCE IN A HOMICIDE SAMPLE

Józef K. Gierowski and Maciej Szaszkiewicz

At the Department of Forensic Psychology at the Institute for Forensic Research in Cracow, research is being carried out with the aim to elaborate an efficient mode of conduct in order to produce a psychological and physical profile of an unknown homicide perpetrator. Further, this is being done to determine such profiles with respect to Polish reality. The first stage of the project will be finalized and summarized soon. It consists of the creation of a large database (1,300 factors) prepared on the basis of files of 100 homicide cases resulting in the conviction of the perpetrator. The most significant variables necessary for efficient profiling are the type and the level of violence of the homicide perpetrators, and the mechanisms which influence them. We shall deal with those variables in this paper.

The estimate of the homicide perpetrators' violence, considered a relatively stable personality variable, was carried out on the basis of three sources:

1) A psychometric examination
2) A life story analysis
3) An observation of behavior

In the psychometric examination, the following tests were used: Buss-Durkee (SABD), MMPI, Wechsler Intelligence Scale, Sachs' Unfinished Sentences Test, and Eysenck's Personality Inventory.

The life story was analyzed by means of a structured clinical interview. The behavior observation was carried out during the psychological examinations. Personal data contained in the files pertaining to the investigation were also used.

After an analysis of the examination results, we divided 100 examined perpetrators into three groups, depending on the level and the kind of violence:

1. 'Non-violent' perpetrators. These perpetrators obtained the lowest level of general violence results. On average, the results were 4.1 sten

(SABD) in comparison with the average of the rest of the perpetrators examined at 6.17 sten (SABD). No characteristic kind of violence as a permanent personality mechanism was found in these people. The group consisted of 38 people.

2. 'Moderately-violent' perpetrators. These perpetrators obtained a high level of general violence results (5.95 sten SABD), and were characterized by the highest level of latent enmity (6.4 sten SABD). Further, the members of this group showed a high inclination to irritation, pronounced negativism, suspiciousness and irritability. They were also characterized by suppression of feelings and emotions, strong self-control and by the inclination to dominate others. The group consisted of 23 people.

3. 'Extremely-violent' perpetrators. These perpetrators reached the highest level of general violence results (6.41 sten SABD), and were prone to direct attack and open violence. Such violence was manifested actively and verbally, directed both at other people and at objects. They were also characterized by auto-violent acts, including suicide attempts, selfishness and domination. They often showed remorse. The group consisted of 38 people.

The estimates, made by means of variant analysis, were to determine whether the three separate groups of perpetrators differed in the level and co-occurrence of the 1300 variables.

INJURIES AND GENETIC CONDITIONING

In the first group, 'non- violent' perpetrators, no serious adverse genetic conditioning or serious injuries were found.

In the second group, 'moderately violent' perpetrators, bed-wetting and neurotic disorders were found in childhood. The members of this group started their sexual life earlier, (in most cases, a very unsatisfactory one) and had distinctly fewer sexual partners.

In the third group, 'extremely violent' perpetrators, the deterioration of psycho-motoric development, inclination to impulsive-aggressive reactions and a higher frequency of occurrence of cranial and cerebral injuries were found.

GENERAL PSYCHIATRIC DIAGNOSIS

The diagnosis of psychosis was found almost exclusively in the 'non-violent' perpetrators. The psychosis was most frequently a delusion-fantasy syndrome or an organic, schizophrenia-like psychosis. Typical schizophrenia or cyclophrenia was not found. The diagnosis of neurosis was found most frequently in the second group, 'moderately-violent' perpetrators, and was characterized by a high level of enmity and fear.

The 'extremely violent' perpetrators were diagnosed as sociopaths. They were also more often diagnosed as mentally disabled. Psychoorganic syndromes, as well as alcoholism and sexual anomalies were found in members of this group.

THE PERSONALITY STRUCTURE, THE EFFICIENCY OF COGNITIVE PROCESSES, AND THE MANIFESTED ADAPTATION DISORDERS IN ADULTHOOD OF THE EXAMINED PERPETRATORS

The general level of intelligence, diagnosed by means of the WAIS Wechsler scale proved to be a variable that significantly differentiated the 'moderately violent' homicide perpetrators group from the two remaining ones. The above-mentioned regularity concerns both the verbal and the non-verbal scale of the test. Thus, the average IQ for the first group was 86 points, for the second group, 101 points, and the lowest IQ average was 82 points, found in the third group.

In the field of personality integration, measured by the MMPI test, the perpetrators in the first and second groups obtained results pointing at a decisively lower level of integration and serious disorders in the regulatory and integrative functions. The perpetrators of the third group, in contrast, obtained significantly lower results within the clinical scales of the test (hypochondria, depression, psychopathy, paranoia, psychasthenia, schizophrenia, hypomania). One may therefore assume, with a high degree of probability, that a high level of violence in homicide perpetrators is closely related to a distorted development of socialization, weak internalization of moral norms and values, and to an identification with criminal sub-culture.

TEMPERAMENT AND CHARACTER SPHERE

The perpetrators in all three groups obtained results suggesting a high level of neuroticism (the average was 7.3 Eysenck sten). One may therefore assume that all of those examined, regardless of the type and the level of violence, were characterized by a high level of emotional arousal and liability, a high level of fear, a low resistance to stress, and a tendency to nervous breakdowns in difficult situations. This confirms the view of some criminologists that neuroticism should be treated as a significant factor of irrationality in criminal acts. A high level of neuroticism intensifies the emotions felt by the perpetrator, lowering, at the same time, the level of self-control. It conditions the inadequacy of criminal behavior to the situation that brings it about. Neuroticism can also be treated as a general indicator of fear. One can therefore assume that fear played a significant role in the etiology of violent acts in those examined, regardless of their normal level of violence. It accompanied almost all direct motives, regardless of their rational or irrational character.

The perpetrators belonging to the first and second groups obtained low results in the field of extroversion (group I-3.97 sten, group II-4.00 sten). One can assume that in these groups, individuals with the introvertive personality structure were dominant. Such a structure makes it more difficult to establish a relationship with other people. Introversion, together with high neuroticism were responsible for the tendency to accumulate emotional tension. Further, they contributed to a suspicious or hostile attitude by the perpetrators towards the society. As a result of this, serious problems occurred in solving conflicts, as well as the tendency to look for substitutes in the sphere of dreams, imagination and fantasies. The third group obtained decisively higher results in the field of extroversion (5.77 sten, on average).

SITUATIONAL MOTIVATIONAL BACKGROUND

Certain external factors, responsible for the tendency to commit a crime, may have a twofold character. On one hand, they can be described as what modern psychology calls 'difficult' situations, which have less influence on the personality. (The term 'difficult' here is characterized by a more objective category). On the other hand, the group of factors constituting situational motivational background is more closely connected with the functioning and the state of personality. What is important here is a temporary state of the personality, conditioned by deprivation of human needs, rather than relatively constant mechanisms and functions of personality. Further analysis may also show the character of conflict as a permanent situation, which is repetitive, but which may also appear suddenly and unexpectedly.

What dominated in all groups was most frequently a long term, growing conflict between the perpetrator and the surrounding society (79% of cases). More significant differences were determined only in the analysis of the types of deprived biological and psychological needs. Thus:

1. In the first group, 'non-violent' perpetrators, weakening factors dominated. These included lack of sleep, lack of food, and tiredness, while somatic diseases were also found. A similar regularity concerns a deprivation of the security need.
2. 'Moderately violent' homicide perpetrators experienced deprivation of the need for affiliation, domination and the need to keep up one's self-esteem.
3. 'Extremely violent' perpetrators manifested more strongly than the others the need to stand out in a crowd.

The personality and the situational motivational background were directly determined by certain chosen features of the motivational processes. Thus, a fully formed motive for the perpetrators' acts occurred significantly more frequently in the second group, perpetrators with a high level of enmity. Among the direct motives, only in the 'non-violent' perpetrators was it possible to find a significantly greater frequency of occurrence of a fantasy motive and the feeling of insecurity.

Statistical cluster analysis, which was based on a separation of homicide perpetrators into 6 groups, yielded quite interesting data. These groups were formed depending on the co-occurrence or mutual exclusion of separated direct motives.

In these groups the following motives were dominant: economic, sexual, fantasy, revenge, feeling of being wronged, and the feeling of being threatened. The general level of violence and enmity differentiated the separated groups of perpetrators. Thus:

1. The lowest level of violence was found in perpetrators with psychotic motives who acted with a feeling of fear.
2. In the group of perpetrators of sexual homicides, the dominant motive was the level of latent enmity.
3. The most violent perpetrators were those with economic motives and those acting because of the feeling of being wronged.

The level of violence turned out to be the differentiating variable for the attitude of the perpetrator toward his victim. In cases of 'non-violent' perpetrators, the victims were most frequently relatives or people who the perpetrators knew. The age of the victims of this group was much lower, with children often the victims. Moreover, it was found that 'extremely violent' perpetrators were more prone to assigning negative values to their victims. They also had a much more clearly pronounced intention to do harm to the victim.

CONCLUSIONS

The research procedure used here, aiming at the comparison between the three groups of homicide perpetrators separated in relation to the level and the type of violence, showed considerable differences. Such differences concerned the level and the structure of cognitive processes, constant features and mechanisms of personality, situational variables and chosen properties of the motivational process. It is quite obvious that the homicide perpetrator need not be a person with an extremely violent personality structure.

In view of the results of the research, people with a low level of violence commit homicides either under the influence of psychotic experiences and fantasies, or as a result of strong situational pressure. In their cases one can point out the contradiction between the character of the act and the permanent personality features.

The accordance between the homicide act and the personality of the perpetrator is characteristic for those perpetrators with a high level of violence. They constitute a relatively homogenous group, as far as the permanent mechanisms and personality features are concerned. The level of their cognitive processes is considerably lowered. They manifest serious social adjustment disorders and their anti-social personality structure is formed in very disadvantageous environments with a large frequency of pathological biopsychical factors. Their violence is often of purely instrumental character.

One may therefore assume, that homicides, treated as symptoms of interpersonal violence, can have clearly different origins, motivations and ways in which they are carried out. It is difficult to imagine that one universal concept of violent behavior wholly explaining its aspects can be created.

The perpetrators, characterized by a high level of suppressed and controlled enmity, are most difficult to deal with. One may surely doubt whether the group is really homogenous.

Some results of the statistical analysis suggest that on the continuum between extreme violence and a lack thereof, homicide perpetrators with a high level of enmity occupy the middle position. It seems that one should rather mention here a different kind of violence, connected with serious disorders of functioning and personality development. Other factors such as strong reactivity to threatening stimuli, and the fear-anger-violence pattern should also be considered.

We hope that the results obtained in this comparative analysis will significantly enhance the reliability of the profiling process. They will also provide information that will make it easier to hypothetically reconstruct a homicide and the motivation of the perpetrator, which in turn, will make detective work more efficient.

Chapter 8

GREYING PRISONERS IN A GREYING SOCIETY: EMPIRICAL
STUDY OF ELDERLY PEOPLE IN GERMAN PRISONS

Arthur Kreuzer and Hein-Juergen Schramke

This study of imprisoned elderly people was conducted from 1993 until 1996[1]. It is a first stock-taking of the imprisonment of elderly people in Germany.

GOALS, THEORETICAL BASES AND METHODS OF THE STUDY

Goals

The fact that drastic changes of the population in the Western industrialized nations, especially in Germany, are taking place, with significant declines in birth-rates and in the number of young people on one hand, and increasing numbers of old people and life-expectancy on the other hand, gave rise to this study. The forensic psychiatrist Cabanis already stated 30 years ago:

> Our century began as the 'century of the child' but seems gradually to change towards a 'century of the old' (Cabanis, 1966, p. 2).

In the course of this demographic development, some thought occasionally to observe increasing criminality rates among elderly people, or even to have discovered a new criminality problem: 'Greying criminality in a greying society', 'White haired offenders—an emergent social problem' (Fattah & Sacco, 1989, p. 21; Kreuzer, 1992, pp. 13, 77). But this was a misconception. The elderly commit crimes much more rarely than the young and are seldomly involved in heavy crimes. Misconceptions may result from the fact that it is much more shocking when elderly people commit offenses because they deviate from their expected roles as 'wise, good, mellow people.' Similar misconceptions existed when new problematic forms of criminality by women occurred, e.g. when homicides committed by female terrorists, whose behaviour diverged just as much from their expected roles as that of the elderly, became known. The similarity of these two phenomena is even more evident when we consider that there are relatively more women among the old, and mainly women among the very old.

In the further course of this discussion, the idea of investigating how criminal courts treated elderly offenders suggested itself, how many old people were imprisoned for the first time in their lives, how many people were growing old in prison on the other hand, how the elderly were treated in prison, what effects imprisonment had on them, whether the establishment of special prisons for the elderly is advisable and whether adequate alternatives to imprisonment existed. This study was supposed to be an initial stock-taking of these questions concerning the imprisonment of elderly people.

Theoretical bases

The study was not based on a particular theory, especially since it was mainly an explorative-descriptive study, but some results and segments of previous theoretical discussions were integrated and combined from two different scientific disciplines: gerontology and criminology, following both psychological and sociological approaches.

The deficit—and decomposition—model prevailed in early gerontological studies of the aging process. Today this process is recognized in its complexity, as being influenced by inner and outer conditions, and definitely as being ambivalent in the sense of losing but also reconstructing or even gaining social abilities. It is not just a decomposition process (Lehr, 1991). Consequently, standard instructions on how to deal with elderly people in society do not exist, like supporting their tendencies to withdraw, excluding them, marginalizing or even simply protecting or sparing elderly people from certain tasks.

Criminological theories traditionally focused on juvenile delinquency. Namely career theories can only be sustained with difficulties today. Progressively developing crime careers following a certain rule are rare. Spontaneous discontinuance and maturing-out processes after age 25 are being observed. From that alone, a decrease of criminality at an older age necessarily follows. But the normality thesis known from research on hidden delinquency (Kreuzer, 1994) can be applied to the criminality of the elderly. Thus mainly minor offenses are generally possible and to be expected from elderly people. Altogether, among imprisoned elderly people, there are likely to be many continuously criminal persons who commit less offenses when growing older, or persons who commit crimes for the first time at an older age by taking advantage of certain social competencies, such as defrauders and members of the organized crime milieu, or, lastly, conflict and casual offenders, who at an older age, partly due to their age, are imprisoned for the first time, such as homicides. An additional question arises from the field of juvenile delinquency, in how far reciprocal developments relevant to criminality and imprisonment at an older age exist in the sense of developing, learning and gaining competencies and independence during youth and the disappearance or change of such competencies at an older age (Kreuzer, 1992). The explaining approach on prison subcultures was introduced from research in the field of corrections.

Methods
Because of methodological and practical reasons, such as limited resources and time, and a small number of elderly inmates, qualitative findings were given priority over quantitative results. A combination of methods was chosen. Intensive interviews were given highest priority, and originally, all inmates above age 60 in Hesse, and within the only special institution for elderly inmates in Singen (Baden—Wurttemberg) were supposed to be interviewed. 20 interviews were conducted in Hesse, 15 in Singen. 17 inmates in Hesse and 12 in Singen refused to be interviewed. The refusal rate of 43.5% was much higher than that of young prisoners and partly due to old age and decrepitude, partly due to skepticism and reservations, which are generally stronger than in young people. 27 of the remaining 35 interviews were completed with the help of files after the consent of the respective inmates was sought. 24 expert intensive interviews with staff members were added. In addition, statistics on imprisonment were evaluated and special countings were performed in North Rhine-Westphalia and Hesse.

The originally planned extension of the study to women in prison and old inmates of therapeutic institutions (committed to psychiatric hospitals, institutions for addicts, preventive detention) had to be omitted. The small number of elderly people in these institutions and the small number of female prison inmates, limits set by data protection and restricted resources, were the decisive factors. Such institutions supposedly open the door to evasive strategies when dealing with elderly delinquents.

SELECTED RESULTS

Statistical primary data
According to police crime statistics (1994), the crime rates were highest among persons between age 18 and 21 in Germany, with 12,513 male and 2,667 female suspects per 100.000 inhabitants for traditional crimes, traffic offenses not included. The rates were lowest for people over age 60 with 989 male and 401 female elderly suspects, that is 1/12 of the crime rate of young adults. Apart from shop-lifting as the dominating offense, there are evidently less cases of fraud as well and very few cases of violent

and drug-related crime. Traffic offenses, such as hit-and-run, driving while intoxicated and negligent bodily harm, have to be added.

According to the statistics on imprisonment, 34,624 persons aged 21–60 and 484 persons over age 60 were in German prisons in 1991. There were, not surprisingly, more elderly inmates among the life-time prisoners, a total of 65, constituting 13.4% of all imprioned elderly persons. 63.2% of all elderly inmates were 60–65 years old, 24.3% between 65 and 70, 12.4% at least 70. According to our target-day counting, there were 47 elderly inmates in Hesse on 9/15/1994, and among those only one woman. A categorization by sentences inflicted brought the result that the biggest group, 21 prisoners, had received a prison term of 2 to 5 years, 13 inmates shorter senteces, 7 sentences between 5 and 10 years, 5 even more. 30 of the 47 elderly inmates had been detained pending trial, 17 of those when they were at least 60 years of age. Elderly inmates had been convicted for theft or fraud in 19 cases, homicides in 8 cases, drug-related crime in 7, robbery in 4 and bodily harm, traffic offenses and sex crimes in 3 cases each. In 1991, one fourth of the elderly inmates in Germany had been committed to 'open prisons' in Hesse.

Typological matters

During these 35 interviews, we recognized many of the biographical developments of prisoners, which are typologically categorized and explained in different ways in criminological theory (Schramke, 1996, p. 88; Fattah & Sacco, 1989, p. 106; Goetting, 1984, p. 14). After a rough categorization of criminal biographies, 16 out of the 35 interviewed inmates had not been convicted previously according to their own statements; on the other hand, 11 had been convicted at least 10 times before. We found inmates who had grown old in prison, but also people who had been imprisoned when they were old, even for the first time. Inmates convicted of property and violent crimes dominated in number. To simplify matters, we will differentiate between two major groups hereafter, 'casual offenders' (20 out of the 35 interviewed inmates) and 'chronic offenders' (12 out of the 35).

a) The 'casual offenders' had a record of very few previous convictions or none at all. Only 9 out of the 20 had been convicted of crimes committed at an advanced age, all of them for the first time, among those were 4 convictions of homicide, 3 for killing their spouses. 11 had been convicted before age 60 and thus grown old while in prison. It can be inferred from files and expert information that age-related factors contributed to the 4 homicides (such as adaptive difficulties after losing a job, senile decay, typical age-related conflicts). Those inmates often do not regard themselves as 'criminals' and feel alienated from the prison population.

b) The 'chronic offenders' comprise a higher number of subgroups, three of which are to be sketched here:

1) First we found the usual 'career offender.' Career here does not equal continuously increasing criminality in the biography of the offender, but only means a course of life with time periods during which criminal acts are committed and prosecuted, often occuring at youth, but repeatedly recurring later on in life. For members of this group, criminal and prison contacts can become part of their self-concept. Part of an interview is given here as an example:

> At that time I was unemployed, I was on the dole and working illicitly at the same time, and of course I stole things... The unemployment pay is of course not enough, and so you try and make some extra money. You work illicitly or you steal... I'm not that kind... to just hang around all the time. I'm not a bum, so to say. OK, I take it easy for two or three days, but then I'll think of something. If I go and work or I go steal something, somehow I'll wake up.

Here theft is viewed in a more positive way than doing nothing, illicit or occasional work.

Chronic offenders, who may definitely have even long-lasting periods in their lives when crimes are not committed, show that common career theories with ideas of progressive courses may be misleading. As one interviewed inmate stated:

> I've said a hundred times: I'll never commit any offense again. I'm so fed up with it now. And ten years later I was here again. This time it took a while. It had never been that long before. I used to come in here every 1 or 1/2 years or I was in prison somewhere else, you know. I was surprised myself that I could make it for so long.

2) Repetitive offenders, burdensome to and standing on the edge of society, form another subgroup. Among them are homeless people with comparatively harmless but continuous violations of the law. They are familiar with the prison conditions and know what to expect. For them, the institution can become a place to spend the winter. But prisons are the wrong place for them to be accommodated;

this is more the sign of a deficit in social politics. Another excerpt from an interview:

> It started in the winter, when it was so icy-cold outside, that's how it started, you know. I didn't have a place to go... the water was frozen up most of the time. So I slept in summer-houses... And there I did something illegal... I said to myself: Now you've had enough rather go to prison for three months, so you're not bothered during the winter.

3) A third group of chronic offenders is formed by those still committing offenses when they are old, but the type of offenses and the culpability of the offenders become less severe. Among those are sexual offenders. They are looked upon by others as 'dirty old men,' but consider themselves as much more harmless, even normal. The following example of an interview shows that at old age crimes may not be committed for sexual satisfaction but rather to get an ego-boost, and that dealing with young, inexperienced 'partners' has nothing to do with perversion but rather with easy access to them at old age:

> If it was an old grandma now, who is as old as I am ... then I'd turn sour. You just sit around all day and watch TV ... You just need the young. That peps you up. Then you're not put aside yet. You believe that you're not thrown on the scrap-heap yet. OK, virility is decreasing now. These past three years it is all more, how can I explain that ... last-minute panic or so ... It is, young people liked me.

Sensitivity to end effects of imprisonment
The effects of imprisonment on elderly people are definitely ambivalent, but altogether imprisonment is more burdensome to old people than to the young. Here is a summary of the results of the study in theses, arranged according to positive and negative effects:

a) The life experience of elderly people can show positive effects during imprisonment. It can help to cope with life in prison, to introduce experiences in the sense of 'survival strategies' developed during former crises, e.g. war captivity, the death of a partner, or former imprisonment. In addition, retired people lose their worries about their financial situation and finding a job after leaving prison.

Elderly inmates are less often the cause of conflicts, even in prison they live more by the rules. Casual offenders have a tendency to look at themselves as 'on the other side,' not on the side of the 'criminals,' thus they have stronger tendencies to cooperate with the prison staff. Chronic offenders tend more to consider things carefully at old age; they create a wider range of autonomy for their actions through their experience. Staff members generally view elderly prisoners in a more positive way because they still live by a 'code of honor' which makes them predictable; they still stick to their word. It has to be left unanswered whether old age is the reason for that or whether it is due to a growing number of negative experiences with young prisoners. As a consequence, the prison staff may grant elderly inmates some more liberties, e.g. they may not always have to be exactly on time.

Obviously elderly inmates enjoy a certain 'old age bonus' with the staff and fellow-prisoners; they receive more respect or pity, as two descriptions by members of the leading staff demonstrate:

> I remember this one elderly man, above 60, who was doing time here after not paying a fine. He obviously had some dogs at home which were not taken care of during his absence. Thus, younger fellow-prisoners started fund-raising and collected the amount of money needed to pay the fine to save him from prison. They were obviously led by the feeling that this old man was in the wrong place here. He was supposed to get out and take care of his dogs.
>
> Pity is not only received from the staff members but also from fellow-prisoners. There is that grandfather who needs to be pampered a little.

The prison culture, in particular, existing at least rudimentarily in all institutions (Bondeson, 1989; Irwin & Cressy, 1964; Sykes, 1964), seems to have less effects on elderly inmates. If at all, old prisoners are only marginally integrated into the prison subculture. For one thing, they are more skeptical, more reserved and disassociated from other prisoners; they feel less attracted by a group (Kratcoski & Babb, 1990; Reed & Glamser, 1979; Panton, 1977). Also, they are not competitors for the power of the subculture and hierarchy, for testing one's strength and possibly sharing power. Elderly inmates are also less interested in subcultural activities, such as participating in the illegal drug-market. This demonstrates again that subculture has to do with gender and age. Elderly inmates may be respected for their life experiences and their enhanced mental and social competencies instead of for their physical superiority, e.g. for their help with petitions, written complaints and the avoiding or settling of conflicts among prisoners as well as between prisoners and staff members, that is, as the 'fatherly type.'

Altogether it is evident that old age is not necessarily combined with a subordinate status in the prison hierarchy and an elevated risk of victimization during imprisonment, as is sometimes assumed by scholars (Bergmann & Amir, 1973; Muthmann, 1981). The existing risk of victimization seems to be small, judged by these interviews. The few reported attacks on elderly prisoners were petty or responses to provocative actions. The fear of being victimized also seems to be smaller than expected. It is mainly existent in inmates imprisoned for the first time and before imprisonment.

b) On the other hand, several heavily burdensome factors concerning life in prison and experiencing prison have to be pointed out.

The old prisoner lives on memories; he has no perspective for the future. For casual offenders the gerontologically important continuancies of life threaten to be interrupted. Now they experience themselves as failures. Or they build up a saving construction to maintain their original vision of self, which may consist of a trivialization or negation of the crime committed or their culpability as well as the construction of a picture contrasting the 'criminal prisoner.' Future legal behaviour in liberty cannot be a saving perspective for elderly inmates anymore.

The sense of time changes for imprisoned elderly people. It is being disputed and supposedly ambivalent whether time passes more quickly for old people, as usual, or more slowly because certain dates to be planned and to live for are lacking. But in any case imprisonment is considered wasted time, a penalty for the remaining time of their lives, a temporary non-existence.

Adaptation to life in prison produces particular difficulties, especially for those imprisoned for the first time in their lives. The conditions at home, relationships, finances, the integration of the partner are wanting. Just recall the problem of the 'co-punished' families and women (Bush et al., 1987; Schafer & Sievering, 1994). Adaptation to a new rhythm of life, new eating and sleeping habits, light and noise conditions is more difficult for old people. One interviewed inmate raised complaints because he was unable to see why he had to be present at the early-morning call although he was in an open institution.

Casual offenders in particular experience the reduction and ending of relationships as problematic. Neighbours and acquaintances terminate contact with them and their relatives. It is almost impossible to build up new relationships.

Outside, but even more in prison, the suicide risk for old people increases.

In the standard prisons, elderly inmates complain about the lack of work options and free-time activities adequate for them. Many would like to work to avoid isolation, although they have reached the age of retirement. Some of them get a job in the institution because of their 'old-age bonus,' some are rejected because of a lack of jobs or because younger prisoners take precedence. Extended collaboration with honarary helpers outside prison could diminish that problem.

Subjectively, elderly inmates see the need for more medical-therapeutical assistance (internal, urological, orthopedic, opthalmo-logical and neurological problems). But they meet with little approval, especially since medical care in prisons is inadequate anyway. Free choice of a doctor is even more important at an older age, but illusory in prison.

To many, the problem of hospitalism and institutional dependance is important (Aday, 1976, 1994; Aday & Webster, 1979). Repetitively imprisoned persons become dependant on the prison, similar to patients committed to psychiatric hospitals repeatedly or for a long period of time. It can come to the point where old people refuse to apply for early release from prison, change to open institutions or leave. One person was actually going to build a hut in front of the prison walls in case of his release. In extreme cases, release from prison can result in suicide; released people feel like expellees. Three examples of interviews illustrate this problem.

The head of an institution:

> We've got one here who is in for about the tenth time. I've got the impression he feels that he belongs here. He always asks to be assigned for window-cleaning. Last time he arrived with special paraphernalia for window-clean-ing... I don't want to go as far as to say that this man repeatedly commits theft to be imprisoned here. But he is evidently very satisfied here....

A social worker:

> There are prisoners who find their real world in prison. they are familiar with the environment. They are able to move most easily in this world. Often they are unable to cope with the world outside. Returning here for them is somewhat like coming home.

A 70-year-old chronic offender on being imprisoned again:

> It was, I would say, partly relieving. When you don't eat on a regular basis, when you try not to do anything wrong, but you go begging... and so on... that costs you an effort in the beginning. But then you get used to it and you say: 'Well, it's still better than prison.' It's that you're free. But then comes the time... when you say: 'You're hungry, cold, wet, you have no real

clothes.' Then you think: 'What are they doing in prison now?' And it automatically follows: 'Well, I now have to...' and then you do something. And then, when they catch you and send you to prison, then you're in, and all of a sudden you can really eat and lie in bed lazily. It's a really snug feeling. You're at home.

Special prisons for elderly inmates

Opinions on special prisons for the elderly vary. Germany has only one such prison in the state of Baden-Wuerttemberg. In other German states, special wings or departments are occasionally found within regular prisons, at the very most also a special department in prison hospitals for patients in the need of special care (Fronmuller, 1989; Kratcoski & Pownall, 1989). Special free-time programs for the elderly do not exist. Therefore TV is also allowed to save personnel nowadays.

The only special institution in Singen was established in 1970. It is set up for 65 elderly inmates and occupied with 49, with numbers decreasing. Originally established for people over 60, inmates over 50 are accepted now as well. Firstly, working prisoners are needed for the small prison workshops. Secondly, the prison would otherwise not be used to its full capacity. Only 29 inmates are at least 60 years old; the average age in October 1993 was 61. It is a 'closed prison' with low security. Generally, elderly prisoners of Baden-Wuerttemberg with a remaining term of 15 months are committed to this institution unless they object or are in 'open prisons' because they work nearby a prison. The institution has 16 staff members as prison guards, one female social worker and three staff members either working in the administrative sector or the kitchen. Numerous free-time activities are offered outside the institution, few inside, but movement is allowed inside up to 22 hrs.

The opinions of the prisoners on such special institutions vary widely; this ambivalence seems plausible with regard to gerontological experiences; even outside, only a few were willing to move to an old peoples' home.

The majority of the prisoners in Singen welcomed the existence of the institution as such but criticized its underequipment with staff. Some missed the 'old inmate bonus' they knew from other prisons. Some showed little sense of group or community, but instead strong mistrust and isolation as well as the feeling of being even more tightly controlled by fellow-prisoners and staff members in such a small institution. The sometimes uttered fear of younger people was mainly based on rumours, as can be seen from these examples of interviews:

> I make much of that. That is because older people are forced into the defensive... by younger people.' 'You know, the young and the old, they say it's the same within families, are not compatible... These quarrels like in other institutions do not exist here.

The majority of the prisoners in Hesse viewed such a prison with disfavor but had not experienced one themselves:

> I personally disapprove of it... I enjoy the company of younger people... if you are only with old people.... then you grow old faster.' 'You become senile that way.' 'I think that's not a good idea. That is because getting old produces a tendency to view things negatively... and on me it would have negative effects if I was constantly with people of my age. When I'm with young people, people younger than myself, although I might think they do crazy things, from my point of view, they in fact have a positive effect on me.

After an overall evaluation, special prisons for elderly inmates cannot be recommended under the circumstances in Germany. Because of the federal competencies and existing local distances, such institutions could only be established in the states ('Lander'). Even then the concentration in one institution would produce long distances for elderly inmates from their hometown. In addition, the number of prisoners is much too small to justify the effort of establishing special, sensibly organized institutions. The number of elderly prisoners would be even smaller if only those prisoners constituting a security risk were grouped together; others should be committed to 'open institutions' according to German law anyway, no matter whether they can hold a job outside prison or not. For the few remaining prisoners small special departments within the regular prisons for men are sufficient; although there, a minimal number of qualified staff members should be available for free-time activities and special care. Moreover, mandatory legal assistance etc. is indicated to safeguard the interests of elderly people during the criminal proceedings and in prison.

The risk of isolation for elderly inmates could be counteracted this way. It is a risk whose tendency is becoming rudimentarily visible in society as a whole.

CONCLUSIONS

More adequate alternatives concerning the punishment and imprisonment of elderly people should be sought on the criminal-political level. One option is prison sentences with probation, combined with certain obligations for the probation period adequate for old people. Improved accommodations and social care as well as support by charitable organizations should replace the imprisonment of elderly homeless people burdensome to society. For some offenders prison sentences could be replaced by, like in the U.S., modified forms of home confinement and other penalties involving the deprivation of liberty (Schramke, 1996). In some cases, community services are another option, such as the duty of walking the dog of another elderly person confined to bed or looking after children on playgrounds. A decision-making strategy similar to 'diversion' as known in juvenile criminal justice should also be taken into consideration to avoid traditional sanctions and the imprisonment of elderly offenders.

Anyway, the existing goals of punishment and imprisonment, i.e. expiation, special deterrence and rehabilitation, are not convincing when it comes to the elderly. Only the most severe crimes may require a prison sentence or its execution for reasons of general deterrence, and even then the inability to follow the trial or to be imprisoned may prevent the completion of the proceedings and the execution of a sentence. This problem became obvious during the recent proceedings against representatives of the former GDR-regime.

NOTES

1   Special thanks are owed to the Hessian Ministry of Justice and the Central Department of Criminology (Kriminologische Zentralstelle) in Wiesbaden for their support and cooperation, as well as to the participating prisons, inmates and staff members for their interviews. This study is published: H.-J. Schramke, Alte Menschen im Strafvollzug, Giessener Kriminalwissenschaftliche Schriften GiKS, Bd. 6, Forum Verlag Godesberg 1996.

PART 3
VICTIM ISSUES

Chapter 9

FEAR OF CRIME: AGE, GENDER AND URBANIZATION.
RESULTS FROM WEST AND EAST GERMANY

Helmut Kury

INTRODUCTION

In recent years, the fear of crime has become one of the major topics in criminology and, because of the mass media, it has also become more and more an issue of public interest. Almost all countries, especially former Eastern bloc states, report a more or less dramatic increase in criminality, but above all, a considerable increase in the fear of crime. After the reunification of the two German states, this has also become true for Germany, particularly in the new German states in the East (Kury et al., 1992; Kury, 1995; 1997).

It has to be taken into account however, that in the USA the fear of crime expressed by citizens has for much longer been a central issue in criminology, as well as in public discussion (Hale, 1996). In the USA, the fear of crime was frequently discussed in the 60s (Hindelang, 1975). Hale (1996) estimated that the number of publications concerned with the fear of crime that have appeared during the past thirty years exceeds 200. This number, without doubt, can be considered an underestimation, especially taking into account that the total number of German language publications in this period amounts to 50. Citizens' fears measured by the key words 'fear of crime' are very much likely to express also general fears caused by societal changes, and not exclusively the fear of victimization.

In general, there are controversies in literature about demographic variables influencing the fear of crime, with one exception. It is almost always agreed upon that women have more fear of crime than men. However, this is the only point which has largely been agreed upon. Relations between age, ethnicity, income, marital status and the fear of crime are discussed very controversially, while single research results are contradictory. It might be generally agreed upon that increasing urbanization is accompanied by an increase in the fear of crime, although there are also contradictory research results in this area.

AGING AND FEAR OF CRIME

After gender, age is the most frequently studied variable in relation to the fear of crime (Adams & Smith, 1976; Clemente & Kleiman, 1977;

Hindelang et al., 1978; Yin, 1980; Warr, 1990; Hale, 1996). While some empirical studies reveal that the fear of crime grows with the advancement of age, there are other studies which find only minor or no relationships between age and fear of crime (Clark & Lewis, 1974; Pollock & Patterson, 1980; Norton & Courlander, 1982; Normoyle, 1987). A few studies have even found that elderly people have less fear than younger people (Hale, 1996, p. 100).

One can look to many recent studies which critically deal with assumed relationships between the fear of crime and age and find this relationship to be differentiated. Such differentiated analyses question simple linear relations (i.e., constant rise in fear of crime corresponding to the advancement of age), and it becomes clear that there exist complex relationship structures between the fear of crime and age. Differentiating variables which seem to modify these relations, partially or to a considerable extent, must be taken into account. Already, Biderman et al. (1967) found a slight or no relationship at all between age and the fear of crime (Ragan, 1977). Box et al. (1988) as well as Braungart et al. (1980) also came to this conclusion. According to LaGrange and Ferraro (1987), the method of measurement leads to an overestimation of the fear of crime with increasing age. They assert that results could basically be caused by measurement artifacts.

Up to now, only a few investigations have been undertaken in German criminological research on the relationship between the fear of crime and age. Those that have been done, for the most part, mirrored the broader cross-currents in international research.

The first large victim survey after the reunification of the two German nations was carried out in 1990 by the Max Planck Institute for Foreign and International Criminal Law, together with the German Federal Bureau of Criminal Investigation (Bundeskriminalamt) (Kury et al., 1992, pp. 234 et seq.). It does not show any homogeneous results with regard to the fear of crime and age. This is in accordance with psychological research on fear, which also does not find any unitary relationship between age and fear. The estimations of security resulting from the survey, taken in various residential areas, were significantly related to age only in East Germany. The group that felt the most insecure in East Germany was the 21 to 29 year-olds, with 35.9% reporting that they were very insecure. With increasing age, the feeling of security in the residential areas rose steadily. Persons 60 years or older reported the highest (85.3%) level of a feeling of security. Thus, *only* the elderly estimated their residential area to be very secure. The results for this item in West Germany were not statistically reliable.

Two other items to test fear that were presented in the survey revealed a slightly more distinct dependence on age, especially in West Germany. In East Germany, with the standard item (a fear of being outside, alone, after nightfall in the residential area), the highest fear rates were reached by the 21 to 29 year old persons. They classified this item into the categories 'very unsafe' and 'rather unsafe.' The 30 to 49 year old persons had lower fear rates, while persons 50 years and older reported slightly higher fear rates. In West Germany, where those under 39 years of age felt slightly more secure, those 40 years and older felt more insecure. Nearly one-third (31.1%) of the persons 60 years or older felt rather or very insecure when alone outside at night in their residential area.

THE PRESENT INVESTIGATION

Here, we will consider the issue of whether an age-related fear of crime is linked with demographic variables, by looking closely at two separate studies conducted in East and West Germany. We will specify how closely the expression of fear is connected with age. In Germany up to now, this question has not been thoroughly examined. Results obtained in the Unites States have been considered valid for Germany only with great criticism (see Boers, 1993 and the criticism offered by Wetzels et al., 1995, 231 et seq.).

The two large victim studies which were effected by the MPI, the German-German victim study 1990 (GG '90), and the German-German victim study 1995 (GG '95), contain some similar or even identical items for testing fear, thus rendering a comparison between the studies possible (Kury et al., 1992). The GG '90 was carried out in 1990 in East and West Germany. 4,999 persons in East Germany, and 2,027 in West Germany were randomly selected. All of the subjects were of at least 14 years of age, and each was interviewed personally. The response rate was 74.6% in East Germany and 70.1% in West Germany.

The GG '95 remains as the largest victim study carried out in Germany thus far. It included 20,695 randomly selected respondents of at least 16 years of age, living in East or West Germany. Here as well, the information was gathered through personal interviews, with response rates of 70.6% in East Germany and 68.3% in West Germany. In East and West Germany 4,202 and 16,493 respondents were interviewed respectively[1].

HYPOTHESES

Considering the wealth of literature resulting from international research, as well as some of our own previous research results (Kury et al., 1992;

Obergfell-Fuchs & Kury, 1996), we started from the following hypotheses in our study and data evaluations:

1 Due to research results available up to now, and the structure of the items presented, the fear of crime can be broken down into an emotional fear and a cognitive estimation of risk. Both dimensions are relatively stable.
2 In East as well as in West Germany, for both fear dimensions, a relationship with demographic variables including gender, previous victimization, and the level of urbanization can be observed. Age however, has only a moderate impact on the fear of crime.
3 The crime-fear-paradox (high fear rates of elderly respondents, especially elderly women, but, at the same time, a low victimization risk) cannot be corroborated by our data.

THE RESULTS

The dimensions of fear

First, we tested the dimension of fear through items presented in both the GG '90 and the GG '95 studies. To this end, the 8 fear items presented in the GG '90, as well as the 6 parallel items in the GG '95 were separately correlated. The two correlation matrices were processed by separate factor analyses of the principle components, and then by varimax-rotation. Each analysis clearly revealed a two-factor solution. While the factor analysis of the 8 fear items in the GG '90 in total explains 57.1% of variance, the 6 fear items in the GG '95 explain 76.0% of variance, a percentage distinctly higher. As expected, both factor analyses yielded an emotional as well as a cognitive fear factor. Hence, this factor structure remains very stable, not only in the single studies, but also in general.

The factor which we called 'emotional fear' consisted of a measurement of the participants' fear of being victimized after nightfall outside of their apartments or houses, their estimations of the level of security in their residential areas, the frequency of their thoughts about victimization, as well as the degree to which they avoid certain places, as a result of a fear of being victimized. The factor 'cognitive sense of risk' consisted of the participants' estimations of the likelihood of becoming victims of such crimes as robbery, theft, burglary, mob action, or those involving bodily injury.

Further, we carried out an item-analysis of those found in both factors, which assessed their internal consistency (reliability), as well as their uniqueness. The results were definitely positive. The uniqueness of the items fell between 0.31 and 0.67, while the values for the reliability on the scale 'emotional fear' came to an Alpha of 0.63 in the GG ´90, and 0.79 in the GG ´95. The scale 'cognitive risk' did even better, with Alphas of 0.80 in the GG ´90 and 0.89 in the GG ´95. If one bears in mind that research scales that are supposed to permit a summary evaluation of single items are frequently used instead of applied test scales, these results fully met our expectations.

The dependence of fear of crime

In order to establish the relationships between both dimensions of fear and a variety of demographic variables, a regression analysis was carried out, keeping both sets of data (GG ´90 and GG ´95) separate. According to the latest research, those variables taken into account are said to exercise an impact on the fear of crime. With respect to this proposal, gender and the level of urbanization are considered the most important. In addition, the variables age and previous victimization, which are controversially discussed with regard to their impact, were also taken into account. Some further, partially atypical independent variables with a theoretically assumed interdependence on the fear of crime, such as going out behavior, estimations of police effectiveness, or contact with the police were also considered. 'Classical' independent variables, such as occupation level, the existence of a federal state, and living in the East or West were additionally considered in the regression analysis in order to elaborate the complex dependence patterns between the fear of crime and the demographic variables as exactly and comprehensively as possible.

In both studies, the GG '90 and the GG '95, the same 14 variables, measured independently from one another, were considered. In the GG '95, contact with the police was added, a variable which was not measured by the GG '90. The number of variables appears to be very large. It can however be fully justified, if one takes the sample sizes into account (approx. 7,000 resp. approx. 20,000 persons). In addition, in both analyses the victim status was considered, which included victimization of specified offenses within the last year, and was divided into three groups according to type and severity of the victimization. The three groups consisted of victims of multiple offenses, victims of contact crimes only (robbery, personal attacks or threats, sexual attacks, or sexual molestation), and victims of non-contact crimes only (theft of a car or bicycle, theft of personal property from a car or another place, damage caused to a car, damage caused without involvement of a car, and fraud).

As these single sub-categories are not inter-independent, regression analyses were always conducted separately.

The regression analysis of the GG ´90 (Table 1) accounts for 18% of the variance in 'emotional fear' and 12% of the 'cognitive risk estimate.' Somewhat greater were the results for the GG ´95 (Table 2) namely 20% of the variance for 'emotional fear' and 17% of the 'cognitive risk estimate.' These levels are not outstanding, but they are comparable to those in other studies.

In both studies, the relationship patterns obtained for the dimensions of fear were relatively constant, although the order of the variables changed. Also in both studies, significant and thus mainly stable predictive factors (ß-weight ≥ .10) could be identified for the construction 'emotional fear.' These variables included gender, community size, victimization and going out behavior. Gender expectedly had the highest predictive impact; the women studied reported higher rates of fear. The results also indicated that emotional fear rises with an increase in community size and previous victimization. With respect to going out behavior, an interesting phenomenon was observed. The predictive factors of both studies are contradictory. In other words, in the GG '90 frequent going out correlated to increased fear, while conversely, in the GG '95 frequent going out correlated to lower fear. However, this rather surprising result may be due to contextual effects, since the item involving going out behavior in the 1990 study was posed within a mainly separate and thus merely neutral context. In the 1995 study, this question was optically close to fear related questions, and therefore was influenced by the surrounding items. This fact was also corroborated by the very high ß-weight.

With regard to age, the predictive value for the level of fear of crime was rather low (Beta-weights: -.08 resp. .08), although the T-values were significant in light of the very large samples. Further, the impact in both studies was reverse. Age, at least with respect to emotional fear, did not play an important role. The variable contact with the police, which was considered in the GG ´95 only, should be mentioned. Here, increased contact seems to be accompanied by lower fear, although these attitude-related variables do not permit any statements to be made about the nature of the relationship. It seems however, to be plausible that an increased contact with the police (except for offender-police-contact which was not measured) exercises a positive influence on feelings of security, and also on the evaluation of police work.

Although the other variables had a partially significant influence, their ß-weights were too low to consider their predictive importance.

Table 1: A Linear Regression Analysis of GG '90

	Emotional Fear				Cognitive Estimate of Risk		
Variable	ß	T	sign. T	Variable	ß	T	sign. T
Gender	.28	21.71	p < .001	Community size	.21	15.96	p < .001
Community size	.25	18.98	p < .001	West/East	.17	10.46	p < .001
Victim	.12	9.27	p < .001	Victim	.12	9.47	p < .001
Multiple victims of various crimes	.12	9.39	p < .001	Multiple victims of various crimes	.12	9.79	p < .001
Victims of contact crimes only	.10	7.55	p < .001	Victims of contact crimes only	.10	8.11	p < .001
Victims of non-contact crimes only	.07	5.37	p < .001	Victims of non-contact crimes only	.06	4.67	p < .001
Frequency of going out	.10	6.74	p < .001	Frequency of going out	.11	8.05	p < .001
Age	-.08	-4.28	p < .001	Age	-.07	-3.78	p < .01
Evaluation of the police	.07	5.56	p < .001	Gender	.06	4.57	p < .001
West/East	.05	2.74	p < .01	Evaluation of the police	.05	3.81	p < .001
Income	-.04	-2.13	p < .05	Living alone/with someone	.04	2.90	p < .01
Occupation level	.04	2.49	p < .05	Income	-.04	-2.22	p < .05
Federal states	.03	2.36	p < .05	Occupation level	.04	2.54	p < .05
Living alone/with someone	.02	1.50	p = .13	Federal states	-.02	-1.50	p = .13
Size of household	.02	1.33	p = .19	School graduate	.02	1.02	p = .31
Occupation	.00	0.18	p = .85	Occupation	-.01	-0.59	p = .56
School graduate	.00	0.16	p = .88	Size of household	.01	0.49	p = .63

R = .43 R² = .18 $F_{(145,152)}$ = 82.38 p < .001

R = .35 R² = .12 $F_{(145,715)}$ = 55.50 p < .001

Table 2: A Linear Regression Analysis of GG '95

	Emotional Fear				Cognitive Estimate of Risk		
Variable	ß	T	sign. T	Variable	ß	T	sign. T
Gender	.32	36.87	p < .001	West/East	.19	14.04	p < .001
Frequency of going out	-.15	-16.40	p < .001	Gender	.17	18.98	p < .001
Contact with the police	-.14	-16.96	p < .001	Evaluation of the police	*.17	20.47	p < .001
Evaluation of the police	.12	15.31	p < .001	Age	.12	11.47	p < .001
Victims	.11	12.89	p < .001	Victims	.12	14.04	p < .001
Multiple victims of various crimes	.12	14.40	p < .001	Multiple victims of various crimes	.13	15.23	p < .001
Contact victims only	.06	7.18	p < .001	Contact victims only	.05	5.68	p < .001
Non-contact victims only	.04	4.77	p < .001	Non-contact victims only	.06	7.56	p < .001
Community size	.10	12.29	p < .001	Contact with the police	-.11	-13.17	p < .001
West/East	.10	7.31	p < .001	Community size	.11	13.01	p < .001
Age	.08	8.46	p < .001	Frequency of going out	-.10	-10.87	p < .001
Income	-.05	-4.46	p < .001	Income	-.02	-1.90	p = .06
Federal state	-.03	-1.87	p = .06	School graduate	-.02	-1.84	p = .07
School graduate	-.01	-0.88	p = .38	Occupation	.01	1.19	p = .24
Occupation	-.01	-0.80	p = .42	Size of household altogether	.01	0.96	p = .34
Living alone/with someone	.00	0.43	p = .67	Occupation level	-.01	-1.00	p = .32
Occupation level	.00	-0.19	p = .85	Living alone/with someone	-.01	-0.58	p = .56
Size of household altogether	.00	-0.14	p = .89	Federal state	.01	0.14	p = .89
R = .45 R² = .20 $F_{(15;13,221)}$ = 221.32			p < .001	R = .41 R² = .17 $F_{(15;13,221)}$ = 182.11			p < .001

For the dimension 'cognitive risk estimates,' under consideration of the relevance criterion of the ß-weights (≥ .10), and the identical results in both studies, only four significant predictive factors were found. These variables included living in East or West Germany (higher risk estimations were obtained in East Germany), community size (estimations of risk rose with increasing community size), victimization, and going out behavior (with the problem though, of a converse predictive factor). The variable gender, which was significant for emotional fear, was only a relevant predictive factor in the GG '95. In the GG '90, its ß-weight amounts to .06. With respect to age, a clear influence was observed, giving this variable a positive predictive factor in the GG '95. This was in opposition to the GG '90, which showed a negative, but at the same time merely low predictive factor. In view of the different predictive factors, no statements can be made on the importance of going out behavior. Here, contextual effects are likely to be relevant, and there is still no answer to the question of a possible relationship with fear.

In the discussion of the fear of crime, age has repeatedly been considered. The central factor of the often quoted crime-fear-paradox consists of the apparent discrepancy between the objective victimization risk of certain age groups, and the subjective feeling of security. Because of this, we intended to analyze the relationships between age and the fear of crime in a more differentiated manner, based on the more recent study (the GG '95) which comprised more than 20,000 persons. To this end, we effected multi-factorial analyses of variance including not only age and the two fear dimensions, but also community size, gender, previous victimization as well as living in East or West Germany. We considered only these variables because they played an important role with respect to the level of fear rates, as was shown by the regression analysis. In order to enhance a uniform approach, the variables mentioned were included in the analyses with both fear dimensions, although this was not absolutely required by the regression analysis.

Fear of crime and age
Figures 1 and 2 show the fear of crime-related results by gender of our victim study which comprised 20,695 persons (GG '95) for East and West Germany. Both dimensions, 'emotional fear' (Figure 1) as well as 'cognitive risk estimates' (Figure 2) reveal a similar picture. In East and West Germany, women have distinctly higher rates of fear than men in both dimensions. Also with respect to gender, East Germans always expressed stronger fear than West Germans.

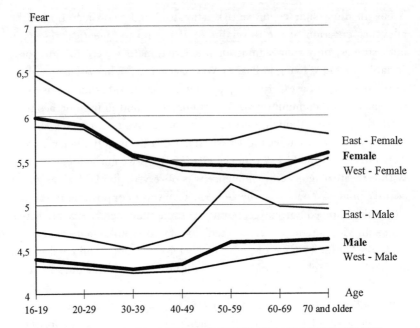

FIGURE 1: EMOTIONAL FEAR IN RELATION TO GENDER AND AGE IN WEST AND EAST GERMANY (GG '95; MEDIANS)

If one looks at emotional fear in relation to the three independent variables gender, age and regional residence (East or West Germany; Figure 1), it can be said that young women, in West as well as in East Germany, comprise the group with the highest fear rates. These rates decrease in accordance with the advancement of age for women in Eastern Germany until the ages 30 to 39, and in West Germany even until the ages 60 to 69. Afterwards, an increase in emotional fear can be observed. In Western Germany this increase occurs rather suddenly, only when the oldest female age group is reached, whereas in Eastern Germany the increase occurs relatively steadily. In both cases, however, the increase observed never reaches the level of fear expressed by the youngest group of women. These results clearly reject the existence of a crime-fear-paradox, a paradox that mainly states that elderly women, with the lowest victimization risk, express the strongest fear.

The curves representing the results obtained for men clearly differ from those of women. Although here, emotional fear also decreases from the youngest age group until approximately the group of 30 to 39 year old men, the decrease is considerably less steep than that observed for females. While fear reported by West German men over the age of 40 steadily

Estimate of Risk

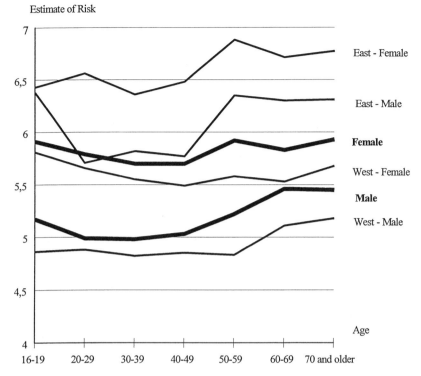

FIGURE 2:: COGNITIVE ESTIMATE OF RISK IN RELATION TO SEX AND AGE FOR EAST AND WEST GERMANY (GG '95; MEDIANS)

increases, fear reported by East German men increases very suddenly and distinctly until the ages 50 to 59. It is then followed by a slight decrease. This clear peak of the fear level for East German men requires closer verification.

With respect to the cognitive risk estimates, the curves are far less homogeneous. Here, the curve for West German women is similar to that obtained for their emotional fear rates: the highest rates are reached by the 16 to 19 year old women, with a decrease observed until the ages 40 to 49. Again, a slight increase is observed thereafter. The curve for East German women oscillates, with the lowest rates for the 30 to 39 year old women, and the highest rates for the 50 to 59 year olds. In general though, the rates increase.

Rates for the cognitive risk estimates of West German men are also similar to those obtained for their emotional fear. After a rather steady development, rates increase for men 50 to 59 years old and older. This increase is, as compared to emotional fear, slightly steeper. East German men however, have a very clear U-shaped distribution. Rates for 16 to 19 year old men are the highest, followed by a steep decrease towards the next age group, 20 to 29 year olds. A generally steady development continues up to the group of 40 to 49 year old men, and then a renewed increase is observed for the 50 to 59 year old men. The distribution then generally remains on the same level. The following discussion of the results will likewise try to explain these rather striking differences in the distribution.

The multi-factorial analysis of variance always yielded highly significant main effects ($p < .001$) with regard to the criterion variable 'emotional fear.' At the same time, differences in the predictive variable gender were the most distinct ($F = 955.31$), followed by the East or West variable ($F = 125.97$), and finally age ($F = 6.20$). The two-way interactions of age with gender ($F = 12.66$; $p < .001$), as well as age with living in the East or West ($F = 3.56$; $p < .01$) were significant as well. No significant result was yielded by the interaction of gender with living in the East or West, or by three-way interactions.

With respect to the 'cognitive risk estimates,' highly significant main effects were also established, with the exception of age/gender: $F = 657.74$; East/West: $F = 691.48$; age: $p < .01$ / $F = 3.22$. The two-way interactions of age with gender ($F = 8.82$; $p < .001$), as well as age with living in the East or West ($F = 3.93$; $p < .01$) were significant as well. No further interaction effects were observed.

Fear of crime and community size

As was shown in the regression analyses, community size played a particularly important role in the fear of crime with both dimensions, emotional fear and cognitive risk estimates. Thus, we will finally confront the question of how strongly community size influences the relationship between the fear of crime and age. Does the crime-fear-paradox especially or exclusively exist within urban areas? In order to give an informative presentation of the results, we established three age groups: 16 to 34 year olds, 35 to 54 year olds, and persons over 55 years of age. We then established, for each of the three age groups, gender specific fear rates for the two dimensions, emotional fear and cognitive risk estimates, with reference to the community size (<20,000, 20,000 – <100,000, 100,000 – < 500,000 and more than 500,000 inhabitants.) The results are presented in Figures 3 and 4.

The results were similar for both genders, for both fear dimensions, and with all three age groups among all four community sizes. Controlling for gender and age, the fear of crime along both dimensions

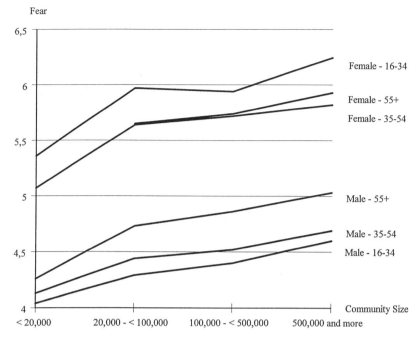

Fear

FIGURE 3: EMOTIONAL FEAR IN RELATION TO GENDER, AGE AND COMMUNITY SIZE
(GG '95; MEDIANS)

increased with community size. With respect to the dimension 'emotional fear,' it was striking that once again young women (16 to 34 years of age) distinctly had the highest fear rates among all four community sizes. The other two age groups however, had mainly similar rates, with an exception of very large cities. Neither here was the crime-fear-paradox corroborated. Again, the group comprised of the youngest women reported the highest fear rates, rather than that comprised of elderly women. The oldest male age group steadily revealed higher fear rates for all four community sizes.

Looking at the dimension 'cognitive risk estimates,' the rates for the oldest male age group (55 years of age and older) in large cities showed an especially distinct increase. This did not similarly appear in the other age groups. Consequently, cognitive risk estimates by men seem to depend thus far on the degree of urbanization. Such estimates increase with the advancement of age, particularly in major urban cities. Here, the differences between the oldest (55 years and older) and the other age groups was the most clear. The oldest age group of women, like men, reached the highest rates of risk estimates, accompanied by a particularly steep

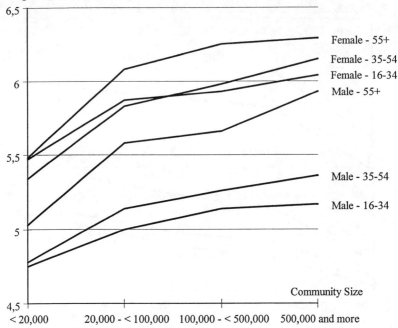

FIGURE 4: COGNITIVE ESTIMATE OF RISK IN RELATIONS TO GENDER, AGE AND COMMUNITY SIZE (GG '95; MEDIANS)

increase from the smallest size category (<20,000 inhabitants) up to the next category of community size (20,000 – <100,000 inhabitants). A striking feature found for the youngest age group of women was that their rates within the smallest communities (<20,000 inhabitants) matched the ones reported by the oldest age group. The following increase was so small though, that already in the category of the next community size, they nearly reached the rates reported by the 35 to 54 year old women, and then fall below in communities with 100,000 to < 500,000 inhabitants. From then on, the group comprised of the youngest women reported the lowest cognitive risk estimates.

These results, of the development of the fear rates, were corroborated again by the results of the variance analysis. With regard to emotional fear, all main effects were again statistically highly significant, but the F-values clearly differed. Gender again had the greatest effect on the fear of crime (F = 1854.50). The effect of community size clearly decreased (F = 156.57) although the increase in fear levels along with increasing urbanization was still statistically highly significant. The effect of age was, in comparison, distinctly lower (F = 10.45) although it was statistically highly significant as well. Two-way interactions yielded considerably lower results. Considering the variables age with community size, they were even found to be insignificant (F = 0.81). In other words, the developments of the fear levels within the single age groups were not influenced by changes in community size. The assumption that especially elderly persons who live in major urban cities have a clearer increase in 'emotional fear,' as compared to other age groups, did not prove to be true at all.

With respect to the dimension 'cognitive risk estimates,' the results differed. In consideration of the main effects, gender again had the greatest effect on the dependent variable (F = 493.00). It was followed by community size (F = 126.73), and finally, as was seen for 'emotional fear,' age (F = 55.04). All F-values were highly significant. The two-way interactions showed a significant interaction on the 1%-level, between age and community size (F = 2.88). So, the results we interpreted above were upheld statistically. With respect to 'cognitive risk estimates,' elderly persons, particularly elderly men, showed a clearly higher perceived risk than did younger persons, in relation to increasing community size.

The widely reported sharp climb in fear among the elderly with increases in urbanization appears here in only one dimension of the fear of crime. It was observed for cognitive risk-estimates of becoming a victim in the future only, not for emotional fear.

DISCUSSION OF THE RESULTS

It was shown through factor analyses performed within the two different studies that the fear of crime splits into an emotional and a cognitive aspect. This distinction, which is frequently made in current research literature, thus proves to be very stable. Hence, it may be stated that hypothesis 1 is confirmed. A standardization of the measurement of the fear of crime throughout different studies is urgently required, indeed.

The regression analyses performed after the scaling of the fear items, in which the formed scales 'emotional fear' and 'cognitive risk estimates' were introduced as criterion variables, yielded for both German studies slightly different predictive influences with respect to emotional fear in comparison to cognitive risk estimates. So, gender, community size and previous victimization proved to be relevant for emotional fear, whereby gender expectedly had the highest predictive value. This result is in accordance with numerous other research results, stating that women, inhabitants of large cities, and victims have a distinctly higher fear of crime. However, the question remains open as to what extent the distinctions between the single groups could also be due to the method of measuring the fear of crime, for example to item phrasing. The 'standard item,' which suggests threat by a sudden criminal attack and describes a situation ('after nightfall, outside the apartment or house, alone'), is also likely to trigger 'learned' fear to some extent. This can be considered a result of the fact that on television and in the cinema, attacks, especially on women, are frequently shown. Similarly, the emotional fear items nearly always involved a certain level of anonymity at the place of residence. This is a situation which prevails in larger cities where informal social control is considerably lower than in rural communities. We justly supposed that the age variable does not play a very important role with respect to the fear of crime. The results even show a reverse effect in both studies. On the other hand, data yielded by the follow-up analyses point to a more complex relation between fear and age than suggested by the results of the regression analysis.

As to 'cognitive risk estimates,' gender was not a homogeneously relevant factor. Instead, besides community size and victimization, the variable 'living in the East or West' prevailed. East Germans, largely inhabitants of big cities and victims, estimated the risk of being victimized within the next 12 months higher than did West Germans, largely inhabitants of smaller cities and non-victims. The higher risk estimation by the cited groups corresponds to the actual situation, and is therefore not surprising. Consequently, a clearly higher incidence rate of offenses (per 100,000 persons) in the Eastern federal states since 1993 points to a rise in crime since the opening of the borders. This was the first year in which the German Federal Bureau of Criminal Investigation (Bundeskriminalamt, 1994) stated that a comparison of the registered crime rates between East and West Germany would be valid. This trend continued until 1996. Hence, it may be concluded, that East Germans actually bear a higher victimization risk than West Germans. Further, East Germany experienced a change in crimes committed within a rather short period of time, and an increased press reporting on crime-related topics. Inhabitants of large cities also run a higher risk in becoming victims of crime, due to the better opportunity structures and the larger number of offenders. A higher risk of victimization was also understandably expressed by persons who were victimized within the past year. The relevant factor 'going out behavior' cannot be interpreted because of the heterogeneous predictive factors and again, the effect of age, which is not homogeneous. These facts lead to a conditional confirmation of hypothesis 2. Only community size and previous victimization proved to be relevant predictive factors with respect to both aspects of the fear of crime. Gender seems to play an essential role, particularly when emotional aspects are considered. Its effect on cognitive risk estimates however, was merely heterogeneous. In accordance with our hypothesis, age is awarded only a moderate role for the explanation of the fear of crime (cognitive and emotional).

The assumption that especially elderly persons express an increased fear of crime has already been doubted in literature because of the contradictory nature of the results (Aromaa & Ahven, 1995; Heiskanen & Aromaa, 1996). Our results as well, do not confirm the crime-fear-paradox at all. On the contrary, it seems that especially young women have the highest fear rates within the dimension 'emotional fear.' It seems plausible that these increased fear rates must be seen in connection with an experienced victimization risk, mainly in the area of sexual offenses, which is particularly high for young women. Further, a sudden criminal attack such as sexual assault or rape, again often shown on television and in the cinema, might especially constitute a permanent threat to the age group of young women who have recently left their parents' home for an apartment of their own. Since on television and in the cinema women mostly belonging to this age group are presented as victims, these crime presentations might develop into factors triggering fear, and thus adapt a model learning function. The slight increase of emotional fear along with age might be traced back to the increased vulnerability of elderly women. On one hand, there is an increased physical vulnerability caused by aging. On the other hand, elderly women often have to cope with a sometimes considerably reduced financial scope. This is partially enforced by widowhood, due to the fact that women have a longer life expectancy than men. These factors have essential negative effects on the quality of life, and are likely to manifest themselves in security estimations (cf., summarizing with regard to age Baltes & Skotzki, 1995; Baltes & Wilms, 1995; Filipp & Schmidt, 1995).

Looking now at men in East and West Germany, the youngest age group had a slightly increased level of emotional fear of crime. This might partially be due to the relatively high victimization risk of that age group. Young men are very often victimized, for reasons including the fact that they are more likely to expose themselves to particularly risky and crime prone situations, as in crowded discotheques, for example. Nevertheless, here the increased fear expressed by young women must, of course, also be taken into account. The young generation, especially, has to cope with manifold problems. At the same time, they have to face reduced resources, not the least of which are financial. Hence, vital personality development is impeded to a considerable extent. This fact may finally result in sharp feelings of insecurity, for which the fear of crime does not mean anything more than some kind of metaphor (Keupp, 1996). The results of the latest Shell-survey also point to the rather bleak future prospects of the young generation, irrespective of the type and level of school training. Among such problems, unemployment is attributed the greatest importance (Münchmeier, 1997).

Regarding emotional fear expressed by men, a clear peak for the 50 to 59 year old East Germans is striking. If this peak did not exist, the curve for East Germany would be very similar to that of West Germany. The crime load borne by this group gives only an unsatisfactory explanation for this phenomenon. If one considers however, this type of fear of crime, once again with respect to the general societal context, possible explanations for this phenomenon become available. For instance, especially in East Germany, the job situation after the German reunification has considerably deteriorated. While in the former German Democratic Republic there was almost no unemployment at all, the situation drastically changed after the reunification. There were firms breaking down, and within a short period of time the unemployment rate even exceeded that in West Germany. The age group of 50 to 59 year old persons, in particular, was likely to be greatly affected by this development. The current study (GG '95) revealed that more than 40% of all East German unemployed men belonged to that age group.

Regarding 'cognitive risk estimates,' the results are not as homogeneous as those for the 'emotional fear of crime.' However, especially with respect to 'cognitive risk estimates,' indications towards the existence of a 'crime-fear-paradox' are very likely to emerge. Here, it is possible to recognize an incorrect estimation of the victimization risk. A cognitive assessment process of that risk is obviously to a lesser extent enforced by general factors which lead to overall feelings of insecurity, factors that partially overlap emotional fear rates. The two aspects of fear are far more independent than has been suggested within the rather artificial separation of presentations up to now. The two scales 'emotional fear' and 'cognitive risk estimates,' for instance, correlate with $r = .57$, thus rejecting any independence.

With respect to West German women, values for cognitive risk estimates were similar to those for emotional fear (a decrease until the 40 to 49 year old women followed by a slight increase). Values for cognitive risk estimates yielded by East German women however, differed considerably. If something like a regression line is applied to the rather oscillating distribution, it would reveal an increase in risk estimates along with age. This however, is done without taking into account the age-depending decrease of the younger age groups. In the present article, due to a lack of research data, we are not in a position to discuss satisfactorily the question concerning to what extent this clear increase in risk estimates along with increasing age might be traced back to women's perceptions of the changed crime situation in East Germany. The frequently shown situation, especially seen in 'reality-TV,' of an elderly woman whose handbag is snatched in the street or who falls victim to a confidence artist, does have an impact that should not be underestimated on the increase in risk estimates of women 50 years of age or older. In West Germany this observed increase is slight, while in East Germany it is quite distinct. In this context, Chiricos et al. (1997) emphasized that it is not so much the general reporting on violence and crime by the media that causes fear, but rather a target-group-specific influence that occurs ('model learning'). 'White women see victims like themselves on TV NEWS and are more fearful' (p. 354).

The male risk estimates are marked by a somewhat distinct increase for the middle aged and older men (in East Germany from 50 to 59 years on, in West Germany not before the age of 60). This might have to do with the fact that particularly in the second half of one's life, weakness and vulnerability increase, bringing about a clearer perception of risks, including the victimization risk. Since former physical strength and agility of youth are gone, it becomes necessary to recognize potential dangers at an earlier stage, which is likely to lead to increased risk estimates.

This possible explanatory hypothesis however, does not explain the extremely high cognitive risk estimate values obtained by the youngest age group of East German men. It is true that especially young men, due to their increased readiness (as compared to persons belonging to older age groups or women) to expose themselves to dangerous situations, have a higher victimization risk. Thus, the estimates made by young East German men are certainly reasonable. The question remains open though, why were the risk estimates reported by young West German men clearly lower? In this context, perhaps socialization effects might play a certain role. Young West Germans, for example, are used to facing a steady change in the scope of their leisure-time activities and in risky situations. Going to discotheques, for example, has always been part of their normal life experience, whereas young East Germans have been confronted with a rather drastic change, especially with respect to such activities. Organized and hierarchically structured activities which were offered in the former German Democratic

Republic are now, after the reunification, replaced by activities to be individually selected. Moreover, they are hardly controllable. To a certain extent, East Germany can be considered an experimental field with respect to leisure-time activities, because of its lack of established structures. In this context, the readiness of the East German juveniles to test what is new may also be linked to a certain caution, rooted in the risks perceived. Another important factor may also be seen in strong feelings of uncertainty, caused by impending unemployment. This is a problem which, in view of the higher unemployment rate in East Germany, concerns East German juveniles more than those in West Germany. In addition, West German juveniles may be more capable of obtaining employment than East German juveniles who are used to the socialistic education system. With respect to age and specific dependence of fear rates with regard to community size, we found out that in the area of emotional fear, young women clearly had the highest fear rates in all size categories. This finding may indeed be seen in connection with the fear already mentioned of falling victim to a sudden violent criminal (sexually motivated, in particular) attack. In the area of cognitive risk estimates however, fear values reported by young women (in comparison to the other two age groups) were marked by a relative decrease with increases in community size. In reality however, the risk for young women to be victims of crime increases with community size. Young women in larger cities mostly experience a special type of socialization which makes them participate in individual and autonomous leisure-time activities. This also gives them more independence and self-confidence, resulting in lower risk estimates. This does not contradict their higher rates of emotional fear, because the items on the 'emotional fear' scale clearly implied a sudden (sexually motivated) criminal attack after nightfall. The anticipation of such an attack on one hand may lead to a clear affective distraction. The risk of experiencing such an incidence though, is, at the same time estimated to be rather low. In addition, such a risk is not exclusively limited to this special type of attack.

In summary, it can be concluded that the frequently cited crime-fear-paradox, declaring that elderly persons are more fearful despite their low victimization risk, cannot be confirmed. Especially with respect to the affective area, even some findings pointing to the reverse can be found. Hence, this confirms our hypothesis 3. We found a broad confirmation of incorrect estimations of victimization risks within the cognitive risk estimates. In this respect, changes in the risk perception caused by the process of aging might play a more important role than an increased fearfulness.

It was also shown that the existing discrepancies of research results, especially concerning the age dependence on the fear of crime, require further and more differentiated research. Hale (1996, p. 103) for example, emphasized: 'Clearly the notion that the elderly are more fearful of crime is one which needs further study.' Before this statement, Eve (1985, p. 406) stressed the necessity for comparative studies, especially on the age dependence on the fear of crime.

Research results available up to now show that on one hand the fear of crime depends on personality variables, such as perceived vulnerability. On the other hand though, the fear of crime has to be viewed within a general societal context, rendering research into this phenomenon quite difficult. The scope of possible intervening variables and their relevance to the fear of crime as already defined, are surely still incomplete and thus subject to further supplementation. 'Every advance that is made ... seems to generate more questions than answers' (Garofalo, 1981, p. 113).

All authors agree (Hale, 1996, p. 132) that it is of major importance to improve research on the fear of crime, especially methodically, as well as to be more precise on the relationship of age and fear. Particularly in Germany, where the fear of crime has become a major issue since the reunification of the two German nations, and in the wake of political change in the former Eastern bloc states, it is necessary to conduct further, more differentiated studies on this topic. In particular, the use of the definition must urgently be standardized.

NOTES

1   Parts of our study were organized in 1995 by the research group 'Community Crime Prevention in Baden-Württemberg' with D. Dölling, Th. Feltes, W. Heinz, D. Hermann, H. Kury, J. Obergfell-Fuchs, Ch. Simsa, and G. Spieß, and by the Institute for Research into Legal Practice of the University of Konstanz study group 'Empirical Criminology: Punitive and Legal Action Research' (W. Heinz); further by the Ministry of the Interior of Baden-Württemberg and the University of Konstanz and carried out by the Opinion Research Institute—GFM-Getas. Special thanks are owed to these research groups for their permission to publish some results of the survey as well as to the Ministry of the Interior of Baden-Württemberg and to the University of Konstanz for their financial support of the survey. We might also acknowledge that the research groups as well as the named individuals who were not listed as authors bear no responsibility for the results reported here.

REFERENCES

Adams, R., & Smith, T. (1976). *Fear of neighborhood*. National Research Center; Chicago.
Aromaa, K., & Ahven, S. (1995). *Victims of crime in a time of change: Estonia 1993 and 1995*. Helsinki.
Baltes M.M., & Skotzki, E. (1995). Tod im Alter: Eigene Endlichkeit und Partnerverlust. In: R. Oerter & L. Montada (Eds.), *Entwicklungspsychologie (3rd. ed.)* (pp. 1137–1146). Weinheim.
Baltes M.M., & Wilms, H.-U. (1995). Alltagskompetenz im Alter. In: R. Oerter & L. Montada (Eds.), *Entwicklungspsychologie (3rd. ed.)* (pp. 1127–1136). Weinheim.

Biderman, A.D, Johnson, L., McIntyre, J., & Weir, J. (1967). *Report on a pilot study in the district of Columbia on victimization and attitudes toward law enforcement and the administration of justice.* Washington, DC.

Boers, K. (1993). Kriminalitätsfurcht. *Monatsschrift für Kriminologie und Strafrechtsreform, 76,* 65–82.

Box, S., Hale, C., & Andrews, G. (1988). Explaining fear of crime. *British Journal of Criminology, 28,* 340–356.

Braungart, M.M., Braungart, R.G., & Hoyer, W.J. (1980). Age, sex, and social factors in fear of crime. *Sociological Focus, 13,* 55–66.

Bundeskriminalamt (Ed.) (1994). *Polizeiliche Kriminalstatistik Bundesrepublik Deutschland. Berichtsjahr 1993.* Wiesbaden.

Chiricos, T., Eschholz, S., & Gertz, M. (1997). Crime, news, and fear of crime: Towards an identification of audience effects. *Social Problems, 44,* (3), 342–357.

Clark, A., & Lewis, M.J. (1974). Fear of crime among the elderly: An explanatory study. *British Journal of Criminology, 22,* 49–62.

Clemente, F., & Kleiman, M.B. (1977). Fear of crime in the United States: A multivariate analysis. *Social Forces, 56,* 519–531.

Eve, S.B. (1985). Criminal victimization and fear of crime among the non-institutionalized elderly in the United States: A critique of the empirical research literature. *Victimology, 10,* 397–408.

Filipp, S.-H., & Schmidt, K. (1995). Mittleres und höheres Erwachsenenalter. In: R. Oerter & L. Montada (Eds.), *Entwicklungspsychologie. (3rd. ed.)* (pp. 438–486). Weinheim.

Garofalo, J. (1981). The fear of crime: Causes and consequences. In: U.S. Department of Justice (Ed.), *Victims of crime. A review of research issues and methods* (pp. 113–135). Washington.

Hale, C. (1996). Fear of crime: A review of the literature. *International Review of Victimology, 4,* 79–150.

Heiskanen, M., & Aromaa, K. (1996). *Victimisation in Finland 1996. Survey findings from the Finnish part of the International Victimisation Survey.* Helsinki.

Hindelang, M.J. (1975). *Public opinion regarding crime, criminal justice, and related topics.* U.S. Department of Justice; Washington, D.C.

Hindelang, M.J., Gottfredson, M.R., & Garofalo, J. (1978). *Victims of personal crime: An empirical foundation for a theory of personal victimization.* Cambridge/Mass.

Keupp, C. (1996). Produktive Lebensbewältigung in den Zeichen der allgemeinen Verunsicherung. *SOS-Dialog, 1,* 4–11.

Kury, H. (1995). Zur Bedeutung von Kriminalitätsentwicklung und Viktimisierung für die Verbrechensfurcht. In: G. Kaiser & J.-M. Jehle (Eds.), *Kriminologische Opferforschung. Neue Perspektiven und Erkenntnisse. Teilband II: Verbrechensfurcht und Opferwerdung. Individualopfer und Verarbeitung von Opfererfahrungen.* (pp. 127–158). Heidelberg.

Kury, H. (1997). Kriminalitätsbelastung, Sicherheitsgefühl der Bürger und kommunale Kriminalprävention. In: H. Kury (Ed.), *Konzepte Kommunaler Kriminalprävention. Sammelband der 'Erfurter Tagung'.* Freiburg.

Kury, H., & Ferdinand, T. (1996). Recent research on victimization and the fear of crime. *Comparative Law Review, 30,* 1–138.

Kury, H., Dörmann, U., Richter, H., & Würger, M. (1992). *Opfererfahrungen und Meinungen zur Inneren Sicherheit in Deutschland.* Wiesbaden.

LaGrange, R.L., & Ferraro, K.F. (1987). The elderly's fear of crime. *Research on Aging, 9,* 372–391.

Münchmeier, R. (1997). Die Lebenslage junger Menschen. In: Jugendwerk der Deutschen Shell (Ed.), *Jugend '97. Zukunftsperspektiven, Gesellschaftliches Engagement, Politische Orientierungen.* (pp. 277–301). Opladen.

Normoyle, J.B. (1987). Fear of crime and satisfaction among elderly public housing residents: The impact of residential segregation. *Basic and Applied Social Psychology, 8,* 193–207.

Norton, L., & Courlander, M. (1982). Fear of crime among the elderly: The role of crime prevention programs. *The Gerontologist, 22,* 388–393.

Obergfell-Fuchs, J., & Kury, H. (1996). Sicherheitsgefühl und Persönlichkeit. *Monatsschrift für Kriminologie und Strafrechtsreform, 79,* 97–113.

Pollock, L., & Patterson, A.H. (1980). Territorial behavior and fear of crime among the elderly and non-elderly homeowners. *Journal of Social Psychology*, *111*, 119–129.

Ragan, P.K. (1977). Crimes against the elderly: Findings from interviews with Blacks, Mexican Americans, and Whites. In: M.A.Y. Rifai (Ed.), *Justice and older Americans* (pp. 25–36).Lexington/Mass.

Warr, M. (1990). Dangerous situations: Social context and fear of victimization. *Social Forces*, *68*, 891–907.

Wetzels, P., Greve, W., Mecklenburg, E., Bilsky, W., & Pfeiffer, C. (1995). *Kriminalität im Leben alter Menschen*. Stuttgart et al.

Yin, P. (1980). Fear of crime among the elderly: Some issues and suggestions. *Social Problems*, *27*, 492–504.

Chapter 10

VICTIMIZATION AND LIFESTYLE AMONG DRUG ABUSERS[1]

Serge Brochu, Isabelle Parent, Anne Chamandy and Line Chayer

The study of victimization among drug abusers is the study of a frontier problem between Law and Psychology. First, in many countries, repressive laws and policies help push the drug market into hidden and potentially dangerous places, leaving the victim little recourse other than retaliation. Second, the lifestyle of many of these victimized drug abusers had already placed them in potentially dangerous situations before they started abusing illicit drugs: many were gang members in their adolescence, or were involved in minor delinquency, or associated with violent people. In a pilot study to gain a better understanding of the victimization of drug abusers, 12 addicts were interviewed and their discourse on victimization related to the drug market was analyzed. The results of the pilot study are presented and analyzed.

INTRODUCTION

Many studies in criminology have addressed the criminal involvement of illicit drug users. However, the victimization[2] of psychoactive substance users has received little attention until recently. It is not surprising that the victimization of socially marginal groups has been studied so little. Research has mainly focused on women and children who are victims of criminal acts or on the so-called 'good victims.' There is often a tendency to dichotomize the roles of aggressor and victim, yet it appears that the two may belong to a relatively homogeneous population. Victims do not usually report a criminal assault because of their own illicit drug use, which leads to a situation where the victimization of users of psychoactive substances is not considered a real social problem. However, when researchers look at the aggressor-drug-victim relationship, they find that the aggressor is not the only one taking psychoactive substances: victimization is often associated with consumption of alcohol or illegal drugs. The aim of this study is to gain a better understanding of the association between the problems of drug use and victimization. Such an understanding is important in societal terms in order to foster the development of intervention strategies adapted to the victim's reality.

This paper first examines various models for understanding the relationship between victimization and the use of psychoactive substances. Then the general framework for the method used in the study is presented. Lastly, there is a discussion of the results.

THE RELATIONSHIP BETWEEN VICTIMIZATION AND PSYCHOACTIVE SUBSTANCES

A review of a study done by one of the authors (Parent, 1997) shows the existence of a relationship between drug consumption and victimization, across all types of data collected (official and self-reported) in both victim and user populations.

However, despite this established prevalence, a conceptual framework for this relationship has yet to be developed. What is the nature of the relationship between use of psychoactive substances and victimization?

All the studies reviewed seem to indicate that the relationship between the use of psychoactive substances and the violence experienced is a complex one. We will now briefly analyze the probable hypotheses.

Several hypotheses have been formulated to try to explain the relationship between use of psychoactive substances and criminal victimization. Some researchers have proposed causal models, while others have suggested correlational models for understanding this relationship.

USE OF PSYCHOACTIVE SUBSTANCES AS A RISK FACTOR IN VICTIMIZATION

For some authors, victimization occurs because of consumption of psychoactive substances. Indeed, many data, such as data from studies of homicide victims, tend to indicate that use of drugs and/or alcohol preceded the victimization.

Some authors have noted that a high percentage of victimization had a drug or alcohol dependency prior to the first assault (Selkin, 1975; Burman et al., 1988; Hussey & Singer, 1993).

Analysis of the temporal sequence between sexual victimization and abuse of psychoactive substances indicates that 23% of teenagers receiving psychiatric treatment had consumed drugs or alcohol before being sexually abused (Hussey & Singer, 1993; Singer, Petchers & Hussey, 1989).

Some authors even suggest that consumption is a factor triggering sexual victimization (Amir, 1971; Burman et al., 1988; Selkin, 1975).

How can this relationship be explained?

Four major models have been proposed showing how use of psychoactive substances may constitute a risk factor in criminal victimization: a model based on the psycho-pharmacological effects of psychoactive substances, a model that emphasizes the prime target for victimization, a model that incorporates the systemic violence related to the market for illegal drugs, and the economic-compulsive model.

The psychopharmacological effects of psychoactive substances
The psychopharmacological model suggests that some people may provoke their victimization through their own intoxication (Goldstein, 1985; Goldstein, 1989; Spunt et al., 1990). As the diagram below shows, the intoxicating properties of psychoactive substances would alter a person's behavior in such a way as to make the person vulnerable to a criminal act. Withdrawal symptoms can also contribute to victimization by provoking irritable or aggressive reactions.

Psychopharmacological model

Use of psychoactive substances	→	Intoxication	→	Psycho-pharmacological effects	→	Victimization

According to Goldstein (1989), 7.5% of the homicides (n = 414) which he classified were caused by the psychopharmacological effects of psychoactive substances.

Several of the specific effects of psychoactive substances could, according to this model, lead to victimization. Intoxication could reduce a person's capacity to identify situations involving risk of victimization, could impair the person's ability to express his or her needs and wishes clearly, could decrease alertness and cloud judgement (Brochu, 1994; Kantor & Straus, 1989; Champagne, 1994; Fattah & Raic, 1970; Hussey & Singer, 1993; Windle 1994) as well as wipe out any ability to take protective measures (Hussey & Singer, 1993). Intoxication could also reduce the resistance of the potential victim. For example, if the victim is in a state of total sedation because of drunkenness, he or she will obviously show no resistance (Fattah & Raic, 1970). It is also likely that the intoxicated victim would be less able to escape their aggressor should a conflict arise (Kantor & Straus, 1989). Furthermore, the effects of psychoactive substances on the central nervous system could diminish the victim's reflexes (Fattah & Raic, 1970; Fattah, 1991). These hypotheses works well for alcohol and drugs considered depressants. However, according to this logic, stimulants would improve reflexes and their use could therefore be considered a protective factor. In short:

> intoxication seems to affect an individual's cognitive sensitivity, reducing a person's ability to adequately discriminate among indicators present within the self and in the external environment, thereby also reducing the range of response (Brochu, 1994, p. 441).

The risk that victimization would occur would therefore be exacerbated.

However, one of the main explanations for this psychopharmacological victimization is that intoxication through use of psychoactive substances could release the victim's aggressive and provocative tendencies (Fattah & Raic, 1970; Fattah, 1991; Goodman et al, 1986). Decreased inhibitions caused by consumption of alcohol could give the person an opportunity to express their frustrations, tensions and emotional conflicts (Wolfgang, 1958). Researchers have observed that consumption of alcohol could precipitate victimization because the victim acted in a provocative manner, and would probably not have done so had alcohol not been consumed (Goldstein, 1989; Welte & Abel, 1989; Wolfgang, 1958; Fattah & Raic, 1970; Lindqvist, 1991). The victim would therefore play an active role in the commission of the crime through physical or verbal provocation. Indeed, in many cases the victim could be considered the initiator of violence since he or she is the first to hit the other person (Fattah & Raic, 1970; Lindqvist, 1991; Silverman & Mukherjee, 1987). Some researchers have studied provocation by victims who had taken psychoactive substances. In almost half of all cases of homicide, the victim seemed in fact to have initiated the aggressive interaction (Lindqvist, 1991; Muscat & Huncharek, 1991). This type of homicide—one provoked by the victim—is more likely to be linked to alcohol than other murders. More specifically, these victims are more likely to have consumed psychoactive substances (Lindqvist, 1991; Wolfgang, 1958) and in greater amounts (Muscat & Huncharek, 1991). Thus, for victims who had consumed alcohol, blood alcohol levels were higher among those who had in some way provoked the commission of the crime (Muscat & Huncharek, 1991).

Yet a detailed examination of this explanation leads one to conclude that the psychopharmacological effects of psychoactive substances depend on the various meanings that users attach to intoxication (Kantor & Straus, 1989). Reactions to psychoactive substances would then depend on the mental and psychological state of the user and the context of use (Brochu, 1994). Studies show that alcohol consumed in medium or heavy doses can induce aggressive behavior only when intoxicated persons find themselves in a provoking or threatening situation (Taylor et al., 1976). In addition, one tends to forget that while it is possible that the effects of some drugs could provoke violent behavior in some people, drug use can also have the reverse psychopharmacological effect and reduce violent tendencies (Goldstein, 1985). Thus, in some cases, people who are prone to violence may self-medicate by using heroin and tranquilizers to control their violent impulses (Goldstein, 1985).

In short, even if a variety of behaviors on the part of the intoxicated person could increase the risk of exposure to criminal victimization, the psychopharmacological properties of psychoactive substances cannot alone explain the appearance of violent behavior in intoxicated persons (Brochu, 1994). The psychopharmacological model does however suggest that individual variations in the victim's behavioral responses to alcohol should be considered.

Psychoactive substance users: prime targets

This model is a slight variation of the preceding one. It suggests that, even though the psychopharmacological effects of intoxication may not lead to provocation by the victim, the potential aggressor will view the psychoactive substance user as a tempting target because of the potential victim's state of intoxication and the fact that he or she uses drugs or alcohol.

The delinquent's selection of a victim could be influenced by the victim's intoxication, even if the victim does not engage in provocative behavior. The victim is chosen because of his or her consumption. Despite the fact that some crimes may be committed on impulse, this model presupposes that, in general, delinquents make subtle distinctions among targets that are likely or unlikely to make good victims, among people who can and cannot be victimized (Fattah, 1991). The victim's intoxication may make the victim appear more physically vulnerable to a potential aggressor, who will then be tempted to try to take advantage of the state induced by the consumption of psychoactive substances (Brochu, 1994; Welte & Abel, 1989), since the possibility of controlling the victim's resistance is one criteria for selecting the victim (Fattah, 1991).

So a person who is often intoxicated in public places becomes an easy target for individuals who are disposed to committing a crime (Simons, Whitbeck & Bales, 1989; Wolfgang, 1958).

Apart from the fact that alcohol/drug use could be a risk factor by making victims less able to identify and express their feelings, for some individuals the consumption of psychoactive substances may justify a sexual assault when the victim is drunk or drugged (Aramburu & Leigh, 1991; Leigh & Aramburu, 1994). Socially, the state of drunkenness may even be interpreted as signifying greater sexual receptivity on the part of the intended victim. Social perceptions reinforce the aggressor's beliefs in this regard. The aggressor receives less blame socially if the act was committed while the victim was intoxicated (Richardson & Campbell, 1982). The aggressor may consider it more acceptable to hit someone who is drunk than to assault a sober person (Aramburu & Leigh, 1991; Leigh & Aramburu, 1994).

Social perceptions of psychoactive substance users are very negative, even when they are victimized. Studies show that an intoxicated victim, of either sex, is considered more responsible and therefore more blameworthy as a victim than a sober victim (Aramburu & Leigh, 1991; Leigh & Aramburu, 1994; Norris & Cubbins, 1992; Richardson & Campbell, 1982).

Such a victim is generally assumed to have played a greater causal role (Aramburu & Leigh, 1991; Leigh & Aramburu, 1994).

Even if the victim did not contribute in any concrete way to his or her victimization, the victim may be considered 'morally tarnished' simply because of the drug use. This social tendency may perhaps be linked to the 'just world' hypothesis, whereby victimization is seen as the penalty inflicted on psychoactive substance users to punish their excesses. To maintain their own feeling of security, people want to believe that they live in a fair society where everyone gets what they deserve (Lerner, 1980).

Consequently, they want to believe that only 'bad people' or people who have 'behaved badly,' suffer (Lerner, 1980). Psychoactive substance users who are victimized are therefore perceived as getting what they deserve (Lejeune, 1977). In short, because of their use of illegal drugs, psychoactive substance users lack the social resources that would protect them against criminal victimization and they cannot rely on official sources to offer the same type of protection that conforming citizens receive, because of social exclusion. By stigmatizing users of psychoactive substances, society is making their victimization legitimate and is implicitly designating them as appropriate targets of victimization (Fattah, 1991). Their victimization therefore meets with a certain tacit approval.

However, there is another side to the coin. Drug users are more likely to resist the commission of a crime or to seek out the offender in order to exact revenge (Johnson et al., 1985). Thus, crimes against deviants are decidedly more risky for the aggressor than crimes against other citizens.

Systemic victimization

Systemic victimization refers to victimization that arises out of typically aggressive interactions within the drug supply and distribution system. To obtain an illegal drug, the user must necessarily enter into contact with the potentially violent world of the drug trade. This model is as follows:

Systemic victimization model

Use of psychoactive substances	→	Drug world (supply and distribution)	→	Victimization

Systemic victimization covers a variety of situations in which violent victimization could occur, such as territorial disputes between rival drug dealers, assaults and homicides committed between various hierarchical levels of the drug world, elimination of informers, punishment of users who do not pay their debts, theft from drug dealers and punishment for selling adulterated or low-quality drugs. Systemic victimization can also occur between drug users, through quarrels over drugs or drug paraphernalia. Illegal drug dealings are often involved in victim-aggressor relations that result in murders. Note that not all psychoactive substance users are involved in the drug market. However, those who are run a high risk of victimization, since violence and the threat of violence are the primary ways of maintaining order in the drug trade (Johnson et al., 1985).

It has been established that in the illegal drug trade, violence is used to enforce respect for the normative code, to settle differences, and as a disciplinary measure (Johnson et al., 1985; Goldstein, 1985, 1986, 1989). One may therefore suppose that the individuals subjected to violence are the ones who deviate the most from these norms.

The data are eloquent in this regard. In some cities, they swell statistics on homicides (Zahn & Bencivengo, 1974). Police reports cite clients killed while negotiating a drug deal or following a violent altercation with a dealer, or clients who are robbed or beaten (Harruff, 1988). Royal Canadian Mounted Police note that drug trafficking or settling of scores linked to drugs played a role in almost 1 out of 10 homicides in 1994 (Fedorowycz, 1995). It therefore appears that drugs and trafficking are the cause of many types of crimes, including homicide (Fedorowycz, 1995).

In an analysis of 414 homicides, Goldstein (1989) found that of the 52.7% of homicides classed as drug-related, 74% could be classified as systemic. A preponderance of systemic homicides was found for all drug categories, except for alcohol, since it is not a prohibited substance (Goldstein, 1989). Note that this research was carried out as crack was gaining in popularity, when the distribution system for this drug was unstable, and this probably increased the number of homicides related to systemic violence (Goldstein, 1986). Of the homicide victims examined by Harruff (1988), 64% of cases did not have detectable levels of cocaine in their blood, but traces of cocaine were found in their urine. This suggests to the authors that victims are at greater risk of being killed during the withdrawal phase, probably due to an active and even dangerous search for their drug dose. The systemic violence experienced arises mainly in relation to money (Johnson et al., 1985). One may therefore suppose that individuals who consume more psychoactive substances are more subject to victimization since they could consume their profits and enter into a spiral of indebtedness. The vast majority of these systemic victims are low-level dealers, that is, individuals involved in the sale of drugs to support their personal habit (Goldstein, 1989).

In conclusion, the victimization experienced because of the drug market is in fact caused by the legal prohibition of drugs. Violent victimization would therefore be more linked to the milieu in which the drug trafficking takes place, than to consumption itself. The demands of the black market therefore contribute to the victimization of those who use psychoactive substances. Because such users must operate outside the law, the market is not subject to commercial conventions. Persons who believe they have been cheated have no conventional recourse for remedying the injustice (Glaser, 1974; Kelly, 1983). Extreme measures are therefore required to control the market.

Economic-compulsive victimization

This model suggests that some psychoactive substance users are compelled to commit crimes in order to support the cost of their drug habit (Goldstein, 1985; Goldstein, 1989; Spunt et al., 1990). Cocaine and heroin, which are expensive substances that can sometimes be used compulsively, may lead to acquisitive criminality. An example might be a person experiencing withdrawal symptoms who commits an armed robbery in order to be able to pay the cost of a daily heroin habit and who is killed by a store owner who is trying to protect him or herself. The following diagram shows that the relationship between drug use and victimization is mediated by the addiction and criminal involvement of the user.

Economic-compulsive victimization model

Drug use	$\rightarrow$	Need for addiction	$\rightarrow$	Money	$\rightarrow$	Crimes $\rightarrow$	Victimization

The most common victims of this type of drug-related crime are other psychoactive substance users, as well as people who have come to the neighborhood to obtain drugs, and prostitutes (Goldstein, 1985). This could lead to some confusion between economic-compulsive victimization and systemic victimization. However, the difference lies in the motivation of the aggressor, which is an essential difference: the choice of target is determined simply by the urgent need to find money to buy the addictive substance or, better still, the drug itself.

Goldstein (1989) holds that only 2% of drug-related homicides are economic-compulsively motivated. It must be noted that this model can therefore only be applied to a certain sub-group of psychoactive substance users: those who have developed a certain addiction and who have few sources of income to support the cost of their habit. This model also assumes a direct causal relation between addiction to psychoactive substances and criminality, while the relation actually appears to be much more complex (Brochu, 1995).

Lifestyle as a factor in victimization

Offenders are known to be at a greater risk of being involved in both drug consumption and victimization. Thus, drug consumers are not necessarily victimized because of their drug use, but rather in connection with their involvement in criminal activities. In addition to their deviant status which may make them easy targets of structural victimization, their chosen lifestyle, including the places where they spend their time, their activities, the subculture to which they adhere, and the peers with whom they associate, contributes to increasing the likelihood that they will be subjected to criminal acts.

Similar activities

Victimization seems to be strongly linked to the person's choice of activities. One of the characteristics of victimized offenders is their willing participation in risky behaviors. This juxtaposition of problems of delinquency, victimization, and drug consumption places such persons in contexts in which the risk of victimization is maximized. Associating with delinquents and being involved in delinquent activities increases the risk of victimization (Mayhew & Elliott, 1990; Killias & Uchtenhagen, 1995). In addition to the delinquency that may be part of the psycho-active substance user's lifestyle, prostitution appears to be an important variable mediating the drugs-victimization nexus (Fedorowycz, 1995; Goldstein et al., 1991). In short, victimization and criminality are part and parcel of the same social process. Additionally, recreational and social pleasure-seeking activities increase vulnerability to victimiza-tion because they take place in socially at-risk contexts (Jensen & Browfield, 1986).

Common environments

Psychoactive substance users choose to spend time in certain specific loca-tions which place them in ecological proximity to potential aggressors (Sampson & Lauritsen, 1990). For example, persons of limited means who are addicted to an illegal substance may choose to live in a disadvan-taged neighborhood (where crime rates are very high) in order to devote a higher proportion of their budget to their favorite drug and probably also to be close to their source of supply of psychoactive substances. Thus, Goldstein & Johnson (1983) and Johnson et al. (1985) found that the most frequent victims of drug-related violence were persons living in the same neighborhood as their aggressors or close to the places where they operate.

Certain situations (bars, parties) are associated both with consumption of psychoactive substances and risks of victimization. Thus, homicide appears to be linked to circumstances in which there is greater likelihood of drinking (Welte & Abel, 1989). These factors do not seem to be causally linked; rather, they coincide, given that people often drink during social gatherings and disputes also often occur in social occasions. The risk of being the target of a criminal act increases with the frequency of evening outings (Sondage canadien sur la victimisation en milieu urbain, 1987). Regular users of psychoactive substances go out more often in the evening and at night than the general population. Common sense suggests that certain public places, such as certain bars and downtown streets, are dangerous, particularly at night. Studies confirm these beliefs: people who regularly go out to bars, for example, run a high risk of multiple victim-ization (Fillmore, 1985; Kennedy & Forde, 1990). More precisely, Fillmore (1985) found that people who said that they went out to bars more than once a week reported seven or more incidents of victimization during the preceding year. This rate is obviously far higher than that pre-vailing in the general population. Risk of victimization does not appear to be related to levels of consumption, but rather to the places where some people go on a regular basis to engage in certain activities. Thus, women who regularly go out to bars are twice as much at risk of being victimized, even if they don't consume large quantities of alcohol. There appears to be an interaction between going out to bars, regular or abusive alcohol consumption, and victimization. Addicts' environment and their subculture bring them in contact with criminals and other people who operate illegally (Kelly, 1983). This seems to create a set of circumstances in which there is a high risk of victimization.

In short, studies suggest that psychoactive substance users' vulnerability to victimization depends largely on their level of exposure (Jensen & Browfield, 1986). All psychoactive substance users are not equally exposed to the risk of victimization.

A high-risk lifestyle

In the present sociopolitical context, illegal drug consumers' lifestyle (behaviors, social contacts, etc.) may expose them to greater risks of victimization. Victimization during childhood also appears to indirectly contribute to adoption of a lifestyle based on participation in high-risk activities or events (for example, girls who experienced incest and who become prostitutes or addicts in order to exorcise their pain). However, a study by Simons & Withbeck (1991) indicates that risks of victimization during adulthood are more closely linked to participation in high-risk activities and interaction with aggressive individuals than to the residual psychological effects of childhood sexual abuse.

Psychoactive substance users socialize and live with other people who abuse alcohol and/or drugs (Fillmore, 1985). Thus, they choose in part to adhere to a certain culture that tolerates both consumption of psychoactive substances and use of violence (Sampson & Lauritsen, 1990). In these subcultures, roles do not seem to be dichotomized between aggressor and victim, but rather to be dynamic and subject to rapid transformations. Johnson et al. (1985) concluded that in many cases, heroin addicts could be seen as victimized victimizers. Thus, victimization of persons considered to be deviants is most often inflicted by other deviants because they associate with each other (Karmen, 1983). The lifestyle theory's principle of homogamy suggests that persons most likely to be victimized frequently associate with aggressive individuals with similar sociodemographic characteristics (Hindelang et al., 1978). Individuals whose lifestyle includes violence run a higher risk of being victimized because of their own aggressive activities and their association with other aggressors. Psychoactive substance users may well be involved in a subculture in which violence is endemic, as weapons are easily available (Zahn, 1975). It is therefore not surprising that conflicts in this setting may result in violent victimization.

Thus, the relationship between addiction and victimization is mediated by aspects of individual lifestyle which expose the person to hazardous events (Simons & Withbeck, 1991). In particular, lifestyles based on desperate survival strategies (prostitution, living on the streets, etc.) are associated with a high risk of criminal victimization (Lasley & Rosembaum, 1988). Such survival strategies involve spending a considerable amount of time in public places in which the risk of victimization is very high. Use of psychoactive substances increases the likelihood that the user may have to resort to desperate survival strategies. Thus, some addicts' lifestyles expose them repeatedly to criminal victimization, and this in turn fosters feelings and attitudes that sap their efforts to attain a less deviant way of life (Simons, Withbeck & Bales, 1989).

To sum up, one may say that deviance and criminal activities lead to a lifestyle that increases the risks of victimization and that the structural constraints of residential or recreational proximity to criminal offenders also have an effect on victimization which is not mediated by lifestyle or individual demographic factors. According to Jensen & Browfield (1986), no measure of conventional lifestyle has been linked to victimization after controlling for indicators of a deviant lifestyle.

METHOD

In a pre-experimental context, 12 of the 13 prisoners living in a therapeutic community at a Quebec minimum security penitentiary were questioned about their experience relating to drugs and victimization. Four themes were explored relating to their experience as an aggressor or a victim: intoxication (psychopharmocological model), needing money to sustain their habit (economic-compulsive model), drug dealing (systemic model), and lifestyle (correlational model).

All the interviews were conducted by the same person. They took place in a closed room at the penitentiary, where there was no risk of being overheard by fellow inmates or prison staff. Although inter-views were taped for transcription purposes, inmates were ensured of confidentiality.

The interviewer did not specify any particular time frame when questioning the respondents about criminal acts they had perpetrated or undergone.

However, for the purposes of analyzing the drug-victimization nexus, only elements present during the consumption cycle were retained.

Verbatim transcripts were then vertically and horizontally analyzed by two of the four authors in such a way as to bring out the essence of what respondents had to say.

The respondents were all men between the ages of 22 and 45 (average of 33.08). The majority (8) were single and childless. Two respondents were serving life sentences, with the average length of sentence being eight years; this group was therefore made up of inmates condemned to long sentences. The majority of the inmates (7/12) had been previously incarcerated and half of them had already undergone treatment for addiction.

Four respondents stated that they had consumed alcohol abusively during the relevant time period, namely before their incarceration. Another third stated that their preferred drug was cocaine, whereas only one respondent was an intravenous heroin user. Finally, four respondents were polydrug abusers.

RESULTS

Intoxication

Victimization may take a wide variety of forms depending on the context in which it occurs. Thus, Luc describes how he was victimized while under the influence of alcohol:

> Well, drunk, yeah, there have been a lot of situations where uh … well, I got beat up, I was drunk and some guys took me as a guinea pig …. Getting robbed, yeah. My car was stolen, that kind of thing, but I wasn't drunk. Well yes, I was drunk, but I was at my friends' place, y'know. (Luc, p. 20, lines 9–12).

For others, however, the situation is less clear; it is more difficult to determine whether it was the drunkenness of the victim or of the aggressor that triggered the victimization incident. Thus, when people are intoxicated, they are more short-tempered, aggressive words come more easily, and they are more prone to be irritable and impulsive:

> Yeah, you get real aggressive. When you're on drugs, I mean, you feel like… you feel like Superman, you feel strong, y'know. You think you're the strongest too and, uh, you'd do anything, y'know. You're aggressive and your mood changes, it's not the same. It can be some minor thing, y'know. It can be just, for example … you go to rent a cottage, O.K., and the guy breaks his beer bottle on the ground. Well just that, it can make you feel like you want to get aggressive with him, throw him out and, I don't know, do something to him. You can be real impulsive. (Éric, pp. 31–32, lines 36–42).

In short, one feels provoked and one provokes others:

> There have been fights in clubs, drink, y'know, too drunk. I got into fights. I was jealous, possessive about my girlfriend. The neighbor, when he looked at her for too long, y'know what I mean, uh, I was damn well looking to pick a fight. Firearms, all that, knives... (Marc, p. 12, lines 29–32).

Sometimes, verbal inflation takes the protagonists further than they had anticipated:

> ...I'm here for manslaughter, caused because of that. Not really for dope, but caused by dope. If I had been sober at the time of the altercation, for sure I wouldn't be here. What happened wouldn't have happened, y'know what I mean, uh ... a shot is fired, and an accident like that is sure to happen. (Jean-Claude, p. 10, lines 3–7).

However, intoxication due to a drug or to a cocktail of psychoactive substances is not the sole factor explaining the sometimes unpredictible behavior of individuals in an altered state of consciousness. One must also take into account the user, his or her consumption habits, and the context of drug use:

> When you're on drugs, you want things to be like they are in the movies. And sometimes, that's not the way things went at parties. One guy was too high, he started setting the woods on fire, or somebody else jumped on the other guy's car because, I dunno, it was his turn to light up and there was none left, there was none left for him. Then he starts thinking that they didn't want to let him smoke and he starts to go nuts.... All kinds of situations that deviate... in the rhythm of life (Éric, p. 31, lines 12–18).

The drug distribution system

The drug distribution system has its laws, its obligations, its norms. When buyers don't 'play by the rules,' all those involved—both buyers and dealers—agree that they must take the consequences:

> Y'know, settling scores. Y'know, guys didn't pay up, well, a hood, a... buck knife, and we break into your place and we beat you up and we kill you, that kind of thing, y'know (Clément, p. 14, lines 3–5).

The interviews indicate that a considerable amount of victimization occurs in the context of the drug trade. There is a significant risk of being robbed:

> So he said 'I'll take twelve hits of acid and two grams of hash', that's OK ... y'know, I had more on me.... Then all of a sudden, the door bust open and two

guys came in with two guns, two sawed-off shotguns, and then they said 'you're gonna give me the drugs right away... and fast.' (Éric, p. 17, lines 16–20).

When individuals contract drug debts but don't pay up, the consequences can be catastrophic. They may be threatened, beaten up, or worse yet:

There are a lot of problems with debts. People who... who sell hash, I can't pay up, I was short, my budget... I went over my budget, I busted my budget. I tried to fix things up, the guys weren't interested, so it led to hitting. Once, I even had to get protection (Gilles, p. 11, lines 8–12).

Paul, a buyer, adds:

There's pressure, at a certain point you get the premonition, you feel the pressure, you get the feeling that you'd better pay up. Otherwise, you might get put to sleep (Paul, p. 15, lines 26–28).

Faced with this risk of victimization and with ferocious competition, people involved in the drug dealing system are ready to do anything. They protect themselves, they arm themselves!

So after that, not long after, we carried out some robberies and we stole some arms. After that, I always had arms with me since that thing happened. I said to myself 'y'know, if that happens again (having money and drugs stolen)... he'll see that... it won't happen twice.' Y'know, I was ready to kill some people, y'know. (Éric, p. 18, lines 11–15).

Dealing drugs led Normand to commit a homicide. The victim entered the place where he was dealing with the intention of stealing the drugs and Normand rapidly used the gun he had obtained in order to protect himself. In his view, violence related to drug dealing also depends on the territory and the type of drug.

In the case of psychopharmacological victimization, whether one ends up as a victim or an aggressor often depends on the circumstances and the intoxication of one's adversaries. Systemic violence, on the other hand, is more systematic: not everyone is equally prone to become a victim. According to Philippe, only individuals with a strong personality manage to survive in this jungle: 'if you show that you're afraid, you become a victim.'

The drug scene, as described by those of its actors whom we met, would appear to be split in two. On one side are the wolves who take advantage of all the opportunities without asking themselves too many questions about their victim; facing them, there are the sheep who are just asking to be fleeced or aggressed:

The other person is your victim, y'know, uh... You screw him around, you do what you want, you manipulate him. You make him do things. When things aren't going the way you want... you get him to go further: 'borrow, borrow,' when the person can't pay any longer, well he's the one that's in the hole, not you, y'know. You gotta be able to come out on top, uh.... (Clément, p. 14, lines 25–29).

Lucrative criminality

For the majority of inmates encountered, lucrative criminality was one of the primary means of meeting the costs of their psychoactive substance use. Lucrative criminality designates drug dealing, robbery, and fraud. Clearly, these are the types of offenses that make the most victims.

For Jean-Claude, who was relatively well-integrated socially—he was self-employed and owned a house and a car—the increase of his level of consumption caused him huge budgetary problems. Unable to resolve this dilemma by legitimate means, he turned to criminal activities. However, this situation is not representative. More commonly, individuals were already involved in criminal activities and the increase in their consumption led them to accentuate their criminal involvement:

> I was stealing a lot and I still couldn't make it. I was selling drugs, stealing, and I wasn't making enough.... I set it up so I would get fired because a week's salary from my job was only enough to pay for one day's worth of drugs, so there was no point in working. So I made sure I got fired, because the law was already applicable at the time: if you quit your job, you lost your right to claim unemployment insurance.... So I made sure I got fired so I could claim unemployment and I continued to steal and to deal drugs (Éric, p. 8, lines 12–21).

The situation is even more catastrophic for individuals who, in addition to increasing their consumption, are unable to adequately manage their financial affairs and who contract debts to obtain their dose of drugs. The pressure from drug suppliers becomes very difficult to deal with and the person may recklessly become involved in criminal activities.

Lucrative victimization may also lead the way to aggressive victimization:

> ...when the person is in withdrawal and is trying to get some, it's very dangerous. It's because the person practically isn't thinking, isn't fully in command of all his faculties, that anything can happen in that situation, the person can do all kinds of dumb things (Pierre, p. 12. lines 5–8).

A high-risk lifestyle

All the respondents viewed criminality and drug use as part of the same lifestyle in which pleasure and luxury are of central importance:

...For fun. I got into drugs like speed, uh, LSD, pot, mescaline. For me, it was the biggest trips. The biggest money, the biggest drugs. Costs more. An apartment, a car, going out to clubs every night, power trips. Money, being seen as important by other people, people around me, ha! ha! ha! (Denis, p. 18, lines 9–13).

However, none of the respondents was shielded from the high-risk lifestyle which they had gradually adopted:

When you get into drugs, you have a whole different lifestyle. You get into marginality, you get into things you wouldn't do if you were thinking. Y'know, when you're straight, you think about it, you say 'it doesn't make sense.' But when you're high, it doesn't really matter. Nothing really matters... And you have the lifestyle... you have a lifestyle that kind of goes with it, yeah... I mean, a lifestyle like... you do drugs, but you have to do that because you do drugs. You listen to it because you do drugs. And, uh... if you do drugs, you mustn't show that you're like a kind of, a straight person. You have to show that you're a person who does drugs.... It's...it's a pretty special lifestyle (Éric, p. 29, lines 5–15).

CONCLUSIONS

Overall, the interviews conducted during this pre-experimental phase of our study tend to confirm the relevance of the conceptual models described at the beginning of this chapter. Thus, there are a broad range of factors pushing our subjects toward aggression and victimization. However, contrary to the image presented in the scientific literature concerning explanatory models of the drug-victimization nexus, this relationship is far from simple.

Thus, what emerges confusedly from the respondents' statements is a mixture of: a) a deviant lifestyle predisposing the subject to become involved in marginal activities and to frequent unsafe places; b) frequent intoxications leading to aggravation of agressive verbal exchanges between individuals who often tend to engage in impulsive behavior; c) an attraction toward expensive drug consumption leading to addiction; d) an involvement in potentially contentious drug transactions. It is therefore difficult to determine the main reason that may have driven an individual to commit criminal acts. Was the person in a state of confusion when the event occurred, did s/he provoke the incident, or was the person simply at the wrong place at the wrong time? One must also keep in mind that the respondents' statements may be shaped, wittingly or not, by a wide variety of motivations and emotions. Feelings such as shame or guilt could have an effect on their statements. One respondent, for example, described himself as an attractive target, an easy prey; is this really accurate, or is he slanting the story to suit his own purposes? In such situations, having the aggressor's version would help to determine which explanatory model is apposite. The data provided by the respondents interviewed in the course of this study strongly suggests that the rate of victimization is very high and practically inevitable. It remains to be seen whether this victimization is so severe that the victims might be motivated to make changes in their lifestyle, more particularly their drug use. Carrying this a step further, it would be worth exploring whether recognition that a person has been victimized might help open the way to intervention, given that it is less threatening than categorizing the person as a criminal.

NOTES

1   This research was funded by Correctional Services of Canada and by FCAR.

2   This study focuses on victimization caused by a criminal act as defined by the Criminal Code, since most studies reviewed define victimization in legal terms. Clearly, this definition of victimization supposes a certain social construction and many types of victimization are therefore excluded. It is, however, evident that drug abusers are, by virtue of their drug dependency, victimizing themselves (Johnson et al., 1985). We are therefore aware that the definition of victimization employed is somewhat reductionist.

REFERENCES

Amir, M. (1971). Patterns in forcible rape. Chigaco: University of Chicago press.

Aramburu, B., & Leigh, B.C. (1991). For better or worse: attributions about drunken aggression toward male and female victims. *Violence and victims, 6(1),* 31–41.

Brochu, S. (1994). Ivresse et violence: désinhibition ou excuse? *Déviance et société, 18(4),* 431–446.

Brochu, S. (1995). *Drogue et criminalité: une relation complexe.* Montréal: Presses de l'Université de Montréal.

Burnam, A.M., Stein, J.A., Golding, J.M., Siegel, J.M. et al. (1988). Sexual assault and mental disorders in a community population. *Journal of consulting and clinical psychology, 56(6),* 843–850.

Champagne, D. (1994). Drogues, sexualité et problèmes sociaux. In: P. Brisson (Ed.), *L'usage des drogues et la toxicoman.* volume II (pp. 31–54). Boucherville: Gaëtan Morin.

Fattah, E.A., & Raic, A.L. (1970). L'alcool en tant que facteur victimogène. *Toxicomanies, 3,* 143–173.

Fattah, E.A. (1991). *Understanding criminal victimization.* Ontario: Prentice-Hall Canada.

Fedorowycz, O. (1995). L'homicide au Canada—1994. *Juristat: Centre canadien de la statistique juridique, 15(11).*

Fillmore, K.M. (1985). The social victims of drinking. *British journal of addiction, 80(3),* 307–314.

Glaser, D. (1974). Interlocking dualities in drug use, drug control and crime. In: J.A. Inciardi & C. Chambers, (Eds.), *Drugs and the criminal justice system.* Beverly Hills: Sage publications.

Goldstein, P.J. (1985). The drugs/violence nexus: a tripartite conceptual framework. *Journal of drug issues, 15(4),* 493–506.

Goldstein, P.J. (1986). Homicide related to drug traffic. *Bulletin of the New York academy of medicine, 62,* 509–516.

Goldstein, P.J. (1989). Crack and homicide in New York city, 1988: a conceptually based event analysis. *Contemporary drug problems, 16(4),* 651–687.

Goldstein, P.J., Bellucci, P.A., Spunt, B.J., & Miller, T. (1991). Volume of cocaine use and violence: a comparison between men and women. *Journal of drug issues, 21(2),* 345–367.

Goldstein, P.J., & Johnson, B.D. (1983). *Robbery among heroin users*. Conférence présentée au congrès annuel de la Society for the study of social problems.

Goodman, R.A., Mercy, J.A., Loya, F., Rosenberg, M.L., Smith, J.C., & Allen, N.H. et al. (1986). Alcohol use and interpersonal violence: alcohol detected in homicide victims. *American journal of public health*, 76(2), 144–149.

Harruff, R.C. (1988). Cocaine and homicide in Memphis and Shelby County: an epidemic of violence. *Journal of forensic sciences*, 33(5), 1231–1237.

Hindelang, M.J., Gottfredson, M.R., & Garofalo, J. (1978). *Victims of personal crime: an empirical foundation for a theory of personal victimization*. Cambridge: Ballinger Publishing Company.

Hussey, D.L., & Singer, M. (1993). Psychological distress, problem behaviors, and family functioning of sexually abused adolescent inpatients. *Journal of the american academy of child and adolescent psychiatry*, 32(5), 954–961.

Jensen, G.F., & Browfield, D. (1986). Gender, lifestyles and victimization: beyond routine activity theory. *Violence and victims*, 1(2), 85–99.

Johnson, B.D., Goldstein, P.J., Preble, E., Schmiedler, J., Lipton, D.S., Spunt, B., & Miller, T. (1985). *Taking care of business: the economics of crime by heroin abusers*. Toronto: Lexington Books.

Kantor, G.K., & Straus, M.A. (1989). Substance abuse as a precipitant of wife abuse victimizations. *American journal of drug and alcohol abuse*, 15(2). 173–189.

Karmen, A. (1983). Deviants as victims. In: D.E.J. MacNamara & A. Karmen, (Eds.), *Deviants: victims or victimizers?*. Beverly Hills: Sage Publications.

Kelly, R.J. (1983). Addicts and alcoholics as victims. In: D.E.J. MacNamara & A. Karmen (Eds.), *Deviants: victims or victimizers?*. Beverly Hills: Sage Publications.

Kennedy, L.W., Forde, D.R. (1990). Routine activities and crime: an analysis of victimization in Canada. *Criminology*, 28(1), 137–152.

Killias, M., & Uchtenhagen, A. (1995). Méthodologie de l'évaluation des essais suisses avec prescription médicale d'opiacés sous l'angle de la délinquance: l'accès sous contrôle médical à l'héroïne réduit-il la délinquance des toxicomanes? *Bulletin de criminologie*, 21(2), 33–48.

Lasley, J.R., & Rosenbaum, J.L. (1988). Routine activities and multiple personal victimization. *Sociology and social research*, 73(1), 47–50.

Leigh, B.C., & Aramburu, B. (1994). Responsibility attributions for drunken behavior: the role of expectancy violation. *Journal of applied social psychology*, 24(1), 115–135.

Lejeune, R. (1977). The management of a mugging. *Urban life*, 6(2), 123–148.

Lerner, M.J. (1980). *The belief in a just world: a fundamental delusion*. New York: Plenum Press.

Lindqvist, P. (1991). Homicides committed by abusers of alcohol and illicit drugs. *British journal of addiction*, 86(3), 321–326.

Mayhew, P., & Elliott, D. (1990). Self-reported offending, victimization, and the British crime survey. *Violence and victims*, 5(2), 83–96.

Muscat, J.E., & Huncharek, M.S. (1991). Firearms and adult, domestic homicides: the role of alcohol and the victim. *American journal of forensic medicine & pathology*, 12(2), 105–110.

Norris, J., Cubbins, L.A. (1992). Dating, drinking, and rape: effects of victim's and assailant's alcohol consumption on judgments of their behavior and traits. *Psychology of women quarterly*, 16(2), 179–191.

Parent, I.(1997). *La victimisation criminelle des usagers de substances psychoactives: aspects théoriques*. Document inédit: CICC, Université de Montréal.

Richardson, D.C., & Campbell, J.L. (1982). Alcohol and rape: the effect of alcohol on attributions of blame for rape. *Personality and social psychology bulletin*, 8, 468–476.

Sampson, R.J., & Lauritsen, J.L. (1990). Deviant lifestyles, proximity to crime, and the offender-victim link in personal violence. *Journal of research in crime and delinquency*, 27(2), 110–139.

Selkin, J. (1975). Rape: when to fight back. *Psychology today*, 71–76.

Silverman, R.A., & Mukherjee, S.K. (1987). Intimate homicide: an analysis of violent social relationship. *Behavioural sciences and the law*, 5, 37–47.

Simons, R.L., Whitbeck, L.B., & Bales, A. (1989). Life on the streets: victimization and psychological distress among the adult homeless. *Journal of interpersonal violence*, 4(4), 482–501.

Simons, R.L., & Whitbeck, L.B. (1991). Sexual abuse as a precursor to prostitution and victimization among adolescent and adult homeless women. *Journal of family issues*, *12(3)*, 361–379.

Singer, M., Petchers, M., & Hussey, D. (1989). The relationship between sexual abuse and substance abuse among psychiatrically hospitalized adolescents. *Child abuse and neglect*, *13*, 319–325.

Sondage Canadien sur la Victimisation en Milieu Urbain (1987). *Caractéristiques du crime avec violence*. Canada: Bulletin, *8*.

Spunt, B.J., Goldstein, P.J., Bellucci, P.A., & Miller, T. (1990). Race/ethnicity and gender differences in the drugs-violence relationship. *Journal of psychoactive drugs*, *22(3)*, 293–303.

Taylor, S.P., Gammon, C.B., & Capasso, D.R. (1976). Aggression as a function of the interaction of alcohol and threat. *Journal of personnality and social psychology*, *34*, 938–941.

Welte, J.W., & Abel, E.L. (1989). Homicide: drinking by the victim. *Journal of studies on alcohol*, *50(3)*, 197–201.

Windle, M. (1994). Substance use, risky behaviors, and victimization among a US national adolescent sample. *Addiction*, *89(2)*, 175–182.

Wolfgang, M.E. (1958). *Patterns in criminal homicide*. Philadelphia: University of Philadelphia press.

Zahn, M.A. (1975). The female homicide victim. *Criminology*, *13*, 409.

Zahn, M.A., & Bencivengo, M. (1974). Violent death: a comparison between drug users and nondrug users. *Addictive Diseases*, *1*, 283–296.

Chapter 11

VICTIM AND OFFENDER MEDIATION IN THE JUVENILE JUSTICE SYSTEM

Anna C. Baldry and Gilda Scardaccione

INTRODUCTION

The Italian juvenile justice system claims to use a Restorative Justice approach, but this is seen in a system that for most of its characteristics is a rehabilitative one. The legislation does not give much space to victims, who are often used only as pieces of evidence. We will now analyse the current legal point of view, and some of the ongoing experiences in terms of what is claimed to be a Restorative Justice approach. A new prospectus project promoted by the Department of juvenile justice will also be presented.

A retributive system wants to hurt the offenders, the rehabilitative one wants to help them, but both ignore the victim. Retributivists claim that victims want offenders to be punished (so mediation is seen as unnecessary); rehabilitators fear that victims want the offender to be punished (so mediation is seen as a dangerous). Both ignore the fact that it is not necessarily what the victims want; in an early Australian project, for example: 'Victims wanted to have their say: they wanted any stolen goods returned; they wanted an apology. But they appeared to have no interest in retributive punishment as such'. (Moore & O'Connell, 1994, p. 56).

By analyzing some of the basic principles of Italian criminal law, opportunities for mediation and reconciliation (for victim-prosecuted offences) will be assessed. The attention will be directed to juvenile law and to Restorative Justice ideals within the Italian practice that is offender-centered.

The object is to address some of the current ongoing criticism in view of the contrast of an attempt to use and refer to some of the basic principles of a Restorative Justice approach, victim/offender mediation, and reparation, in a system that is still offender-oriented.

ITALIAN LAW AND RESTORATIVE JUSTICE

Mediation, in criminal justice, can be defined as any neutral restorative process in which victim(s) and offenders communicate with the help of an impartial third party, either directly (face-to-face) or indirectly via the third party, enabling the victims to express their needs and feelings, and offenders to accept and act on their responsibilities.[1]

But the Italian Legal system was not designed to provide opportunities for mediation, especially in criminal cases, perhaps for cultural and political reasons including:

1. The Italian law based on mandatory prosecution of known offences (article 112 of the Italian Constitution Declaration) does not divert cases from court trials, therefore does not admit any pre-trial mediation. The Juvenile Justice system, however, allows at some stages, victim/offender mediation.
2. The 'Legality Principle' states that adult offenders' personality characteristics can not be taken into account for establishing their responsibility.
3. The victims have a marginal role in the Italian Criminal Justice System especially with young offenders (14–18 years); in these cases, for example, victims do not have the right to start a civil action linked to the criminal prosecution.

Generally speaking, the philosophical juridical background of the Italian system is based on the offender conviction as a protection and defense of the rights of the victim and the citizens.

In Italian law, certain offences such as assaults, slander, and insults can be prosecuted only by the victim, and are the only opportunity for diverting cases from the trial into reconciliation. In these cases the Public Prosecutor may try to bring the two parties to an agreement (art. 564 Penal Code): in successful cases the victim withdraws the complaint against the accused and the case is closed. Gatti & Marugo (1994) underline that rather than a structured and planned reconciliation between the parties, these cases often end up with the police trying to convince victims not to apply their legal rights for vindictive purposes.

There are at least two reasons to encourage and develop, in a structured and defined way, reconciliation between victims and offenders on the basis of this legislative norm. Most minor offences that can be prosecuted only by the victim are committed against someone known to the accused often living in the same neighbourhood or community. Both victims and offenders might benefit from reconciliation because it gives them the opportunity to improve their communication and relation. Another advantage of this way of dealing with petty crimes, is to reduce the burden of work within the criminal justice system, resolving disputes outside courts.

Unlike the adult system, the Italian juvenile justice system allows the personality of the young offender to be taken into account at any time during the criminal justice procedure, and influence the legal decisions. As has been mentioned before, this is the opposite of the 'legality principle' for adult offenders that prevents the personality assessment of the accused from being considered in any legal action, therefore preventing it from influencing the sentence.[2]

The assessment of the young offender's personality aims to establish the degree of responsibility of the accused in terms of his or her own maturity; moreover, it aims to establish the best solution and most adequate criminal sanction. The assessment of the young offender's personality is based on the level and degree of responsibility in relation to the crime committed and on the personal, social and family resources; at this stage of the proceeding it would be possible for the offender to meet the victim, and possibly to achieve reconciliation or reparation.

The law defining the assessment of the young offender's personality (art. 9 D.P.R. 448/88, Decree of the President of the Republic,[3]) provides the pattern to establish what kind of victim/offender mediation could be promoted at this stage of the process: there is currently valuable experience taking place within the Juvenile court in Turin (Bouchard, 1992). The present situation in other parts of the country is mixed and still not clear.

The judge can make a probation order, and the law refers at this point to the possibility of victim and offender mediation (art. 28, D.P.R. 448/88). Juvenile probation is a new device in the Italian criminal juvenile justice system but has quite a different form from most of the existing probation orders around the world. It is based on the suspension of the trial, not of the sentence. But as Palomba (1992) indicates, it follows the same philosophical principle of probation given, whose aim is to try to avoid imposing a punitive sanction on the young offender, provided that he or she behaves satisfactorily during a specific period. In order to benefit from this opportunity given to the young offender, the social workers of the juvenile justice administration and the community service workers jointly develop a project that the offender has to agree to fulfil. The implementation of the project is based on several aims that show the complexity of this alternative sanction. Besides the basic aim of all probation orders, that is to avoid a sanction and implement rehabilitation, another one is to achieve psychological development based the social adjustment of the young offender and to develop his or her own sense of responsibility. In order to do this, the juvenile is given the opportunity to restore the damage caused by the offense through reparation or reconciliation with the victim.

How does this compare with the concept of Restorative Justice as it has been developed in recent years? Restorative Justice is a form of justice based on the principle of healing the injuries caused by the crime: restoring victims as far as possible to their former condition, or improving it if they were in need and requiring offenders to take part in this, or to make reparation in other ways, but also restoring them to full membership in the community. In a Restorative Justice approach, reparation ('restitution' in the American system) in the context of victim and offender mediation, is the contribution that can be made by the offender to the victim, to help to make right the harm (physical or emotional) caused by the crime. If the victim does not wish to receive it personally, or in victimless crimes, reparation may be made to the community (the so called 'community service orders' as defined in the Anglo-American system). Reparation may include an apology, financial payment, practical work, return and/or repair of goods, and the undertaking of future behavior or voluntary participation in education, treatment or training programs. This decision should be oriented towards the victim as well as towards the offender. That means that the victim, in those cases where there is one, should be heard and should show satisfaction. But the Italian juridical system is offender-oriented. All activities and decisions taken are mainly done in the interest of the juvenile: the victim is often left out. The opportunity given to a young offender to 'pay back' for the harm caused mainly excludes the victim whose opinion is rarely taken into account. Victims are not directly considered and the decision is taken without hearing them. As will be demonstrated from the results of the study conducted, it is a common practice used in several parts of the country, in Rome, Campobasso and Messina.

As mentioned, any Restorative Justice attempt of dealing with crime is forced within a rehabilitative system that is 'offender-oriented'. The aim and concern are to fulfil the psychological development of the juveniles and to hold them responsible. It is important therefore, at least to guarantee in those cases where mediation takes place, that full attention is given to victims and their needs are taken into account. This is an important issue with regard to the training of mediators, especially if they are recruited from the juvenile justice services.

According to Palomba (1992), reparation can take place without reconciliation and reconciliation can take place without reparation: it depends on the crime committed and the willingness of the victim.

There is another contradiction in this law when mediation takes place as part of the probation order: during the specific time that has been established, the young offenders are checked and supervised to see whether they are fulfilling the activities of the project and enhancing their sense of responsibility, psychologically preparing themselves to make amends to the victim. On the other hand, the victims need practical and emotional support and require time and recognition of their state in order to be able to elaborate the impact and consequences of the victimization (Coppola De Vanna, 1996). This is another important point that has to be taken into consideration when implementing mediation and when training mediators. This applies particularly in a country such as Italy, where victim support services are not yet widely developed.

The Project of the Department of Juvenile Justice

The Department of Juvenile Justice has recently gathered a group of experts to define possible experimental projects of victim and offender mediation in the whole country on the basis of the juridical dispositions that have been previously outlined and the extensive experience gained in other countries (Scardaccione, 1996). These are not yet in practice but are in the process of getting started.

There are two operative levels in which victim and offender mediation could be put forward. In both of them social workers working as probation officers for the Juvenile Justice Department would play a central role. The first level is during the investigative stage. When social workers are assessing the young offender's personality and writing up a report during the first stage of the proceeding, they would have to consider whether there are conditions to promote victim and offender mediation. These conditions should be based on the possibility of getting in touch with the victim, on the willingness of both the victim and the offender to participate in a mediation session, and on the existing resources of the family and in the community and social services.

The second level is during the probation order which we have previously referred to. Social workers, when developing the plan would also have to consider whether there are conditions for mediation between the victim and the offender.

The implementation of mediation programmes would be the duty of professionally trained staff in mediation, one in each jurisdiction of the country. Both community social workers and juvenile justice social workers would form this group, specially trained for mediation practice. They would act as the mediators. This group of experts would work accordingly with the judicial authority, the juvenile justice social service and the community social services. The reason for including professionals of the community services in these groups is to give mediation a broader meaning next to the juridical one: that is to reduce conflicts and re-establish social and emotional communication between the parties. In all cases, the juvenile justice social services would play an intermediate role between the judicial authority and the mediators.

This project does not exclude any type of crime; even most serious ones can be considered for mediation. But preference would be given for those crimes where victim's rights have been usually violated (in all cases of brawls, personal injuries) and for those with a high social significance and impact (damage in schools). Mediation is conceived for reducing social conflicts especially in those cases, quite frequent among juveniles, where the victim and the offender belong to the same peer group.

The present project is still in its preparation stage. It is therefore not possible yet to provide any figure on cases and evaluation results. What has been done so far in terms of victim/offender mediation in Italy is very limited and often disorganized. There are some very few exceptions and Turin, as we will be able to see shortly, is an example.[4]

Moreover, it is interesting to assess and see what is done on the basis of another possible way of dealing with offense through reparation and evaluate in these cases, too, what part victims play.

In this regard, we will present results from research that was conducted in two Italian cities: Messina and Campobasso.

THE RESEARCH

Aims of the study

The present study was intended to analyze to what extent victim/offender mediation takes place in Italy and what forms of restitution or reparation the young offender has made in favour of the victim.

Data was collected from the files of the local social services of the Department of Criminal Justice, acting as a Probation Office responsible for supervision of probation of young offenders in two Italian cities, Campobasso (a small provincial town in Central Italy not far from Naples) and Messina (an industrialised city on the east side of Sicily). During 1994 and 1995, a total of 39 cases in Campobasso and 30 in Messina were referred to these social services. These cases were the ones where the judge had ordered 'suspension of trial with probation' (art. 28, D.P.R. 448/88). From these, we extracted the ones where the offender had to fulfil some symbolic or material restitution or reparation and those cases where the judge requested the social workers to explore the possibility for the offender to 'conciliate with the victim'. On this basis, a total of 29 cases were extracted from Campobasso and 10 from Messina. The aim of the study was to investigate the level of attention paid to the young offenders in terms of holding them accountable for the harm caused, by giving them the opportunity to reintegrate in society and make amends to the victim and to the community, without a purely retributive or rehabilitative approach. This is possibly done with a confrontation of the harm caused, either by meeting directly the victim or making amends. Another aim of the study was to assess the part victims played in the whole process (i.e., whether they were actually asked if they were willing to have their damage repaired or meet the offender and receive apologies, and whether reparation was made in the victim's interests).

The study presented here is purely descriptive. Because of the small sample size, results are not intended to be representative, but can provide useful information regarding the risks of trying to use a Restorative Justice approach in a rehabilitative system that is mainly offender-oriented

The sample

A total of 39 cases was analyzed. There are no significant differences between the two sample cities under investigation, therefore the results and figures will be presented jointly. All young offenders were Italian males and their mean age was 16 years-old. Most of them (71.8%) attended school and the remaining (22.2%) had a stable job; a total of 32.1% of those that attended school also worked occasionally. Of the whole sample, 61.5% lived in a quiet, residential area, 28.2% in a quiet, rural area and 10.3% lived in a poor area of the city. Half of them belonged to a poor family but with no serious problem of social deprivation; 44.4% belonged to a middle class family and 5.6% to a single-parent family with quite a lot of economic problems.

Regarding their crime records, 27.8% had already committed at least one previous offense. Regarding the type of current offense, theft was the most common (46.2%). See table 1 for more details.

Table 1: Number and percentage of current crimes

Crime committed	N	%
theft	18	46.2
illegal possession (drugs, arms)	8	20.5
personal injuries	8	20.5
threat	2	5.1
receiving of stolen goods	2	5.1
manslaughter	1	2.6
Total	39	100.0

Plan in the probation order

The next step was to analyze the type of reparation or restitution that was part of the plan of the probation order that young offenders had to fulfil, and to see whether it included some forms of direct or indirect reparation and/or restitution and reconciliation with the victim. In all cases but two, where only reconciliation in favour of the victim took place, the young offender was supposed to make amends for the harm caused. Only in one case reparation was a material one; in all remaining cases reparation was intended in a broader sense: volunteer work for a charitable organization or for people in need. These activities are referred to as 'community service orders.'

So, reparation through community service took place in 36 cases, material reparation to the victim, in just one case, apology only in two cases, and apology combined with reparation in 13 cases.

In 61.5% of all cases, the judge requested the social workers to explore the possibility for the offender to 'conciliate with the victim.' Of these, victim and offender conciliation (the juvenile made his apologies to the victim) took place in 28.2% of the cases. In another 3 cases the young offender made his apologies to the victim although this was not mentioned in the judge's order. Altogether, the young offender made his apologies to the victim only in 33.3% of all cases. There is no significant difference related to the crime committed and whether reconciliation took place or not. Excluding 'illegal possession,' where no direct victims were involved, reconciliation took place in 7 of the 18 cases of theft, in 3 of the 8 personal injuries crimes and in one of the two cases of receiving stolen goods. In both threat cases and in the manslaughter one no reconciliation took place.

The next step was to analyze what degree of attention was paid to the victims and what part they played in the whole proceeding. In only 24 cases (corresponding to 54.5%) where the judge recommended an apology, was the victim asked whether this was what he or she wanted, and this in just over half of those cases (13); thus in the remaining cases victims were not given the opportunity to consider apology until after the offender had been asked. In those 3 cases where it was not mentioned in the probation order, the victim willingness to receive apologies was then obtained by the social workers (corresponding to 20% of the total).

It should be mentioned that in some victim/offender mediation services, it would be for the victim's sake that the offender is asked first, because it is felt that victims would be disappointed if they agreed to receive an apology and the offender was then unwilling to make it. Conversely, if the offender offers to make an apology but the victim does not wish to accept it, the offender should be allowed the opportunity to make reparation in another way, for example through community service.

Where the victim was approached first, an apology was offered and accepted in 55.6% of the 16 cases; but where the offender was approached first, this only happened in one case (corresponding to the 8.3%; $c^2 = 6.9$, df = 1, p < .01). This could mean that victims are more likely to accept an apology when they feel that their position has been recognized by being asked first; it could also mean that offenders are more willing to offer an apology if they have the reassurance that it is likely to be accepted.

In only 10.3% of all cases the symbolic reparation of the offender was related to the target victim (in one case where a boy insulted a man for his racial origin, he then agreed to do volunteer work in a charitable association that hosted immigrants).

DISCUSSION

From this brief study some conclusions can be drawn. Offering the victim the opportunity to meet the offender and possibly receive reparation and/or an apology, is not one of the main practices used when a young offender has committed a crime even if this has been recommended by the judge as part of the probation order. In those cases where the offender made his apology to the victim, the social worker of the Department of Criminal Justice was covering the role of the mediator. Numerous research studies have shown that mediators should belong to independent bodies to guarantee neutrality (Bouchard, 1992; Gatti & Marugo, 1994; Umbreit, 1994; Wright, 1995). The current situation in Italy does not provide this independent body. It could be possible in some cases that social workers act as mediators, as it is conceived in the project promoted by the Juvenile Justice Department but in these cases they should not be the same ones that are also acting as probation officers. If a mediator works for this Department, then the necessary neutrality might not be always guaranteed for the people involved, especially in the victim's perception, therefore a lot of attention has to be paid to the training of these professionals. This is one of the main risks, that also other countries such as England had to face when mediation started to be introduced as part of probation orders (Marshall & Merry, 1990), when trying to fit some of the Restorative Justice principles into a system that is mainly offender-oriented as the one for juveniles.

The Restorative Justice approach refers to indirect or direct reparation and mediation as a possible response to the harm caused to the victims. Thanks to symbolic restitution, the young offender has the opportunity to show regret and willingness to pay back for the harm caused. Social workers acting as probation officers are not yet prepared for victim and offender mediation. Often the victim's willingness to mediate is not even ascertained and the victim might feel forced to give the young offender the opportunity to express regret.

From the study conducted it emerges that some of the basic principles that are part of the Restorative Justice approach are gradually being introduced in the current way of dealing with young offenders. Punishing the offender does not contribute to the reduction of criminal offenses. Giving them the opportunity to commit themselves in a socially useful activity (e.g., work for the community) might contribute both to their social and psychological development, but it also helps to give the community the opportunity to realize that the offender is accepting responsibility and has the capacity to contribute to the welfare of the community.

The project developed by the Department of Juvenile Justice and the results of the study indicate that in the current juvenile justice system there is the possibility to reach a Restorative Justice approach. But the focus is still too much on the offender's side. Full attention has to be paid so that the victim also has a central part in the process. To guarantee these basic rights, it should be possible to give victims the opportunity to take an active part during the proceeding, having the opportunity, if they want to, to meet the offenders and share with them their feelings. Things are gradually changing in our system but a lot of work still needs to be done.

NOTES

1   Mediation is the process, the outcome and the possible decisions that the two parties involved might have agreed on, and can include reconciliation, indicating apology, or restitution or reparation either in symbolic terms or corresponding to the loss caused. It is up to the victim and to the offender whether any kind of these agreements are reached. In the Italian criminal law there is no indication of 'mediation' as it has been defined here. The law refers to '(re)conciliation' or 'reparation' but does not specify what these terms mean. Generally speaking, it can be said that the aim of '(re)conciliation' is to bring, as far as possible, the relation between the two parties to the stage before the commission of the crime. We agree with Martin Wright (1996) in underlining that the term might have an idealistic religious viewpoint. In the following part of the paper we will use the term used by the law: '(re)conciliation,' when this is actually the word used, but we will refer to (victim/offender) mediation to include the possibility of both (re)conciliation and reparation.

2   In the Italian criminal justice system there is no distinction between the 'verdict' and the 'sentence' that are carried out jointly. The assessment of the personality is forbidden before the sentence, but is taken into consideration for the treatment of the convicted person. In the juvenile justice system, the personality of the juvenile is assessed before the sentence, which is based on this assessment as well.

3 The Decree of the President of the Republic, that differs from a 'law decree', that has to pass through Parliament to be approved, is a law directly approved by the President of the Republic.

4 At present v/o mediation is taking place also in Mileu, Bari and Rome.

REFERENCES

Bouchard, M. (1992). Mediazione: dalla repressione alla rielaborazione del conflitto. (Mediation: From repression to the reelaboration of conflict). *Dei Delitti e delle Pene, 2*, 191–202.

Coppola de Vanna, A. (1996). Messa alla prova, conciliazione e mediazione. (Probation, conciliation and mediation). *Minori Giustizia, 1*, 59–63.

Gatti, U., & Marugo, I. (1994). La vittima e la giustizia riparativa. (The victim and Restorative Justice). *Marginalità e Società, 4*, 12–32.

Marshall, T., & Merry, S. (1990). *Crime and accountability—Victim/offender mediation in practice.* London: Home Office. HMSO.

Moore, D. B., & O'Connell (1994). Family conferencing in Wagga Wagga: A communitarian model of justice. In: C. Adler & J. Wunderstitz (Eds.), *Family conferencing and juvenile justice: The way forward or misplaced optimism?* Canberra: Australian Institute of Criminology.

Palomba, F. (1991). *Il sistema del nuovo processo penale minorile.* (The New penal procedure code for juveniles). Milano; Giuffrè.

Scardaccione, G. (1996). Programmi di mediazione (Mediations programmes). *Minori, Diritto e Giustizia, 1*, 33–48.

Umbreit, M. S. (1994). *Victim meets offender. The impact of Restorative Justice and Mediation.* (pp. 53–64). Criminal Justice Press: N.Y.

Wright, M. (1995). Alternatives to the Criminal Justice Process. *Iuris, 4*, 47–58.

Wright, M. (1996). *Justice for victims and offender. A restorative response to crime.* 2nd ed. Winchester: Watrside Press.

PART 4
TESTIMONY AND WITNESS ISSUES

Chapter 12

THE COGNITIVE INTERVIEW IN FORENSIC INVESTIGATIONS: A REVIEW

Mark R. Kebbell, Rebecca Milne and Graham F. Wagstaff

INTRODUCTION

When investigating criminal acts, witness testimony is often very important. For example, a recent survey of 159 United Kingdom (UK) police officers showed 36% of respondents believed that witnesses 'always' or 'almost always' provide the major leads for an investigation. A further 51% believed that witnesses 'usually' provide the major leads (Kebbell & Milne, in press). However, the survey also revealed that 53% of police officers believed that witnesses 'never' or 'rarely' provided as much information as they wanted. Consequently, maximizing the accurate testimony of a witness is an important aim for many police officers.

One technique that has been shown to successfully improve eyewitness performance is the 'cognitive interview' (Fisher & Geiselman, 1992). The initial or 'original' version of this technique involved four instructions; these required the witness to:

1) reinstate mental context;
2) report everything;
3) recall events in different orders;
4) change perspectives (Geiselman, Fisher, Firstenberg, Hutton, Sullivan, Avetissian & Prosk, 1984).

Later, Fisher and Geiselman developed an 'enhanced' cognitive interview (Fisher, Geiselman, Raymond, Jurkevich & Warhafig, 1987a; Fisher, Geiselman & Amador, 1989). This sought to redress problems that routinely occur in 'standard' police interviews, described later in this chapter. Essentially the 'enhanced' cognitive interview is an original cognitive interview with additional instructions to ensure that:

1) rapport is established;
2) control of the interview is transferred to the witness;
3) questions are compatible with the witness's mental operations;
4) the witness is encouraged to use focused retrieval;
5) the witness is encouraged to use imagery.

(For reviews and more detailed descriptions of the cognitive interview see Bekerian & Dennett, 1993; Fisher, 1995; Fisher & Geiselman, 1992; Memon & Bull, 1991; Memon & Kohnken, 1992; Kohnken, Milne, Memon & Bull, in press; Memon & Stevenage, 1996). Research indicates that both forms of the cognitive interview have the potential to enhance recall compared to control interviews in laboratory situations. The original version of the cognitive interview produces approximately 25% to 35% more information than controls (Kohnken, Thurer & Zoberbier, 1994), and Fisher et al. (1987a) have found further improvements with the enhanced cognitive interview. These memory enhancements have been shown to occur without adversely influencing accuracy rates (i.e. the proportion of correct to incorrect information, Geiselman, 1996; but see Memon & Stevenage, 1996), increasing susceptibility to leading questions (Geiselman, Fisher, Cohen, Holland & Surtes, 1986; Milne & Bull, 1995), or disrupting confidence-accuracy relationships (Geiselman et al., 1984; Kebbell & Wagstaff, 1997).

The effectiveness of the cognitive interview has meant that most UK police forces have incorporated the cognitive interview into police recruit training and taken steps to train serving officers in its use. This training has been called the 'National Interviewing Package' (Central Planning and Training Unit, 1992). Typically, training lasts for five days, two on cognitive interviewing for witnesses and the remainder on ways of interviewing suspects. Given this investment of resources, it is obviously important that the cognitive interview should be evaluated not only in the laboratory, but also in the field. The aim of this chapter, therefore, is to evaluate the effectiveness of cognitive interviews compared with standard interviews in real investigations.

THE 'STANDARD' POLICE INTERVIEW

To compare cognitive interviews with standard interviews it is first necessary to describe standard interviews and associated problems. Whilst most UK police officers received no formal training in witness interviewing before the introduction of the cognitive interview (George, 1991), police officers did seem to conduct interviews in a similar way (Clifford & George, 1996; Fisher, Geiselman & Raymond, 1987b; George, 1991; Memon, Holley, Milne, Koehnken & Bull, 1994; Yuille, 1984). However, the 'standard police interview' left much to be desired. Fisher et al. (1987b) provide the most detailed description and critique as follows.

Interruption of witness's responses

Police interviewing is characterized by frequent interruption of witness' responses by the interviewing officer. After introducing themselves, the interviewer typically asks the witness to tell him or her what happened. However, when the witness starts to provide an account, he or she is frequently interrupted.

Interruptions cause two problems. First, they break the concentration of witnesses when they are trying to retrieve information. If the interviewer's questions break the witness' concentration, then the witness must switch attention from trying to recall information to the interviewer's questions. Then the witness must go back to his or her memory to answer the question. This makes the task much more difficult and such constant shifting of attention prevents optimal recall of the event. This is particularly unfortunate as free recall (i.e. uninterrupted recall) typically produces very accurate recall (Yuille & Cutshall, 1986). Further, the increased difficulty of trying to recall information despite constant interruptions may stop the witness from trying so hard to recall information.

The second drawback of interruption is that after the witness has been interrupted several times he or she begins to expect interruption through-out the interview. As the witness expects to have only a short period to respond, he or she shortens responses accordingly. Clearly, any response that is shortened will not produce as much information, and may exclude information, important to an investigation.

Use of question-answer format

Police interviewing relies heavily on the use of a question-answer format. Most questions used in forensic interviews are closed questions (e.g. 'what colour was the attacker's shirt?'). Such questions may have the advantage of eliciting information that the interviewer feels is relevant and prevent the witness from wandering off the point, but they can also cause problems.

Closed questions produce a less concentrated form of retrieval. Witnesses take less time to respond to closed questions than open-ended questions, which may be due (at least in part) to less time being spent actively trying to retrieve information. In addition, both closed and open questions are asked quickly fired at witnesses; thus, there is only a short time between a ques-tion-answer and the next question, giving no opportunity or encouragement to the witness to elaborate or extend an answer. This use of questions also changes the nature of the witness's task from that of free recall. When closed questions are used, the interview takes on the format of the interviewer asking a closed question and the witness giving a brief answer, the interviewer asking another closed question, and so on.

This means that the interview changes from being directed by the witness to being directed by the interviewer. Fisher et al. comment, 'It is difficult enough for the witness to retrieve detailed events from memory when actively trying; it is virtually impossible when he remains passive' (p. 181). Using a question-answer format also means that the only information elicited is that which is requested. Thus, if the interviewer forgets to ask a certain question, no information in that area is recorded.

Inappropriate sequencing of questions
The next problem is that, typically, questions are sequenced in an inappropriate manner. This causes problems similar to those associated with excessive use of question-answer format; both impair recall performance through shifts in attention. Many questions asked by interviewers are in a seemingly arbitrary order that may adversely influence witnesses through shifting their retrieval efforts from one area to another. For example, an interviewer may ask a visually orientated question about the suspect's face, then follow with an auditory question about the suspect's voice, then return to a visual target, such as the suspect's clothes. This shift in retrieval attention from one area to another and from one sensory modality to another may impair performance. Indeed, alternating retrieval in this way has been shown in one study to produce a 19% decrease in witness's performance (Fisher & Price-Rouch, 1986). Further problems can be caused by asking what Fisher et al. term 'general knowledge' questions, such as 'why do you think he did that?' or 'was he married?', in among questions concerning the crime. Again, shifting from the recall of crime details to general knowledge questions, then back to crime details can cause decreases in the witness' performance.

Other problems
Other problems occur in some interviews but not all. These include negative phrasing, leading questions, inappropriate language, judgmental comments, lack of following potential leads, and underemphasizing auditory cues.

Negative phrasing occurs when questions are asked in the negative form. For example, 'you don't remember if..?' Phrasing questions in this form may actively discourage the witness from trying hard to retrieve information.

Leading questions are questions that subtly suggest that a certain answer is required. Not only are the demand characteristics of the situation likely to produce compliance, but Loftus (1975) found that leading questions may bias witnesses' later recollections of an event.

Inappropriate language is found where interviewers use overly formal sentences or words, which are difficult for the witness to comprehend (e.g. 'what was the index number of the vehicle?'). Such language may not only prevent the witness from understanding the question, but also creates a barrier between the interviewer and the witness that is not conducive to optimal performance. Judgmental comments are occasionally made, often about the witness' role in an incident (e.g. 'you shouldn't have been carrying so much cash'). These may make the witness defensive or offend the witness, and it is difficult to see how they can enhance recall.

Furthermore, police officers often fail to follow up on leads that they are given. For instance, a suspect may be described as looking like 'a gangster' without any attempt being made to follow up the comment, to elicit why the witness felt that the suspect looked like a 'gangster'. Thus, information that might help produce a more objective description is again missed. Finally, auditory clues are often underemphasized. Officers rarely enquire about what a suspect may have said or if they had an accent.

Clearly, the standard police interview has many potential areas for improvement, and any interview procedure that addresses these problems is likely to lead to enhanced recall. It is important to recognize, therefore, that in real-life investigations the cognitive interview may have advantages over standard interviewing procedures that go beyond the use of the specialist mnemonics memory retrieval aids. It also follows, that if we are to maximise the effectiveness and efficiency of the cognitive interview in the field, attention must be paid to the relative efficacy of these various components in enhancing recall.

USE OF THE COGNITIVE INTERVIEW IN REAL-LIFE INVESTIGATIONS

Most research on the cognitive interview has been conducted in the laboratory and field studies are rare (see also, McGurk, Carr & McGurk, 1993; for an evaluation of the PEACE approach as a whole). There are, however, two notable exceptions, one in the USA and one in the UK. In the first, Fisher, Geiselman & Amador (1989) conducted a field study with 16 experienced detectives from a robbery division in the USA. Preliminary recordings were made of witness interviews conducted by detectives before any training in the cognitive interview. Subsequent recordings were made after seven officers had been trained in the cognitive interview while the remainder were assigned to a control condition. In all, 88 interviews were recorded before training, and 47 interviews were conducted after training; 24 by officers trained in the cognitive interview and 23 by officers in a control group. Interviews were selected so that each crime was severe enough that time would be made available to conduct a thorough interview.

Effectiveness of the cognitive interview was tested in two ways:

1) by comparing the number of 'facts' elicited before and after training in the use of the cognitive interview, and
2) by comparing the number of facts elicited by the trained detectives using the cognitive interview and the control group of detectives who were still using standard techniques.

Detectives who were not going to be trained in the cognitive interview were compared with the detectives who were to be trained in the cognitive interview. There were no significant differences between the two groups before training. However, after training there was a significant improvement; 63% more information was recalled by witnesses interviewed by detectives trained in use of the cognitive interview compared with those interviewed by the 'control' detectives. Moreover, detectives in the cognitive interview trained group showed a 47% increase in the amount of information that they elicited from witnesses compared with their previous performance before training.

Fisher et al. (1989) were able to estimate accuracy by comparing each witness report with what they term another 'reliable' source, when possible. In 22 cases this source was another witness, in one case a confession, and in one case information was supplied by a video camera. They found a 93% corroboration rate for information produced by detectives untrained in the cognitive interview, and a 94.5% corroboration rate for detectives using the cognitive interview. No significant difference was found between the two. However, as Fisher et al. (1989) note, just because two witnesses correlate an item, does not necessarily mean that they are accurate: both may be wrong. Clearly though, this study shows that the cognitive interview has the potential to lead to dramatic enhancements in witness recall.

However, it is also notable that of the seven detectives trained in the cognitive interview, one produced a decrease in performance of 23%. On the basis of such a small sample it is difficult to estimate whether this was a curious anomaly or whether this represents a potential problem. Fisher et al. (1989) comment of this detective:

> Not coincidentally an analysis of the post-training interviews showed that he was the only one of the seven detectives who did not incorporate the recommended procedures into his post-training interviews (p. 724).

However, they provide no details to show how he did not incorporate the recommended procedures. For instance, did he keep interrupting witnesses? Did his method of instructing witnesses to reinstate context cause confusion? Also, because the cognitive interviews are not described, it is not possible to identify the elements in the cognitive interview responsible for improvements, or even if all the elements of the cognitive interview were used. As we shall see next, these are important points. Furthermore, the detectives were aware that they were evaluating a new technique, which they had been specially trained to use. The training for, and use of, a new technique may have produced improvements in the police officers' performance, by motivating them to try harder and in turn, to motivate the witnesses to try harder too.

Of relevance here, is the field investigation in the United Kingdom by George (1991), which is also summarised by Clifford & George (1996). In this study, 28 police officers were evaluated in one of four conditions, seven in each. A recording of an interview performed by each officer was evaluated before each was trained in an interview technique or placed in the control group. The interview techniques were: 1) the cognitive interview, 2) conversation management (a procedure developed to open channels of communication, see Shepherd, 1988), 3) conversation management combined with the cognitive interview, and 4) an untrained control group. The results indicated that the cognitive interview showed an improvement when compared to the standard police interview control group of 14% more information. When compared to performance before 'enhanced' cognitive interview training, this improvement was 55%. This advantage was for all kinds of information (i.e. who, what, when, where, how and why). Neither conversation management nor the combination of conversation management and cognitive interview produced more information than the untrained group. These results would suggest that it was not 'training' *per se*, or novelty alone that accounted for the improvements that occurred with the cognitive interview.

Clifford and George (1996) provide a detailed account of the form of the cognitive interview. Interestingly, of the four original mnemonic strategies, three were hardly used; instructions to report everything, change orders or change perspectives. A similar pattern of results has been found by Memon, Holley, Milne, Koehnken & Bull (1994) in a laboratory study. George (1991) notes that it is unsurprising that officers rarely used the change of perspective mnemonic as:

> ...it is not an easy concept to ask someone to put themselves in someone else's shoes to review an event asking them to say what they think they would have seen, and remain confident that there will be no confabulation (p. 117).

Critics have also suggested that the use of the change perspectives mnemonic may make it difficult to use such statements in court, especially if children are interviewed, again because of a danger of confabulation (Boon & Noon, 1994); although it appears to have little impact on jurors' judgements of guilt or innocence (Kebbell, Wagstaff & Preece, in press). The police officers in this study may have had an intuitive grasp of this and so did not use the technique. Similarly officers and witnesses may find it difficult to use change order instructions, although it is not clear why officers did not use instructions to report everything.

The fourth mnemonic strategy, reinstatement of context, was used more frequently and to good effect. Information retrieved with an open question was significantly greater when that question was presented with a request to reinstate context. Instructions for focused retrieval (i.e. to work hard) also appeared to significantly increase recall. Imagery, while used relatively frequently in the cognitive interview condition, failed to enhance recall on its own.

Importantly, this field study documented the questioning style used by the interviewers. This revealed a dramatic change. Officers in the cognitive interview condition asked far fewer questions. What questions they did ask were more likely to be open and they asked far fewer leading or closed questions. While the number of questions decreased to one third of the pre-training levels, the amount of information elicited from a witness, per ten minutes, increased dramatically. Why, however, the effects of the cognitive interview should be eliminated when it is combined with another procedure (conversation management) remains something of a mystery.

POLICE PERCEPTION OF THE COGNITIVE INTERVIEW

Whilst the two field studies show that the cognitive interview may enhance witness memory, they tell us little about police officers' perceptions of the cognitive interview. Clearly, officers must have a positive attitude to a technique if it is to be successful, particularly after its novelty value has worn off. To investigate this issue, Kebbell, Milne & Wagstaff (in press) surveyed police officers' perceptions of the effectiveness of the cognitive interview in witness interviews.

Ninety-six UK officers trained in the cognitive interview were surveyed as well as a control group of 65 untrained officers. Officers were asked to rate how useful and how frequently they used the components of the cognitive interview.

Trained officers were significantly more likely to say that they use instructions to mentally reinstate context, use different orders, change perspectives and use imagery than untrained officers.

The responses of the trained officers also showed that some components of the cognitive interview were used more frequently and were rated as more useful than others. Rated as most useful, and most frequently used, were instructions to establish rapport, report everything, encourage concentration, witness-compatible questioning, and mental reinstatement of context.

Rated as less useful and less frequently used were different orders, imagery, change perspectives and transfer control. However, it must be born in mind that officers' reports of how they interview may be very different from how they actually interview (Robson, 1993).

The fact that officers rated establishment of rapport as the most important technique to use when interviewing seems particularly important. In our experience, witnesses often do not provide information because of a reluctance to talk to the police rather than memory problems. This is particularly the case when a witness has been a victim of abhorrent and embarrassing acts or may be construed as having been partly culpable for an offense. Establishment of rapport is likely to increase witnesses' inclination to provide information to the police, and a point police officers seem to have understood.

Further data indicated that the cognitive interview was generally perceived to be a useful procedure that increases correct recall; for instance 89.4% of officers indicated that the cognitive interview produced 'more' or 'much more' information than a standard interview. Typical positive comments concerning the cognitive interview were as follows:

> Extracts more information and appears a fair system to a third party as full explanations are usually arrived at which may save problems later in court with the defense. The interview is more structured and detailed. And there is less chance of forgetting to mention an item. A better quality of evidence is obtained.

These positive perceptions of the cognitive interview do not appear to be simply due to novelty value; the average time since cognitive interview training for the trained group was nearly two years.

Kebbell et al. also questioned officers about their perception of how much incorrect information is generated with the cognitive interview. They found that officers did not have an exaggerated perception of the ability of the cognitive interview to enhance accurate recall; only 8.5% stated that the cognitive interview produces much less incorrect information than a standard interview. (This contrasts, for example, with the exaggerated credulity that tends to be shown in interviewing with hypnosis, which may, in fact, have a detrimental effect on overall accuracy, see Wagstaff, 1993; Wagstaff, Vella & Perfect, 1992). Significantly, however, Kebbell et al. found that many officers reported that they simply do not have the time to conduct a cognitive interview (see also, Kebbell & Wagstaff, 1996b). For instance 54% of cognitive-interview trained officers reported that they 'never' or 'rarely' had enough time to conduct what they believed was a good interview. This problem was compounded by the fact that 93% of officers believed that the cognitive interview took longer to conduct than a standard interview; a finding supported by the results of some laboratory studies (Kohnken et al., 1994; Mello & Fisher, 1996). Typical negative comments were as follows:

> Time consuming which is a problem in a busy sub-division with other demands on your time. Requires a lot of practice and learning to do it well. There is no doubt that cognitive interviews are a far more effective means of interviewing than SI. However, regrettably the cognitive interview is time consuming if it is to be done properly and unfortunately time is limited and you simply cannot spend as much time with victims/witnesses as you would like, certainly when you are a uniformed officer. However, CID who have time probably have a better opportunity to practice it than uniformed officers.

In fact, of the 74 negative comments, 64 (86.5%) concerned time constraints.

CONCLUSIONS

Clearly, the cognitive interview has the potential to enhance witness memory. Furthermore, the importance of witnesses' to criminal investigations makes the enhancement of witnesses recall extremely worthwhile (Kebbell & Milne, 1996; Rand, 1975). However, there are two particularly important issues associated with its use in real-life investigations that require further study.

First, in practice, the components of the cognitive interview are not used equally frequently. Some are used more frequently than others and are perceived to be more useful than others. Second, police officers often do not have as much time as they would like to conduct a cognitive interview. Taken together, these factors strongly suggest that time should be spent discovering what parts of the cognitive interview are most responsible for enhancements in recall, and ensuring that officers are trained in those techniques that are most effective (Bekerian & Dennett, 1993; Kebbell & Wagstaff, 1996b).

For instance, Memon & Stevenage (1996) point out that in many laboratory studies a cognitive interview without mnemonic instructions produces similar recall to a full cognitive interview. In his field study, George also concluded that memory enhancements were mainly due to an absence of the problems typically associated with standard police interviews plus instructions to reinstate context. And, significantly, Mello & Fisher (1996) have recently commented:

> ..the cognitive interview may be a tool that works primarily by facilitating communication rather than or in addition to, one that facilitates memory retrieval (p. 415).

It could be the case, therefore, that valuable training time is perhaps best spent training officers in the social components of the cognitive interview and context reinstatement. This might be more worthwhile than spending some of that valuable time training officers to use instructions to change orders or change perspectives which will not be used, and which may have little or no effectiveness in enhancing recall (Boon & Noon, 1994; Mello & Fisher, 1996).

It is also important that 'quick' interviews are developed (Kebbell & Wagstaff, 1996; 1997). For instance, if a mugger has recently run off and the police wish to search for him in the immediate area, it might not be appropriate to conduct a full cognitive interview, all that is required is a brief description. In these situations the problems with standard interviews described earlier may not be as clear as they first seem because as a method of conducting a rapid, succinct interview it may be effective. However, even when time is at a premium, improvements over standard interviews might possibly be achieved through a compromise between standard interviews and the cognitive interview. For example, a full cognitive interview using context reinstatement and uninterrupted free recall may in some situations take too long. A standard interview with frequent interruption and closed questions may take less time but not produce enough accurate information. A compromise might be to ask the witness a direct, open question (e.g., 'describe the mugger in as much detail as you can') and then allow them to respond.

REFERENCES

Bekerian,, D.A., & Dennett, J.L. (1993). The cognitive interview: Reviving the issues. Applied Cognitive Psychology, 7, 275–297.

Boon, J. & Noon, E. (1994). Changing perspectives in cognitive interviewing. Psychology, Crime and Law, 1, 59.69.

Central Planning and Training Unit (1992). Investigative Interviewing: A Guide to Interviewing. London: Home Office, Central Planning and Training Unit.

Clifford, B.R. & George, R. (1996). A field evaluation of training in three methods of witness/victim investigative interviewing. Psychology, Crime and Law, 2, 231–248.

Fisher, R.P. (1995). Interviewing victims and witnesses of crimes. Psychology, Public Policy, and Law, 1, 732–764.

Fisher, R.P., & Geiselman, R.E. (1992). Memory Enhancing Techniques for Investigative Interviewing: The Cognitive Interview. Springfield: Charles C. Thomas.

Fisher, R.P., Geiselman, R.E., & Amador, M. (1989). Field test of the cognitive interview: Enhancing the recollection of actual victims and witnesses of crime. Journal of Applied Psychology, 74, 722–727.

Fisher, R.P., Geiselman, R.E., & Raymond, D.S. (1987b). Critical analysis of police interview techniques. Journal of Police Science & Administration, 15, 177–185.

Fisher, R.P., Geiselman, R.E., Raymond, D.S., Jurkevich, L.M., & Warhaftig, M.L. (1987a). Enhancing enhanced eyewitness memory: refining the cognitive interview. Journal of Police Science & Administration, 15, 291–297.

Fisher, R.P. & Price-Roush, J. (1986). Question order and eyewitness memory. Unpublished manuscript, Department of Psychology, Florida International University, USA.

Geiselman, R.E. (1996). On the use and efficacy of the cognitive interview. Psychology, 7 (6), witness-memory.2.geiselman.

Geiselman, R.E., Fisher, R.P., Cohen, G., Holland, H., & Surtes, L. (1986). Eyewitness response to leading and misleading questions under the cognitive interview. Journal of Police Science & Administration, 14, 31–39.

Geiselman, R.E., Fisher, R.P., Firstenberg, I., Hutton, L.A., Sullivan, S.J., Avetissian, I.V., & Prosk, A.L. (1984). Enhancement of eyewitness memory: An empirical evaluation of the cognitive interview. Journal of Police Science and Administration, 12, 74–80.

George, R. (1991). A field and experimental evaluation of three methods of interviewing witnesses and victims of crime. Unpublished Master's Thesis, Polytechnic of East London, London, UK.

Kebbell, M.R. & Milne, R. (in press). Police officers' perception of eyewitness factors in forensic investigations: A survey. The Journal of Social Psychology.

Kebbell, M.R., Milne, R. & Wagstaff, G.F. (in press). Applying the cognitive interview: Police officers' perceptions of its usefulness. Psychology, Crime and Law.

Kebbell, M.R. & Wagstaff, G.F. (1996a). The influence of item difficulty on the relationship between confidence and accuracy: Does a cognitive interview or hypnosis alter this relationship? Proceedings of the British Psychological Society, 4, 89.

Kebbell, M.R. & Wagstaff, G.F. (1996b). Enhancing the practicality of the cognitive interview in forensic situations. Psychology, 7(16), witness-memory.3.kebbell.

Kebbell, M.R. & Wagstaff, G.F. (1997). Why do the police interview eyewitnesses? Interview objectives and the evaluation of eyewitness performance. The Journal of Psychology, 131, 595–601.

Kebbell, M.R.,Wagstaff, G.F. & Preece, D. (in press). The effect of knowledge that testimony was elicited with a cognitive interview on jurors' judgments of guilt. Psychology, Crime and Law.

Kohnken, G., Milne, R., Memon, A., & Bull, R. (in press). A meta-analysis of the effects of the cognitive interview. Psychology, Crime and Law.

Kohnken, G., Thurer, C. & Zoberbier, D. (1994). The cognitive interview: Are the interviewers' memories enhanced, too? *Applied Cognitive Psychology, 8*, 13–24.

Loftus, E.F. (1975). Leading questions and eyewitness report. *Cognitive Psychology, 7,* 560–572.

McGurk, B.J., Carr, M.J. & McGurk, D. (1993). Investigative interviewing courses for police officers: an evaluation. *Police Research Series, 4.* London: Home Office Police Department.

Mello, E.W. & Fisher, R.P. (1996). Enhancing older adult eyewitness memory with the cognitive interview. *Applied Cognitive Psychology, 10*, 403–418.

Memon, A., & Bull, R. (1991). The cognitive interview: its origins, empirical support, evaluation and practical implications. *Journal of Community & Applied Social Psychology, 1,* 291–307.

Memon, A., Holley, A., Milne, R, Koehnken, G., & Bull, R. (1994). Towards understanding the effects of interviewer training in evaluating the cognitive interview. *Applied Cognitive Psychology, 8*, 641–659.

Memon, A., & Kohnken, G. (1992). Helping witnesses to remember more: the cognitive interview. *Expert Evidence, 2,* 39–48

Memon, A. & Stevenage, S. (1996). Interviewing witnesses: What works and what doesn't? *Psychology, 7 (6),* witness-memory.1.memon.

Milne R. & Bull R. (1995). Children with mild learning disability: The cognitive interview and suggestibility. Paper presented to the *Fifth European Psychology and Law Conference*, Budapest, Hungary.

Rand, Corporation (1975). The Criminal Investigation Process. *Rand Corporation Technical Report R-1777,* 1–3. Santa Monica, California.

Robson, C. (1993). *Real World Research*. Oxford: Blackwell.

Shepherd, E. (1988). Developing interview skills. In P. Southgate (Ed.), *New Directions in Police Training*. London: HMSO

Wagstaff, G.F. (1993). What expert witnesses can tell courts about hypnosis: A review of the association between hypnosis and the law. *Expert Evidence, 2,* 60–70.

Wagstaff, G. F., Vella, M. & Perfect, T. J. (1992). The effect of hypnotically elicited testimony on juror's judgements of guilt and innocence. *Journal of Social Psychology, 31,* 69–77.

Yuille, J.C. (1984). Research and teaching with the police: A Canadian example. *International Review of Applied Psychology, 33,* 5–23.

Yuille, J.C. & Cutshall, J.L. (1986). A case study of eyewitness memory of a crime. *Journal of Applied Psychology, 71,* 291–301.

Chapter 13

'TRY AGAIN': THE COGNITIVE INTERVIEW OR FREE RECALL?[1]

Laura Campos and Maria L. Alonso-Quecuty

Adams (1985) in her paper 'Improving Memory: Can Retrieval Strategies Help?' showed that employing different mnemonic strategies at the time of retrieval can enhance the completeness and accuracy of memory. In a legal context, the elicitation of complete and accurate statements from witnesses and victims is essential. An interview technique that agrees with Adams' proposal is the Cognitive Interview (CI) (Geiselman et al., 1984). The CI is a package of mnemonic strategies which asks witnesses to think about what happened and encourages them to make as many retrieval attempts as possible (Memon & Bull, 1991). Is the effectiveness of the original CI due to the use of different mnemonic strategies, or is it simply a result of multiple retrieval opportunities throughout the interview? Our results showed that the CI is more than the simple action of repeating the retrieval of information four times.

INTRODUCTION

Although research on human memory shows that the use of various mnemonic strategies has beneficial effects at the time of obtaining complete and accurate memory accounts (see Adams, 1985), people do not normally spontaneously use retrieval strategies in an effective way (Williams & Hollan, 1981).

Adams (1985) explores the possibilities of improving memory accounts by employing different strategies at the time of retrieval. In her paper, Adams considers four mnemonic strategies which are supported by research on human memory:

a) Recreating information about the learning environment: subjects remember more when they are tested in the acquisition environment or when they are instructed to mentally recreate the original environment (Burns, 1981; Frerk et al., 1985; Godden & Baddeley, 1975; Krafka & Penrod, 1985; Malpass & Devine, 1981; Smith, 1979, 1984; Smith, Glenberg & Bjork, 1978).

b) Establishing landmarks: when subjects are provided with common landmark events, such as locations or activities used as contexts within which to search for target information, (e.g., Since New Year's Day, has anyone tried to rob you?) or when they generate their own land-marks, more accurate responses are elicited than when they are asked using a general format question (e.g., During the last six months, did anyone steal anything that belonged to you?) Subjects given landmarks also show a lower tendency to 'forward telescoping' (Baddeley, 1979; Lindsay & Norman, 1972; Loftus & Marburger, 1983; Neter & Waksberg, 1964; Sudman & Bradburn, 1973; Williams, 1976; Williams & Hollan, 1981).

c) Taking multiple perspectives: when different perspectives (e.g. concep-tual) or positions (e.g. physical) are taken at the time of retrieval, a greater accuracy in recall is also obtained (Anderson & Pichert, 1978; Bereiter & Scardamalia, 1980, 1982; Bower, 1981; Bower, Black & Turner, 1979; Bower & Gilligan, 1979; Firstenberg, 1983; Hasher & Griffin, 1978).

d) Recreating the temporal order of events: both the sequence and posi-tion of information can have a powerful effect on leading subjects to elicit accurate memory recall even if the test items are presented in random order (Bekerian & Bowers, 1983; Bower & Morrow, 1990; Burns, 1981; Loftus, 1979; Loftus & Loftus, 1980; Mandler, 1967; McCloskey & Zaragoza, 1985; Whitten & Leonard, 1981).

Coinciding with Adams' work, Geiselman and his colleagues (1984) for-mulated what they termed the 'cognitive interview' (CI). It is an interview procedure, devised to improve police interviewing, which is essentially comprised of the retrieval strategies outlined in Adams' paper.

The CI, in its original form, is composed of four techniques and some ways of helping witnesses to recall specific details. These include:

a) cognitive reinstatement of the context: witnesses have to mentally rein-state the physical (external) and personal (internal) contexts which existed at the time the incident took place;

b) emphasis on reporting everything: witnesses are advised, throughout the interview, to mention absolutely everything they remember, although some things may not seem important;

c) recount events in a different order: witnesses have to report what happened from different starting points (e.g. starting from the end and going backwards to the beginning of the event);

d) change of perspective: witnesses have to position themselves in another place of the scene, so that they report what they could have seen from that perspective.

After obtaining this final version of what occurred, a series of auxiliary techniques are employed where appropriate, for the recollection of details concerning physical appearance, names, objects, conversations and features of speech.

Research on the CI has generated a large amount of published information. Thus, a considerable number of variables have been examined (see Bekerian & Dennett, 1993; Memon & Stevenage, 1996 for a review). However, the priority treatment given to the study of factors that can modulate the success of the CI as an interview procedure has left aside the focus of attention on the theoretical examination of that success, with few exceptions (e.g. Aschermann, Mantwill & Köhnken, 1989; Köhnken, Thürer & Zoberbier, 1994; Mantwill & Andres, 1990; Mantwill, Aschermann & Köhnken, 1992; Mantwill, Köhnken & Aschermann, 1995).

Some questions concerning the CI remain unanswered. For example, why are more complete and accurate statements obtained when eyewitnesses are interviewed by means of the CI as compared to the Standard Interview (SI)? Further, is the improvement in recall due to the use of the different mnemonic strategies included in the CI, like Geiselman and his colleagues claim (e.g. Fisher & Geiselman, 1992; Fisher & McCauley, 1995; Fisher et al., 1987; Fisher, Geiselman & Amador, 1989; Geiselman & Fisher, 1988; Geiselman & Padilla, 1988; Geiselman et al., 1984; 1985; 1986a; Geiselman, Saywitz & Bornstein, 1990), or is it simply a result of multiple retrieval opportunities throughout the interview within the CI instructions? (Thomson, personal communication).

Recently, some experiments have been performed to test the effects that multiple retrieval attempts could have on eyewitnesses' memory when they are interviewed using the CI or the SI (e.g. Alonso-Quecuty & Hernandez-Fernaud, 1997; Memon et al., 1996; Turtle & Yuille, 1994.) Memon and her colleagues (1996, cited in Memon & Stevenage, 1996) found that the CI was only effective at the first questioning phase, that is, the first time it was used, in comparison to when it was applied several times across different interview sessions. As Memon & Stevenage (1996) pointed out, it appears that the CI advantage could be related to the number of retrieval attempts.

Nevertheless, in our opinion, in order to isolate the effects that multiple retrieval attempts could have on eyewitnesses' memory, it would be better to compare the level of recall obtained by means of a single CI applied in just one interview session, to that obtained as result of multiple free recall tasks also in a single interview session. The aim of this paper was to demonstrate that contrast. We took into account the theoretical explanations given by Adams (1985) and proved by the experimental research on human memory, with respect to each of the mnemonic strategies which make up the CI. Our hypothesis is favourable to the existence of significant differences between the level of recall obtained by making multiple retrieval attempts without using mnemonics, and the recall obtained by means of the CI, in which mnemonics are used.

METHOD

Subjects
One hundred seventy undergraduate students from the University of La Laguna volunteered to participate in the experiment. There were 92 females and 78 males. In both cases their ages ranged from 19 to 21 (mean 19.65).

Materials
A video-recording of a simulated incident was made in the parking area of the University of La Laguna. The event depicted two young men approaching a parked car. After an attempt to open the car door in a very suspicious manner, several people appeared shouting that they did not have the right to open the car. Among them, the car owner and, later, an accomplice of the suspects appeared. The sequence culminated in a physical and verbal exchange between the three young men (the two suspected thieves and the accomplice), the owner of the car (who was threatened with a knife), and a witness. The dispute came to an end with the arrival of the police, and the flight of the three suspects. The incident lasted 15 minutes. Its length and high level of action differed substantially from the event traditionally used in CI research (a four-minute-event with only two characters: the owner of the Liquor Store and the assailant) (Fisher et al., 1987; Geiselman et al., 1985; 1986a). A protocol for the analysis of the dependent variables was also devised.

Design
A factorial design of the type of interview was used: a cognitive interview (n = 102) and a standard interview which was applied four times in sequence (n = 68.)

The following dependent measures were employed:

1. Correct Information: exact information given by the subjects. Correct responses were classified into three categories according to whether the exact detail mentioned referred to persons, objects or events. The total number of correct responses was also considered.
2. Errors: information given by the subjects which, although it was featured in the recording, was in some way distorted (e.g., a description of the car including the correct make, but incorrect model). Errors were classified into three categories according to whether they referred to persons, objects or events. The total number of details incorrectly reported was also considered.
3. Confabulations: information given by the subjects that did not appear in the film (e.g. the mention of a motorbike.) Once again, confabulations were classified into three categories: persons, objects and events. The total number of confabulations was also considered.

Procedure

All subjects underwent two experimental stages. In the first phase, the subjects received the following instructions:

> Now you are going to watch a film on video. You will watch an incident which took place in the parking area of the University of La Laguna. Your task consists of paying attention to everything that happens, as if you were real eyewitnesses.

The subjects watched the video tape sequence in groups. Thereafter, they entered individual cubicles where the second phase of the experiment took place. Subjects were randomly distributed into two experimental groups according to the interview type.

Thus, subjects in group 1 were questioned using a narrative Spanish traditional interview (STI) (Hernandez-Fernaud & Alonso-Quecuty, 1997). It consisted of asking the single question: 'What happened?' After their first statement, subjects were asked to 'try again' for three more times. Therefore, we obtained four statements from each subject, in a narrative form. In the second group subjects were questioned using a cognitive interview. Here, the subjects gave a first statement after the cognitive reinstatement of the context.

A second statement was elicited when subjects changed perspective and reported what they could have seen from that point. A third statement was obtained when subjects tried to recall events in a different order. Finally, a fourth statement was given when subjects had to attend to a series of auxiliary techniques for the recollection of various details. Therefore, four statements were also obtained from each subject to whom the cognitive interview was applied.

RESULTS AND DISCUSSION

As a preliminary step towards the analysis of the dependent variables (correct information, errors and confabulations), a description of the sequence to be watched by the witnesses was devised. This transcription, in the form of a script, listed the elements of the action.

One-way analyses of variance (ANOVAs) were performed on each of the dependent variables. The ANOVAs showed some significant effects.

The results confirmed our hypothesis. We found significant differences between the level of recall obtained using the STI applied four times in sequence, and that obtained using the cognitive interview. Thus, with respect to the *total number of correct responses*, statements obtained by means of the CI were more accurate than statements obtained by means of the STI ($F(1,168) = 49.081$, $MS_e = 230.50$, $p < .01$; CI mean: 44.23 and STI mean: 27.57.) Furthermore, statements obtained by means of the CI contained significantly more correct information for *persons* ($F(1,168) = 39.836$, $MS_e = 23.97$, $p < .01$; CI mean: 9.62 and STI mean: 4.78) and *events* ($F(1,168) = 39.956$, $MS_e = 141.68$, $p < .01$; CI mean: 32.97 and STI mean: 21.19) than statements obtained by means of the STI. In relation to the *total number of errors*, no significant differences were found between the interview groups ($F(1,168) = 3.797$, $MS_e = 4.49$, ns). Moreover, no significant differences were found between interview groups for either *errors for persons* ($F(1,168) = 0.157$, $MS_e = 1.22$, ns) or *errors for objects* ($F(1,168) = 0.003$, $MS_e = 0.29$, ns). However, statements obtained by means of the CI contained significantly less *errors for events* than statements obtained by means of the STI ($F(1,168) = 9.614$, $MS_e = 2.14$, $p < .01$; CI mean: 1.07 and STI mean: 1.78.) Finally, with respect to *confabulations*, no significant differences were found between the interview groups in relation to the *total number of confabulations* ($F(1,168) = 0.298$, $MS_e = 5.80$, ns.) Moreover, no significant differences were found between interview groups for *confabulations for persons* ($F(1,168) = 2.390$, $MS_e = 1.73$, ns.) However, statements obtained by means of the CI contained significantly less *confabulations for events* (F(1,168) = 6.445, MS_e = 2.85, p < .05; CI mean: 0.96 and STI mean: 1.63) but more *confabulations for objects* (F(1,168) = 6.512, MS_e = 0.13, p < .05; CI mean: 0.18 and STI mean: 0.03) than statements obtained by means of the STI.

These results fall along the same lines as those previously obtained in CI research. The cognitive interview produces more complete and accurate accounts than the STI without an increase in the number of errors (Alonso-Quecuty & Hernandez-Fernaud, 1997; Aschermann, Mantwill & Köhnken, 1991; Fisher & Geiselman, 1992; Geiselman et al., 1984; 1985; 1986a; 1986b; 1986c; Hernandez-Fernaud & Alonso-Quecuty, 1997; Perry & Chapman, 1992). Nevertheless, a greater number of confabulations for objects was obtained by means of the CI. A possible explanation for this result could be that the auxiliary techniques used in the final stage of the CI are mainly employed for the recall of objects. It is here that witnesses may feel themselves forced to answer without being sure of what they are stating (Hernandez-Fernaud & Alonso-Quecuty, 1997).

As we pointed out in the introduction, some questions concerning the cognitive interview had remained unanswered. Thus, we wondered if the success of the original CI was due to the four-time repetition of the retrieval of information, or if its effectiveness was the result of the use of different cognitive strategies. The experiment discussed in this paper answers this question. The results obtained show that the cognitive interview is more than the simple process of repeating the retrieval of information four times. Thus, this fact leads us to stress the theoretical background underlying the mnemonic strategies which make up this interview procedure.

Thanks to experimental research on human memory, we rely on specific techniques that can be used in the field of forensics. Thereby, these strategies can be used to improve the retrieval of information from witnesses. Now, we know that the mnemonic strategies which make up the cognitive interview are really effective (e.g. Anderson & Pichert, 1978; Malpass & Devine, 1981; Norman & Bobrow, 1978; Smith, 1979; Tulving, 1983; Tulving & Thomson, 1973), and that asking witnesses to 'try again' is not enough to obtain a complete and accurate report of what happened.

NOTES

1   This research was supported by the Spanish Ministerio de Educación y Ciencia (DGICYT grants PB89-0170-CO3-01 and PB93-0566-C03-01) and the Canary Government grant (93/171) of the second author, and a postgraduate grant (Canary Government) of the first author

REFERENCES

Adams, L.T. (1985). Improving Memory: Can Retrieval Strategies Help? *Human Learning, 4*, 281–297.

Alonso-Quecuty, M.L., & Hernandez-Fernaud, E. (1997). Tócala otra vez, Sam: Repitiendo las mentiras. *Estudios de Psicología, 57*, 29–37.

Anderson, R.C., & Pichert, J.W. (1978). Recall of previously unrecallable information following a shift in perspective. *Journal of Verbal Learning and Verbal Behavior, 17*, 1–12.

Aschermann, E., Mantwill, M., & Köhnken, G. (1989, March). *Diagnostik von Wissensstrukturen* [Assessment of knowledge structures]. Poster session presented at the 31st Conference of Experimental Psychologists, Bamberg, Germany.

Aschermann, E., Mantwill, M., & Köhnken, G. (1991). An independent replication of the cognitive interview. *Applied Cognitive Psychology, 5*, 489–495.

Baddeley, A. (1979). The limitations of human memory: Implications for the design of retrospective surveys. In: L. Moss & H. Goldstein (Eds.), *The recall method in social surveys*. London: University of London Institute of Education.

Bekerian, D.A., & Bowers, J.M. (1983). Eyewitness testimony: Were we mislead? *Journal of Experimental Psychology: Learning, Memory and Cognition, 9(1)*, 139–145.

Bekerian, D.A., & Dennett, J.L. (1993). The cognitive interview technique: Reviving the issues. *Applied Cognitive Psychology, 7*, 275–297.

Bereiter, C. & Scardamalia, M. (1980, October).*Cognitive coping strategies and the problem of 'inert knowledge'*. Paper presented at the NIE-LRCD Conference on Thinking and Learning Skills, Pittsburgh, Pa.

Bereiter, C., & Scardamalia, M. (1982). From conversation to composition: The role of instruction in a developmental process. In: R. Glaser (Ed.), *Advances in instructional psychology, Vol. 2*. Hillsdale, N. J.: Lawrence Erlbaum Associates.

Bower, G.H. (1967). A multicomponent theory of the memory trace. In: K. W. Spence & J. T. Spence (Eds.), *The psychology of learning and motivation, vol 1*. New York: Academic Press.

Bower, G.H. (1981). Mood and memory. *American Psychologist, 36(2)*, 129–148.

Bower, G.H.; Black, J.B., & Turner, T.J. (1979). Script in Memory for Text. *Cognitive Psychology, 11*, 177–220.

Bower, G.H., & Gilligan, S.C. (1979). Remembering information related to one's self. *Journal of Research in Personality, 13*, 420–431.

Bower, G.H., & Morrow, D.G. (1990). Mental models in narrative comprehension. *Science, 247*, 44–48.

Burns, M.J. (1981). *The mental retracing of prior activities: Evidence for reminiscence in ordered retrieval*. Unpublished doctoral dissertation, University of California, Los Angeles. Dissertation Abstracts International, 42, 2108B.

Firstenberg, I. (1983). *The role of retrieval variability in the interrogation of human memory.* (Doctoral dissertation, University of California, Los Angeles, 1983). Dissertation Abstracts International, 44, 1623B.

Fisher, R.P., & Geiselman, R. E. (1992). *Memory-Enhancing Techniques for Investigative Interview.* Illinois: Charles C. Thomas Publisher.

Fisher, R.P., Geiselman, R. E., & Amador, M. (1989). Field test of the cognitive interview: Enhancing the recollection of actual victims and witnesses of crime. *Journal of Applied Psychology, 74(5)*, 722–727.

Fisher, R.P., Geiselman, R.E., Raymond, D.S., Jurkevich, L.M., & Warhaftig, M.L. (1987). Enhancing eyewitness memory: refining the cognitive interview. *Journal of Police Science and Administration, 15*, 291–297.

Fisher, R.P., & McCauley, M. (1995). Improving eyewitness testimony with the cognitive interview. In: M. Zaragoza, J.R. Graham, G.C. N. Hall, R. Hirschman, & Y.S. Ben-Porath (Eds.), *Memory and testimony in the child witness* (pp. 141–159). Thousand Oaks, CA: Sage.

Flexser, A.J., & Tulving, E. (1978). Retrieval independence in recognition and recall. *Psychological Review, 85*, 153–172.

Frerk, N., Holcombe, L., Johnson, S., & Nelson, T. (1985). *Context-dependent learning in a classroom situation*. Unpublished paper, Gustavus Adolphus College.

Geiselman, R.E., & Fisher, R.P. (1988). The cognitive interview: an innovative technique for questioning witnesses of crime. *Journal of Police and Criminal Psychology, 2*, 2–5.

Geiselman, R.E., Fisher, R.P., Cohen, G., Holland, H., & Surtes, L. (1986c). Eyewitness responses to leading and misleading questions under the cognitive interview. *Journal of Police Science and Administration, 14*, 31–39.

Geiselman, R.E., Fisher, R.P., Firstenberg, I., Hutton, L.A., Sullivan, S.J., Avetissian, I. & Prosk, A. (1984). Enhancement of eyewitness memory: an empirical evaluation of the cognitive interview. *Journal of Police Science and Administration, 12*, 74–80.

Geiselman, R.E., Fisher, R.P., MacKinnon, D.P., & Holland, H.L. (1985). Eyewitness memory enhancement in the police interview: cognitive retrieval mnemonics versus hypnosis. *Journal of Applied Psychology, 70*, 401–412.

Geiselman, R.E., Fisher, R.P., MacKinnon, D.P., & Holland, H.L. (1986a). Eyewitness memory enhancement in the cognitive interview. *American Journal of Psychology, 99*, 385–401.

Geiselman, R.E., Fisher, R.P., MacKinnon, D.P., & Holland, H.L. (1986b). Eyewitness memory enhancement in the police interview: Cognitive retrieval mnemonics versus hypnosis. *Journal of Applied Psychology, 70*, 401–412.

Geiselman, R.E.; Saywitz, K.J. and Bornstein, G.K. (1990). *Cognitive questioning techniques for child victims and witnesses of crime*. Report to the State Justice Institute.

Geiselman, R.E., & Padilla, J. (1988). Cognitive interviewing with child witnesses. *Journal of Police Science and Administration, 14*, 31–39.

Godden, D.R., & Baddeley, A.D. (1975). Context-dependent memory in two natural environments: on land and underwater. *British Journal of Psychology, 66*, 325–332.

Hasher, L., & Griffin, M. (1978). Reconstructive and reproductive processes in memory. *Journal of Experimental Psychology: Human Learning and Memory, 4(4)*, 318–330.

Hernandez-Fernaud, E., & Alonso-Quecuty, M.L. (1997). The Cognitive Interview and Lie Detection: A New Magnifying Glass for Sherlock Holmes. *Applied and Cognitive Psychology, 11*, 55–68.

Köhnken, G., Thürer, C., Zoberbier, D. (1994). The cognitive interview: Are the interviewers' memories enhanced, too? *Applied Cognitive Psychology, 8*, 13–24.

Krafka, C., & Penrod, S. (1985). Reinstatement of context in a field experiment on eyewitness identification. *Journal of Personality and Social Psychology, 49*, 58–69.

Lindsay, P.H., & Norman, D.A. (1972). *Human information processing: An introduction to psychology*. New York: Academic Press.

Loftus, E. (1979). *Eyewitness Testimony*. Cambridge. Mass: Harvard University Press.

Loftus E., & Loftus, G. (1980). On the permanence of stored information in the human brain. *American Psychologist, 35*, 409–420.

Loftus, E.F., & Marburger, W. (1983). Since the eruption of Mt. St. Helens, has anyone beaten you up? Improving the accuracy of retrospective reports with landmark events. *Memory and Cognition, 11(2)*, 114–120.

Malpass, R.S., & Devine, P.G. (1981). Guided memory in eyewitness identification. *Journal of Applied Psychology, 66*, 343–350.

Mandler, G. (1967). Organization and Memory. *The Psychology of Learning and Motivation, 1*, 327–372.

Mantwill, M., & Andres, J. (1990). Die wirkung des kognitiven interviews bei nicht-episodischem stimulus material. *Unveröffentlichte Untersuchung am Institut gür Psychologie*. Kiel.

Mantwill, M., Aschermann, E., & Köhnken, G. (1992). *Das kognitive interview und schemageleitete Erinnerung* [The cognitive interview and schema guided retrieval]. Universität Kiel, Kiel, Germany.

Mantwill, M., Köhnken, G., & Aschermann, E. (1995). Effects of the Cognitive Interview on the Recall of Familiar and Unfamiliar Events. *Journal of Applied Psychology, 80 (1)*, 68–78.

McCloskey, M., & Zaragoza, M. (1985). Misleading postevent information and memory for events: Arguments and evidence against memory impairment hypotheses. *Journal of Experimental psychology: General, 114(1)*, 24–31.

Memon, A., & Bull, R. (1991). The cognitive interview, its origins, empirical support, evaluation and practical implications. *Journal of Community and Applied Social Psychology, 1,* 291–307.

Memon, A., & Stevenage, S. V. (1996). Interviewing witnesses: what works and what doesn't? *Psychology,* APA.

Memon, A., Wark, L.; Bull, R., & Koehnken, G. (1996). *Isolating the effects of the cognitive interview.* Paper presented at The British Psychological Society Cognitive Conference.

Neter, J., & Waksberg, J. (1964). A study of response errors in expenditures data from household interview. *Journal of the American Statistical Association, 59,* 18–55.

Norman, D., & Bobrow, D. (1978). Descriptions: an intermediate stage in memory retrieval. *Cognitive Psychology, 11,* 107–123.

Perry, D.J., & Chapman, A. J. (1992). *Applying the cognitive interview procedure to road accident witnesses.* Paper presented at the Annual Conference of the British Psychological Society.

Smith, S.M. (1979). Remembering in and out of context. *Journal of Experimental Psychology: Human Learning and Memory, 5,* 460–471.

Smith, S.M. (1984). A comparison of two techniques for reducing context-dependent forgetting. *Memory and Cognition, 12,* 477–482.

Smith, S.M., Glenberg, A.M., & Bjork, R.A. (1978). Environmental context and human memory. *Memory and Cognition, 6,* 342–353.

Sudman, S., & Bradburn, N.M. (1973). Effects of time and memory factors on response in surveys. *Journal of the American Statistical Association, 68,* 805–815.

Tulving, E. (1974). Cue-dependent forgetting. *American Science, 62,* 74–82.

Tulving E. (1983). *Elements of episodic memory.* New York: Oxford University Press.

Tulving, E., & Thomson, D.M. (1973). Encoding specificity and retrieval processes in episodic memory. *Psychological Review. 80, 5,* 352–373.

Turtle, J., & Yuille, J. (1994). Lost but not forgotten details. Repeated eyewitness recall leads to reminiscence but not hypermnesia. *Journal of Applied Psychology, 79,* 260–271.

Whitten, W. and Leonard, J. (1981). Directed search autobiographical memory. *Memory and Cognition, 9,* 566–579.

Wickens, D. (1970). Encoding categories of words: An empirical approach to meaning. *Psychological Review, 77,* 1–15.

Williams, M.D. (1976). *Retrieval from very long-term memory.* Unpublished doctoral dissertation, University of California, San Diego.

Williams, M.D., & Hollan, J.D. (1981). The process of retrieval from very long-term memory. *Cognitive Science, 5,* 87–119.

Chapter 14

MENTAL REINSTATEMENT AS A TECHNIQUE TO ENHANCE CHILDREN'S RECALL

Paul M. Dietze and Donald M. Thomson

This paper presents two experiments that investigate the effectiveness of mental reinstatement in enhancing children's free recall of live events[1]. Mental reinstatement is designed to enhance recall performance by increasing the amount of feature overlap between the testing session and the original setting in which the target event was experienced (Flexser & Tulving, 1978). This increase in feature overlap is thought to derive from increased availability of contextual cues resulting from the subject's use of the reinstatement instructions. Mental reinstatement has potentially important applications in the forensic setting, specifically in relation to the investigatory process. Indeed, mental reinstatement is regarded as an important component of innovative investigative interviewing techniques such as the cognitive interview (Geiselman, Fisher, Firstenberg, Hutton, Sullivan, Avetissian & Prosk, 1984).

Previous research has produced mixed results with respect to the effects of mental reinstatement upon children's and adults' recall performance; some studies show strong effects of mental reinstatement (e.g., Smith, 1979) while others have not shown any effects (e.g., Memon, Cronin, Eaves & Bull, 1992). In relation to children's recall performance, previous research has shown that mental reinstatement can enhance recall when stimuli such as films have been used (e.g., Dietze & Thomson, 1993). In contrast, when live events have been used as stimuli, mental reinstatement has been shown to be of only limited utility in enhancing recall (Memon et al., 1992). The two experiments reported in this paper examine the effectiveness of mental reinstatement in enhancing children's free recall of two different types of live events, namely, a participant and an observer live event. In addition, they examine some important issues raised in the literature with respect to the types of mental reinstatement procedure which should be used with children and the baseline against which the effects of mental reinstatement should be compared.

EXPERIMENT 1

Experiment 1 was designed to examine the effects of two different types of mental reinstatement upon children's free recall of a 'participant' live event. The event was a 'participant' live event in the sense that it consisted of a series of activities that were undertaken by the children during their school class. These activities were given the label 'Monash activities' so as to allow for easy identification of the target event during subsequent memory testing. The Monash activities consisted of two games and a story reading. The children were unlikely to have come across any of the activities before as the games were made up specifically for this experiment and the story was obtained prior to widespread publication.

METHOD

Design

Experiment 1 used a 2*3 factorial design with age and interview condition manipulated as between-subject variables. Two age groups were included: 6-year-old and 12-year-old children, and three interview conditions were used: free recall, mental reinstatement and mental reinstatement-verbalization.

The three interview conditions all used the 'report everything' mnemonic of the cognitive interview as the nominal free recall instruction (see Saywitz, Geiselman & Bornistein, 1992). The free recall interview was comprised of only this 'report everything' instruction. The two mental reinstatement conditions, mental reinstatement and mental-reinstatment-verbalization, included additional instructions designed to help subjects mentally reinstate the environmental and affective context surrounding the target event. These instructions were: 'Now please close your eyes. Picture that time when you did the Monash activities as if you were there right now. Take your mind back to the place where you were—the place where you did the Monash activities. Try to think about what the place was like. Think about things like what was around you; about the furniture, the other kids, if there were things on the walls and if there were things that were hanging from the roof. Just about the place for a minute.'

The two mental reinstatement conditions differed only in the instructions for the mental reinstatement-verbalization condition, in which the children were asked to verbally describe their mental activity while reinstating the context. This condition was included to examine claims within literature that children need to verbalize their reinstatement to ensure that they reinstate the context properly (Saywitz et al., 1992).

Participants

There were 48 participants who were recruited from a primary school in suburban Melbourne.

Interviews

All interviews took place one week after the children participated in the Monash activities. The interviews were conducted by an adult male interviewer in a small room which the children rarely, if ever, frequented and that was different from the room in which the activities took place.

Scoring

Videotapes of the Monash activities were made for both age groups to aid in the development of a coding criterion. A group of six adults viewed the videotape for the 6-year-old group and another group viewed the videotape for the 12-year-old group. After viewing the tapes these adults were asked to write down all they could remember of the stimulus event they had seen. An exhaustive list of salient items was then created for both events. Items common to both lists were then compiled to create a coding criterion. All interviews were transcribed and scored according to the coding criterion. A reliability check was carried out whereby one third of the transcripts were coded by a second scorer who was kept blind to the hypotheses under investigation. The mean percent agreement between the two scorers across all scored measures was 88%. Two measures from the criterion are reported in this paper: correct responses and errors of commission.

RESULTS

Correct responses

Figure 1 shows the mean number of free recall correct responses for the three interview conditions as a function of age. There was an effect of age upon the correct responses in that the 12-year-olds recalled more correct responses than the 6-year-olds. Inspection of Figure 1 also suggests a trend for increased correct responses in the mental reinstatement conditions. However, the effect of interview condition was not significant.

Error of commission

Figure 2 shows the mean number of free recall errors of commission for the three interview conditions as a function of age. Inspection of figure 2 suggests that few errors of commission were made in any of the experimental conditions. Nevertheless, there was an effect of age, whereby the 12-year-olds made fewer errors of commission than the 6-year-olds.

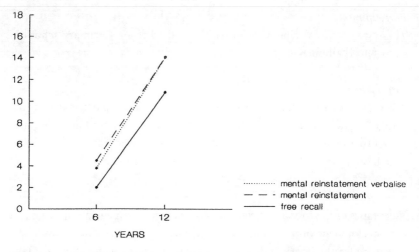

FIGURE 1: MEAN CORRECT RESPONSES AS A FUNCTION OF AGE FOR THE THREE INTERVIEW CONDITIONS USED IN EXPERIMENT 1

DISCUSSION

Experiment 1 revealed three major findings. First, there was a consistent effect of age where correct recall increased, and errors decreased, as a function of increasing age. This replicates similar findings reported in literature (e.g., Rudy & Goodman, 1991). Second, the only effect of either form of mental reinstatement upon correct recall or errors was a non-significant trend for increased correct recall in the mental reinstatement conditions. This

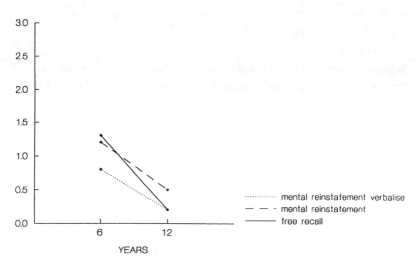

FIGURE 2: MEAN ERRORS OF COMMISSION AS A FUNCTION OF AGE FOR THE THREE INTERVIEW CONDITIONS USED IN EXPERIMENT 1

second finding may relate to the type of event and the recall instructions used in Experiment 1. In previous research, positive effects of mental reinstatement upon children's recall have been reported in studies where target events such a films have been used (e.g., Dietze & Thomson, 1993). In contrast, other studies using live events where children were participants in the target event have shown few significant effects of mental reinstatement (Memon et al., 1992). The outshining hypothesis (see Smith, 1988), developed to explain inconsistent findings with regard to context effects in the adult literature, can account for this apparent inconsistency. The outshining hypothesis essentially states that the retrieval cues provided by mental reinstatement can aid performance only when the effectiveness of nominal retrieval cues (in this case the recall instruction) provided at testing is limited. It may be that any possible effects of mental reinstatement may have been masked by participants easily accessing the live participant event through the nominal retrieval cue (in this case the 'report everything' mnemonic from the cognitive interview). Such easy access may derive from either excellent memory for the participant event, or the effectiveness of the nominal retrieval cue. These possibilities were examined further in Experiment 2, in which an observer live event was used in combination with recall instructions which, according to the outshining hypothesis, should increase the ability of mental reinstatement to enhance recall in comparison to Experiment 1.

The third main finding of Experiment 1 was that there was no evidence of any difference in the effects of the two types of mental reinstatement instructions. As a consequence of this finding, the mental reinstatement-verbalization condition was used in Experiment 2.

Experiment 2

As was the case with Experiment 1, Experiment 2 examined the effects of mental reinstatement upon children's free recall of a live event. Experiment 2 was designed to maximize the possibility for the effects of mental reinstatement to emerge. The major contrasts between Experiments 1 and 2 were in the type of live event, and the free recall instructions that were used. In Experiment 1 the children were active participants in the target event, while in Experiment 2 the children witnessed the target event as bystanders. The target event for Experiment 2 consisted of a staged disruption of a film that the children were being shown in class. The disruption occurred when an experiment confederate entered the room and claimed that she was supposed to be presenting the film to the children. An argument ensued, after which the experimental confederate realized that she had made an error and left. According to arguments in literature, this type of bystander event should be remembered less clearly than the participant event in Experiment 1 (Baker-Ward, Hess & Flanagan, 1990).

Therefore, according to the outshining hypothesis, any effects of mental reinstatement should emerge more easily.

Experiment 1 used the 'report everything' mnemonic of the cognitive interview as the free recall baseline against which the effects of mental reinstatement were measured. This mnemonic has been shown to be effective in enhancing recall performance in comparison to typical free recall instructions (Geiselman, Fisher, MacKinnon & Holland, 1986). Therefore, the effectiveness of the 'report everything' mnemonic may have masked any effects of mental reinstatement upon participants' recall of the stimulus event in Eexperiment 1. In order to counter this potential effect, Experiment 2 used typical free recall instructions which, according to the outshining hypothesis, should also allow the effects of mental reinstatement to emerge more easily.

METHOD

Design

Experiment 2 used a 3*2 factorial design with age and interview condition manipulated as between-subject variables. Three age groups were included: 6-year-old, 8-year-old and 12-year-old children, and two interview conditions were used: free recall and mental reinstatement.

The two interview conditions used typical free recall instructions as the nominal recall instruction. The free recall interview was comprised of only this instruction. The mental reinstatement condition used the identical mental reinstatement instructions as those used in the mental reinstatement condition of Experiment 1. The procedure used for interviewing the children was also the same as that used in Experiment 1.

Participants

There were 60 participants who were recruited from a primary school in suburban Melbourne. The use of 10 participants in each cell allowed for a small increase in statistical power in comparison to Experiment 1.

Scoring

The scoring criterion was developed differently from that used in Experiment 1. Two experimenters compiled a list of 'salient' items which were considered exhaustive of the main features of the staged disruption. As in Experiment 1, all interviews were transcribed and scored according to this criterion with a reliability check carried out.

RESULTS

Correct responses
Figure 3 shows the mean number of correct responses for the two interview conditions as a function of age. There was an effect of age such that correct recall increased as a function of increasing age. However, in accordance with the findings of Experiment 1, there was no significant effect of interview condition.

Errors of commission
Figure 4 shows the mean number of errors of commission for the two interview conditions as a function of age. There were no effects of either age or interview condition upon errors of commission.

DISCUSSION

The findings of Experiment 2 are consistent with Experiment 1. There was an effect of age such that correct recall increased as a function of increasing age. While the effect of age in relation to errors of commission was not significant, it should be noted that few errors of commission were made in any of the age groups.

As in Experiment 1, there was no evidence of any benefit of mental reinstatement upon free recall performance. This finding emerged in spite

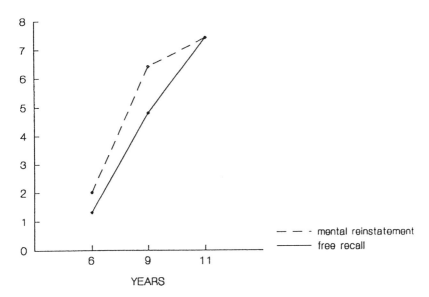

FIGURE 3: MEAN CORRECT RESPONSES AS A FUNCTION OF AGE FOR THE TWO INTERVIEW CONDITIONS USED IN EXPERIMENT 2

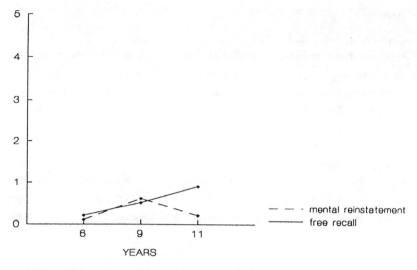

FIGURE 4: MEAN ERRORS OF COMMISSION AS A FUNCTION OF AGE FOR THE TWO INTER-VIEW CONDITIONS USED IN EXPERIMENT 2

of using an event and free recall instructions which, according to explanations offered in the adult literature such as the outshining hypothesis, would be expected to maximize the effects of mental reinstatement upon recall. Instead, the results of both experiments suggest that mental reinstatement may not be particularly effective in enhancing children's recall of live events.

CONCLUSION

The results of the two experiments presented in this paper suggest that mental reinstatement offers few benefits for children's free recall of live events. These findings are perhaps not surprising given the inconsistent effects of environmental and affective context reinstatement reported in adult memory literature (e.g., Fernandez & Glenberg, 1985). However, the findings have implications for innovative investigative interviewing procedures advocated for use with children. Some of these procedures, such as the cognitive interview, include mental reinstatement as an important component of the protocols that relate to free recall. On the basis of the experiments presented here, there is little evidence to suggest that the use of mental reinstatement instructions during investigative interviews with children will produce any major benefit for recall.

The findings presented in this paper have significant implications for research on the cognitive interview. Previous research with children suggests that the cognitive interview can be an effective means of enhancing children's recall performance (e.g., Geiselman & Padilla, 1988; Saywitz et al., 1992). This is a serious problem given that there are concerns that the cognitive interview is responsible for producing this performance enhancement (but see Memon et al., 1992). This is a serious problem given that there are concerns over the evidential acceptability of some of the 'cognitive' parts of the procedure (see Bekerian & Dennett, 1993). The results of the experiments presented here suggest that the effects of the cognitive interview reported in developmental literature may not derive from its mental reinstatement components. Clearly then, further research is necessary to identify the locus of the effects of the cognitive interview upon children's recall that have been reported in previous research.

NOTES

1   The experiments reported in this paper are currently being prepared for journal submission—this paper presents only a small subset of the data collected in the experiments.

REFERENCES

Baker-Ward, L., Hess, T.M., & Flanagan, D.A. (1990). The effects of involvement on children's memory for events. *Cognitive Development, 51(1),* 55–69.

Bekerian, D.A., & Dennett, J.L. (1993). The cognitive interview technique: Revising the issues. *Applied Cognitive Psychology, 7,* 275–297.

Dietze, P.M., & Thomson, D.M. (1993). Mental reinstatement of context: A technique for inteviewing child witnesses. *Applied Cognitive Psychology, 7,* 97–108.

Fernandez, A., & Glenberg, A.M. (1985). Changing environmental context does not reliably affect memory. *Memory and Cognition, 13,* 333–345.

Flexser, A.J., & Tulving, E. (1978). Retrieval independence in recognition and recall. *Psychological Review, 85,* 153–171.

Geiselman, R.E., Fisher, R.P., MacKinnon, D.P., Holland, H.L. (1986). Enhancement of eyewitness memory with the cognitive interview. *American Journal of Psychology, 99,* 385–401.

Geiselman, R.E., & Padilla, J. (1988). Cognitive interviewing with child witnesses. *Journal of Police Science and Administration, 16(4),* 236–242.

Memon, A., Cronin, O., Eaves, R., & Bull, R. (1992). *An empirical test of the 'mnemonic components' of the CI: Can they explain the apparent memory enhancing effects of the CI?* Paper presented at the Third European Conference of Law and Psychology, Oxford, september.

Rudy, L., & Goodman, G.S. (1991). Effects of participation on children's reports: Implications for children's testimony. *Developmental psychology, 27(4),* 527–538.

Saywitz, K., Geiselman, R.E., & Bornstein, G. (1992). Effects of cognitive interviewing, practice, and interviewing style on children's recall performance: *Journal of Applied Psychology, 77,* 744–756.

Smith, S.M. (1979). Remembering in and out of context. *Journal of Experimental Psychology: Human Learning and Memory, 5(5),* 460–471.

Smith, S.M. (1988). Environmental context-dependant memory. In: G.M. Davies & D.M. Thomson (Eds.), *Memory in context: Context in memory* (pp. 13–34). Chichester: Wiley.

PART 5
STUDIES OF LEGAL PROCESSES

Chapter 15

THERAPEUTIC JURISPRUDENCE IN A COMPARATIVE LAW CONTEXT[1]

David B. Wexler

INTRODUCTION

Therapeutic jurisprudence—the study of the role of the law as a therapeutic agent—is an interdisciplinary enterprise designed to bring insights from the clinical behavioral sciences into the development of the law (Wexler & Winick, 1996). The therapeutic jurisprudence perspective suggests that the law itself can be seen to function as a kind of therapist or therapeutic agent. Legal rules, legal procedures, and the roles of legal actors (such as lawyers, judges, and often therapists) constitute social forces that, like it or not, often produce therapeutic or antitherapeutic consequences. Therapeutic jurisprudence proposes that we be sensitive to those consequences, rather than ignore them, and that we ask whether the law's antitherapeutic consequences can be reduced, and its therapeutic consequences enhanced, without subordinating due process and justice values.

Therapeutic jurisprudence does not suggest that therapeutic considerations should trump other considerations (Schopp, 1996); therapeutic considerations are but one category of important considerations, as are autonomy, integrity of the fact-finding process, and community safety. Therapeutic jurisprudence also does not purport to resolve the value questions; instead, it sets the stage for their sharp articulation. In addition, the therapeutic jurisprudence lens generates empirical questions: one may speculate on the therapeutic consequences of various legal arrangements or law reform proposals, but empirical research is often necessary to determine with confidence whether the law actually operates in accordance with the speculative assumption.

The reach of therapeutic jurisprudence is by no means confined narrowly to mental health law. Instead, therapeutic jurisprudence serves as a therapeutic perspective on the law in general and has been applied to mental health law, criminal law and procedure, sentencing and corrections law, family and juvenile law, sexual orientation law, health law, disability law, workers' compensation law, personal injury and tort law, labor arbitration law, and even to contract law. As a field of inquiry, therapeutic jurisprudence brings together a number of topics that have not generally been recognized as related: how the criminal justice system might traumatize sexual battery victims, how workers' compensation schemes might create the moral hazard of prolonging work-related injury, how a fault-based (rather than a no-fault) tort compensation scheme might enhance recovery from personal injury, and how the current law of contract might operate to reinforce the low self-esteem of disadvantaged contracting parties.

DOING THERAPEUTIC JURISPRUDENCE

There seem to be two basic ways of 'doing' therapeutic jurisprudence, which may be called the Law-Based Approach (LBA) or the Psychology-Based Approach (PBA). It seems to me that the approach followed in any particular instance has somewhat less to do with an investigator's professional affiliation or disciplinary identification, and somewhat more to do with how a therapeutic jurisprudence inquiry happens, in a given case, to be triggered. The Law-Based Approach turns the therapeutic jurisprudence lens on a particular law and contemplates its likely therapeutic or antitherapeutic consequences. The Psychology-Based Approach, on the other hand, looks through the therapeutic jurisprudence lens at promising psychological/clinical literature, and contemplates how the particular psychological advance may be brought profitably into the law and the legal system.

Law-based approach

A rather recent example of the LBA is Kay Kavanagh's therapeutic jurisprudence analysis of the 'Don't Ask, Don't Tell' legal policy regarding homosexuals in the United States military (Kavanagh, 1996; for a discussion of the British law, see Rubin, 1996). Kavanagh's take on the law is that, in practice, it likely does more than lead to gay service members merely keeping quiet about their sexual orientation; instead, it probably chills the discussion of many daily life events that might raise questions about one's sexual orientation—such as where one went for the holidays, and with whom. Accordingly, Kavanagh claims the policy will promote isolation, anomie, and superficial social relationships for gay and lesbian service members.

Psychology-based approach

The Psychology-Based Approach to therapeutic jurisprudence, although in no way more important than the LBA, tends to be a bit tidier: it springs from a somewhat more defined literature—that addressed to mental health professionals and the like (Wexler, 1996)[2]—and that literature may also contain suggested outcome measures for assessing the therapeutic efficacy of a legal system that opts to incorporate the psychological/clinical insight.

I have used the PBA to consider how the literature on the psychological principles of health care compliance—such as patients signing behavioral contracts and making a public commitment to comply—can be brought into the legal system to improve a probationer's compliance with the terms of conditional release (Wexler, 1996). Similarly, I have used the PBA in looking at the literature regarding the 'cognitive distortions' of sex offenders, and in considering how the various judicial styles of accepting guilty pleas in American law might hinder or help later rehabilitation efforts by, in turn, perpetuating or challenging the cognitive distortions of the guilty-pleading defendants (Wexler, 1996).

Most recently, Allison Shiff and I used the PBA to look at some work on reducing recidivism through empathy training. Daniel Goleman, a psychology-trained *New York Times* journalist, recently received much attention in the United States for his book entitled *Emotional Intelligence* (Goleman, 1995). In it, Goleman discusses some promising results obtained by William Pithers, a prison psychologist who developed a 'perspective-taking' therapy in the context of working with child molesters.

As Pithers explains, '[e]mpathy with the victim shifts perception so that the denial of pain, even in one's fantasies, is difficult' (Goleman, 1995). Teaching a former offender empathy for his victim helps combat his distorted thinking about his crime and its effect on the victim, motivating him to resist the temptation to repeat his crime.

Pithers attempts to convey victim empathy through a variety of processes:

> The offenders read heart-wrenching accounts of crimes like their own, told from the victim's perspective. They also watch videotapes of victims tearfully telling what it was like to be molested. The offenders then write about their own offense from the victim's point of view, imagining what the victim felt. They read this account to a therapy group and try to answer questions about the assault from the victim's perspective. Finally, the offender goes through a simulated reenactment of the crime, this time playing the role of the victim (Goleman, 1995).

The empathy training literature, like the literature on the psychological principles of health care compliance and the literature on the cognitive distortion of sex offenders, in and of itself has nothing to do with the law. The PBA, however, looks at the literature with an eye to bringing it into the legal process. How might we promote empathy training through the operation of the legal system itself?

Shiff and I thought of grafting a 'perspective-taking' approach onto American 'teen court' diversion programs (Shiff & Wexler, 1996). Although juvenile court might in many respects itself be regarded as a diversion of youths from the criminal justice system, a number of American jurisdictions divert even from juvenile court those first-time minor offenders who admit to their crime. Those offenders are diverted from juvenile court into 'teen court'—a rehabilitative-oriented sentencing proceeding presided over by an adult judge, but with sentencing decision making, within carefully circumscribed limits, resting with a teenage jury, which deliberates after hearing arguments by a teen prosecutor and a teen defense counsel. The teen jury is composed of volunteers as well as former teen court defendants who are required as part of their sentence to participate at least once as a teen court juror.

Shiff and I thought the rehabilitative potential, and especially the empathy-training element, of the process could be enhanced by creating the role of *victim's* attorney:

> While some courts currently focus on developing victim empathy by use of mandatory apology letters and restitution tailored to the crime, we believe the emphasis on empathy can perhaps best be expanded by the appointment of a third teen attorney in the process—a victim's attorney. A teen attorney could represent the victim, help prepare a victim impact statement, brief the victim for testifying, or help prepare a videotaped interview and impact statement.
>
> The role of victim's attorney could itself be particularly therapeutic for at-risk teens—and for former defendants (who, in addition to being sentenced to serve on a teen jury, might also be sentenced to serve as victim's attorney in the future). Serving in the real-life role of victim's attorney would force the teen to identify with the crime victim's perspective—seemingly accomplishing, through the operation of the legal system itself, something closely akin to the 'perspective-taking' empathy therapy proposed by Pithers. Since lack of empathy appears to be a major factor in the development of criminal behavior, the use of the legal system to teach empathy to youths may be a particularly fruitful enterprise—perhaps even more fruitful than teaching empathy to adult offenders who lack it (Shiff & Wexler, 1996; Wiebe, 1996; Ashworth, 1993).

COMPARATIVE THERAPEUTIC JURISPRUDENCE

With its emphasis not so much on technical legal doctrine but instead on law-in-action regarding legal arrangements and therapeutic outcomes, therapeutic jurisprudence invites, and can profit mightily from, a comparative law approach (Wexler & Winick, 1991; Winick, 1996; Carson & Wexler, 1996; Carson, 1995; Carson, 1996)[3]—something to which American lawyers, at least, are not very accustomed (Glendon et al., 1994).

American lawyers—even academic lawyers—tend to think of 'the law' as pronouncements from the United States Congress, the United States Supreme Court, and the various state courts and legislatures. But we can surely profit from examining legal arrangements that lie beyond our borders. For example, it has been suggested that certain features of the continental criminal justice system might, as compared with the Anglo-American system, better promote acceptance of responsibility and rehabilitation (Moskovitz, 1995; Tomlinson, 1983; Wexler, 1996; Shiff & Wexler, 1996; Jacob et al., 1996).[4] A Law-Based Approach to therapeutic jurisprudence could certainly benefit from an infusion of knowledge, experience, and scholarly discussion of other legal systems.

A Psychology-Based Approach to therapeutic jurisprudence could, of course, equally benefit from an international perspective. A personal experience may help drive the point home.

I recently met with Judge William Schma, of Kalamazoo, Michigan, who shares an interest in therapeutic jurisprudence and who is active in the National Association of Drug Court Professionals (Lehman, 1995).[5] I referred him to a study I had come across in a psychiatric journal discussing the relapse proneness of methadone clients receiving lump-sum payments of disability benefits (Herbst et al., 1996); the article concluded that the relapse potential was substantially reduced for recipients who had a 'representative payee' (a guardian of sorts) as a money manager. Reading the article for its therapeutic jurisprudence implications, I discussed with the judge the possibility of a drug court diversion program functioning, with the client's consent, as a representative payee.

What I most recall of the conversation, however, is not the specifics of the substantive discussion, but rather how taken aback I was by the judge's question about how I *located* the relevant psychological/clinical literature. I told him that, virtually as a hobby, I browsed some of the relevant journals, but readily conceded that the process of finding the pertinent material was largely a 'hit-or-miss' procedure.

What is painfully clear to me in the current context, however, is that the browsing procedure is 'hit-or-miss' regarding the *American* materials; with respect to promising psychological/clinical material originating elsewhere, the procedure is overwhelmingly a 'miss.' Paul Gendreau captured it well when, writing recently on offender rehabilitation, he remarked:

> More blatant examples of ethnocentrism are the fact that American reviews on treatment effectiveness almost never reference the literature from foreign countries where different approaches to the 'crime problem' exist (e.g., less incarceration) (Gendreau, 1996).

How can we begin to remedy this situation? David Carson has raised the possibility of a joint meeting of the European Association of Psychology and Law and of the American Psychology-Law Society. I think it is a superb idea. We should also explore meeting with the Australia-New Zealand Association of Psychiatry, Psychology, and Law. If and when such joint meetings occur, I recommend that we schedule as part of them a Comparative Therapeutic Jurisprudence Symposium, at which we could use both a Law-Based Approach and a Psychology-Based Approach to discuss, from a therapeutic jurisprudence perspective and on an international level, interesting legal developments and promising psychological/clinical findings (Wexler, 1996).[6]

Indeed, I think we should seek to hold comparative therapeutic jurisprudence conferences regularly. Moreover, we should seek regularly to publish a special issue of an interdisciplinary journal devoted to the systematic exploration, at the international level, of the therapeutic implications of legal developments (LBA work) and of the legal implications of therapeutic developments (PBA work). Perhaps updates could also occur by establishing an electronic bulletin board or web site, and by having representatives from different nations agree to communicate important legal or psychological/clinical developments emanating from their own countries. International exchanges of this sort could benefit the field enormously—and should presumably benefit the domestic law of the nations of participating academics, practitioners, and policy makers.

A DIAGRAMMATIC CONCEPTUALIZATION

Therapeutic jurisprudence basically treats the law as an independent variable and is interested in studying the relationship between legal arrangements and therapeutic outcome or response. When we engage in *comparative* therapeutic jurisprudence, we will presumably be comparing the law of two different jurisdictions (e.g., two nations or two political entities within a single nation), and we will be contemplating or studying the therapeutic impact of those laws.

The two laws may either be similar to each other or different from each other. Further, taking into account such factors as culture and demographics, we might either expect the two jurisdictions to yield a similar therapeutic outcome to a given law (e.g., basically an issue of external validity and generalizability), or to respond differently even to similar laws. Accordingly, the various situations of legal arrangements and anticipated or actual therapeutic outcome can be captured by the four cells produced by the following 2-by–2 diagram (Markovits, 1989):[7]

Legal Arrangement

		Same	Different
Therapeutically-Relevant Outcomes	Same	A	B
	Different	C	D

Cell A

If, as in Cell A, a researcher is commenting on a law in nation X that is similar to a law in nation Y, and if the cultures and demographics of the two nations are sufficiently similar so that the therapeutic outcome in nation Y is not likely to be different from the therapeutic outcome ascertained in nation X, policymakers in nation Y may wish to pay particular attention to the presentation. The comparative perspective as applied to Cell A, therefore, potentially increases the human resources dedicated to tackling therapeutic jurisprudence problems. A possible example is how patient perception of the fairness of psychiatric testimony at civil commitment hearings influences later treatment compliance by a committed patient. The ongoing work of Alexander Greer, Mary O'Regan, and Amy Traverso, first undertaken in a highly exploratory fashion in Massachusetts and now being conducted both in Massachusetts and in Ontario, seems illustrative (Greer et al., 1996).

Greer et al's preliminary work, performed at Worcester State Hospital, suggests that, of all the participants in the commitment hearings (e.g., judge, lawyers, physicians), patient-respondents interviewed after commitment were by far most distrustful of their treating/testifying physicians—a finding surely suggestive of potential problems in the ensuing therapeutic enterprise. These results, if confirmed by a later full-scale study, would be suggestive of the likelihood of similar problems in other culturally/demographically similar jurisdictions operating under a similar system and structure of civil commitment. The research seems, therefore, illustrative of Cell A.

Cell B

In Cell B, the cultures or psychological factors are again sufficiently similar so that we would expect a given legal arrangement to yield the same therapeutic outcome in both jurisdictions (i.e., generalizability of results). But in this cell, the particular law, legal procedure, or other pertinent legal arrangement is different in nation X and in nation Y. If the investigated law in nation X yields a particularly powerful therapeutic response—one that is known or strongly assumed to be far superior to the result achieved in nation Y as a result of nation Y's legal arrangement—then the issue arises of nation Y possibly 'importing' or 'transplanting' (Watson, 1993; Kahn-Freund, 1974) the legal feature in issue. Possible transplantation will raise a number of fascinating questions—practical, constitutional, normative—but grappling with them is likely to be a rewarding experience both intellectually and in terms of possible fruitful law reform (Winick, 1996).[8]

Actually, certain implications of Greer's civil commitment work, discussed above under Cell A, slides comfortably into Cell B, where we compare situations with assumedly similar cultures/psychological responses but where the legal schemes are, on at least some important dimension, different. In discussing likely issues for future research, Greer et al. ask:

> what impact—on patient perceptions of fairness and on treatment outcome— might result from changing the process so that the testifying physician is not the treating physician of the given patient-respondent, but is instead merely (vis-a-vis that particular patient) one who evaluates and testifies? (Greer et al., 1996).

In actuality, the differences in physician roles (treating/evaluating/ testifying) noted by Greer are probably grounded more in practice than in law, and accordingly might well be manipulated for experimental purposes, obviating the need for cross-jurisdictional cooperative research. But without manipulating the situation, the research could occur in two otherwise similar jurisdictions that happen to follow different practices regarding the permissibility of treating physicians participating in commitment hearings. And a cross-jurisdictional study (across states or provinces or even between jurisdictions in different nations—such as the United States and Canada) would be truly *required* if the difference in physician roles were technically grounded in law rather than merely in practice.

Such a cross-jurisdictional study—comparing patient perceptions of fairness and ultimate treatment compliance or efficacy in jurisdictions that differ, by law or legal practice, on whether testifying physicians serve only as evaluators or serve also as healers—would be representative of Cell B research: the legal schemes or practices would be importantly different, but the assumption is that the therapeutic response to a *given* legal arrangement would be the same across the two jurisdictions.

If the research yielded significant results—e.g., that treatment is ultimately far more successful when the physician roles of evaluator and treater are sharply separated—then the normative, practical, constitutional debate can begin regarding possible 'transplantation' of the law of jurisdiction Y to the supposedly similar jurisdiction X (Wexler & Winick, 1991).[9] The debate could be an interesting one.

For example, isn't it likely that the treating physician will know the patient far better than would a physician who saw the patient solely to perform a prehearing evaluation? Are we sacrificing efficiency and even possibly shortchanging the fact-finding mission of the judicial process by disabling the treating physician from testifying at the patient's civil commitment hearing?

Another reason for performing Cell B research may be to re-examine the wisdom of a legal arrangement that, because of embedded local law, cannot readily be experimented with domestically. Law in the United States, for example, operates within a constitutional context that often limits the potential for legal experimentation or change. Indeed, sometimes even *dicta* (a judicial statement lacking precedential value) may create the appearance of a constitutional straightjacket that, in practical terms, will prevent domestic reconsideration.

For example, in the United States, Winick's proposal—to allow marginally incompetent defendants to stand trial or plead guilty—may be considered impossible to implement without violating constitutional doctrine (Wexler & Winick, 1991). At least this has been the received wisdom, as a result of the Supreme Court's dicta in *Pate v. Robinson.*[10] *Pate* has broadly been assumed to stand for the proposition that the Constitution places an absolute prohibition on trying the incompetent defendant. This assumption has hampered empirical research in the competency-to-stand-trial area. Winick has criticized the assumption that the Constitution imposes an absolute prohibition on the trial of an incompetent defendant wishing to be tried, but few states will be willing to experiment with the trial of such defendants for fear that any ensuing convictions would be vulnerable to due process attack.

Although Winick suggests that there would be therapeutic and other advantages of permitting the trial of such defendants, it is thus unlikely that this aspect of his proposal will be testable in a domestic laboratory. Other countries, however, dealing with the incompetency-to-stand-trial problem without the restrictions of the *Pate v. Robinson* gloss on due process, are more free to experiment with Winick's proposal. The experience in these jurisdictions could accordingly be looked to in order to probe the wisdom of Winick's suggestions, and they could be used as laboratories for empirical research on the question. Should such research document the existence of therapeutic value and other advantages in Winick's proposal, then it would be open for American courts to discard the *Pate v. Robinson dicta*.

The research suggested above is surely Cell B research: two nations differ with regard to the propriety of adjudicating marginally incompetent criminal defendants who wish to proceed with the judicial process. The research would be undertaken in a nation permitting adjudication and the operating assumption would be that the therapeutic response to the researched law is similar to what it would be in the United States, were such a law to be operative there.

If the results demonstrate therapeutic superiority, the constitutional/normative/practical debate would then ensue: Should the *dicta* in *Pate* be discarded? If a defendant is incompetent, even marginally so, how fair is it to proceed with adjudication? On the other hand, if the defendant wishes to proceed, and if proceeding appears likely to yield therapeutic benefit, isn't the system simply shooting itself in the foot by barring adjudication? But should the defendant's incompetent assent be entitled to any weight at all? Should it make a difference that defense counsel is also eager to proceed? Of the four cells, Cell B research may be the one that best combines intellectual excitement with the real possibility of practical law reform.

Cells C and D

Cells C and D both deal with the situation of a particular jurisdiction where, for cultural, demographic, or related reasons, we should expect the therapeutic response to a given law to be quite different from the response that would result from that law in our own country. In Cell D, the law of that country is also quite different from our own. In Cell C, however, the law in the two societies is similar, but the therapeutic outcome is different.

To put the matter in context, let us assume that nation Y, a tightly-knit, homogenous country, has a sentencing law that routinely permits the imposition of sanctions that involve 'shaming' or 'shunning'—such as requiring defendants 'to apologize publicly to their victims or to wear signs listing their offenses' (Massaro, 1991). Let us assume further that an investigation indicates that such sanctions serve a substantial rehabilitative—or at least a deterrent—function in nation Y.

Nation X is a heavily urbanized, heterogenous country with a substantial crime problem and a more 'standard' sentencing code. If nation X considers 'importing' nation Y's sentencing scheme as a means of curtailing criminality, it will need to confront substantial constitutional/normative concerns.

Even if those normative objections are overcome, however, the question of efficacy remains. Perhaps nation Y's sentencing law is effective only because nation Y is tightly-knit and homogeneous (Kahan 1996; Wexler & Winick, 1991).[11] If so, then compared with nation X, the situation in nation Y would fall into Cell D: the legal arrangement is different in nations X and Y, and the therapeutic response to nation Y's law is also different from the response that same law would produce if it were imported into nation X.

Similarly, if nation Y's law somehow were brought into nation X (Watson, 1993), the situation would *then* fall within Cell C: The legal scheme (regarding this particular matter) in nation X would now be similar to that of nation Y, but, because of differences in the two societies in homogeneity/ heterogeneity, the therapeutic response in nation X would be different (i.e., less efficacious) than it is in nation Y. These two cells, then, counsel some caution in the law reform prospects of our comparative work (Wexler & Winick, 1991).[12]

Cells A and B obviously present the most fruitful—or, in any event, the least complicated—opportunities for sensible law reform through comparative therapeutic jurisprudence. But Cells C and D should teach us to propose law reform recommendations carefully and with humility, and they should also give us food for thought regarding the issue of therapeutic efficacy in a world composed increasingly of multicultural societies.

CONCLUSION: A PROPOSED PARTNERSHIP WITH THE COMPARATISTS

If the diagrammatic conceptualization regarding legal 'transplantation' seems commonsensical, even painfully obvious, it should nonetheless not be confused with the *actual* process of law reform through borrowing. True, transplantation of laws from one legal system to another has been commonplace. In fact, 'borrowing is the main way law develops (Watson, 1993).' The principal selection criterion for borrowing, however, seems not at all to be shared social conditions between the two legal systems involved. As Alan Watson explains:

> Obviously, a society is unlikely to accept a wholly inappropriate rule, but is it possible to establish criteria that determine which rules are borrowed? Is there a determined search for the best solution; are systems selected for scrutiny on the basis of shared social, political, and economic values and conditions? I have found no determining social criteria. Rather, the main criterion is simply accessibility. An outsider's system of law is accessible above all when it is (a) in writing, (b) in a form that makes it relatively easy to find and understand (and this includes the language in which it is written) and (c) readily available.
>
> * * *
>
> A further criterion is habit and fashion. Once a system becomes used as a quarry, it will . . . be borrowed from again, and the more it is borrowed from, the more the right thing to do is to borrow from that system, even when the rule that is taken is not necessarily appropriate (Watson, 1993).

To me, Watson's words underscore the importance of a therapeutic jurisprudence approach that is at once academic and practical and that is both interdisciplinary and international in its perspective. Therapeutic jurisprudence is in no sense restricted to a study of legal doctrine or 'legal science' (Jacob et al., 1996), but is keenly interested in the law-in-action. As noted at the outset of a leading comparative law text, comparatists share that law-in-action interest: 'The need to see our own and other legal institutions in context means that comparative law by its very nature is an interdisciplinary field, one that depends heavily on empirical work (Glendon et al., 1994; Markovits, 1986).[13]

In collaboration, therapeutic jurisprudence scholars and comparatists could engage in a vigorous Law-Based Approach to therapeutic jurisprudence, subjecting legal arrangements to a sophisticated scrutiny that should increase appropriate legal transplants and decrease inappropriate ones. Further, what Watson found to be the key with legal borrowing—accessibility in acquisition and comprehension—seems also to explain the 'hit-or-miss' phenomenon in our use of promising developments in the clinical behavioral sciences (Davis, 1987; Melton, 1987; Rogers, 1983).[14] A systematic, international attempt regularly to locate and synthesize that material, and to brainstorm the ways in which that material might be used in shaping or applying the law, would invigorate the Psychology-Based Approach to therapeutic jurisprudence. The participation of comparatists in that project would ensure that the promising clinical literature could be creatively incorporated into a variety of legal systems.

Just as therapeutic jurisprudence must be constantly vigilant in considering the consumer perspective (Petrila, 1996; Wexler & Winick, 1996), it should not lose sight of a comparative law perspective. Indeed, I hope in short order, for reasons given by Emile Durkheim about comparative sociology, we will not need even to speak of *comparative* therapeutic jurisprudence: 'Comparative sociology is not a particular branch of sociology; it is sociology itself' (Glendon et al., 1994; Durkheim, 1964; Lempert, 1986; Nijboer, 1993).[15]

NOTES

1 Under permission of Behavioral Sciences & the Law, vol. 15, 233–246, 1997. Copyright John Wiley & Co.

2 [I]t will be helpful to the therapeutic jurisprudence community if a relatively discrete literature is regarded as principally relevant to the enterprise. Rather than the whole of social science, or even the whole of psychology, of special interest should be those articles, whether expressly related to law or not, that are written on cognitive-affective—behavioral topics by and for mental health professionals—psychiatrists, psychologists, social workers, counselors, and criminal justice and correctional professionals. In that way, efficiency will be promoted, for therapeutic jurisprudence scholars will have a handle on the kind of literature they need to keep up with and examine through the legal lens of therapeutic jurisprudence. David B. Wexler, *Reflections on the Scope of Therapeutic Jurisprudence* in LAW IN A THERAPEUTIC KEY, chapter 41, at 822.

3 DAVID B. WEXLER & BRUCE J. WINICK, ESSAYS IN THERAPEUTIC JURISPRUDENCE 317–320 (1991) (calling for a comparative law approach). Law in a Therapeutic Key contains several chapters that touch on comparative law matters. *See especially* Bruce J. Winick, *The Jurisprudence of Therapeutic Jurisprudence*, in LAW IN A THERAPEUTIC KEY, chapter 32; David Carson & David B. Wexler, *New Approaches to Mental Health Law: Will the UK Follow the US Lead, Again?*, in LAW IN A THERAPEUTIC KEY, chapter 31. *See also* David Carson, *Therapeutic Jurisprudence for the United Kingdom?*, 6 J. FORENSIC PSYCHIATRY 43 (1995); David Carson, *Therapeutic Jurisprudence: An Alternative Approach to Issues Affecting the Criminal Justice System*, in DOES PUNISHMENT WORK? 72 (James McGuire ed., 1996).

4 Myron Moskovitz, *The O.J. Inquisition: A United States Encounter with Continental Criminal Justice*, 28 VAND. J. TRANSNAT'L L. 1121 (1995). Of course, that does not mean the United States should—even if constitutionally it could—move toward such a system. *See, e.g.,* Edward A. Tomlinson, *Nonadversarial Justice: The French Experience*, 42 MD. L. REV. 131 (1983) (criticizing certain aspects of the French system). Nonetheless, some attractive features of the Continental system have already received some mention in the therapeutic jurisprudence literature. *See, e.g.,* David B. Wexler, *Therapeutic Jurisprudence and the Criminal Courts*, in LAW IN A THERAPEUTIC KEY, chapter 9, at 158 n.5; Allison R. Shiff & David B. Wexler, *Teen Court: A Therapeutic Jurisprudence Perspective*, in LAW IN A THERAPEUTIC KEY, chapter 14, at 298; David B. Wexler, *Justice, Mental Health, and Therapeutic Jurisprudence*, in LAW IN A THERAPEUTIC KEY, chapter 36, at 728. For a discussion of some of the rehabilitative features of the Japanese criminal justice system, see HERBERT JACOB ET AL., COURTS, LAW, AND POLITICS IN COMPARATIVE PERSPECTIVE 342-47 (1996).

5 For a discussion of drug courts, see Judge Jack Lehman, *The Movement Toward Therapeutic Jurisprudence: An Inside Look at the Origin and Operation of America's First Drug Courts*, 10 NJC ALUMNI 13 (Spring 1995).

6 In an article on the teaching of therapeutic jurisprudence, David B. Wexler, *Some Thoughts and Observations on the Teaching of Therapeutic Jurisprudence*, 35 REVISTA DE DERECHO PUERTORRIQEÑO 273, 285–86 (1996), I gave the following example of subjecting psychological

literature to therapeutic jurisprudence scrutiny: For instance, I have been intrigued by the possible relevance to law of the work of James Pennebaker on the healing power (on mental and physical health) of writing and speaking about traumatic events. Most of Pennebaker's findings have been synthesized in his book *Opening Up: The Healing Power of Confiding in Others*. Pennebaker's work is just now barely beginning to find its way into the therapeutic jurisprudence literature. Although his book does not itself deal with the law, its possible legal implications are evident to anyone who reads it from the perspective of therapeutic jurisprudence. Seminar students reading it could explore the relevance of Pennebaker's thesis to such matters as the drafting and processing of victim compensation claims, the preparation and presentation at sentencing of victim impact statements, the importance of a psychotherapist-patient privilege, the debriefing of jurors in traumatic trials, and even the role of the federal government in interviewing victims of natural disasters. Of course, the discussion of the possible application of Pennebaker's work to the legal arena would be even richer if the legal arena included a variety of legal systems.

7 Of course, a similar dichotomous classification could be constructed to conceptualize comparative law/behavioral science work generally, not only comparative therapeutic jurisprudence. To construct that diagrammatic scheme, we would not limit the outcome axis to clinically-related 'therapeutic outcomes' but would speak instead of 'behavioral consequences' generally. For a discussion of the use of dichotomies for bringing order to comparative law analysis, see Inga Markovits, *Playing the Opposites Game: On Mirjan Damaska's The Faces of Justice and State Authority*, 91 STAN. L. REV. 1313 (1989). Of course, despite their strength as a tool of organization, dichotomies typically oversimplify the real world. Thus, matters classified here as either the 'same' or 'different' often are in fact situated along a continuum. Similarly, when matters such as population concentration and ethnicity are taken into account, the effect of a given law may well vary even within a single jurisdiction. In this first-cut analysis, I have resisted the temptation to break down further the classification. In addition, some reviewers of an earlier draft of the manuscript have suggested that social/cultural/ demographic/historical matters similarly deserve to be classified along a same/different dimension. I have not done so primarily for the following reason: If psychology is in fact a science—and the entire endeavor postulates that it is—then if the legal arrangements are (i.e., the law and its administration) and the overall cultural factors in two jurisdictions are truly identical, the therapeutically-relevant outcomes should likewise be identical. Likewise, if the legal arrangements are truly identical and the therapeutic outcomes are different, we should postulate that the differential results are due to differences that lie within the overall cultural domains of the two jurisdictions.

8 Sometimes, although we may be unwilling on normative grounds to import another nation's legal scheme, a familiarity with the other nation's situation may lead us to at least modify or tinker in interesting ways with our domestic law: For example, research in another country showing that a high degree of communal involvement in the raising of children increases the mental health of children and their families would not cause us to reexamine due process protection for a sphere of family privacy that allows a significant degree of parental autonomy, free of government control, over the rearing and education of children. It might, however, make us think about ways, consistent with parental autonomy, of providing services and opportunities to parents (that they could be free to accept or reject) that might increase the degree of participation by grandparents, neighbors, and teachers in the child-rearing process. Bruce J. Winick, *The Jurisprudence of Therapeutic Jurisprudence*, in LAW IN A THERAPEUTIC KEY, chapter 32, at 674.

9 Another example of [Cell B] comparative therapeutic jurisprudence could look at the use of psychological health care compliance principles to enhance a conditionally released mental patient's chances of taking prescribed medication.

> We know, for instance, that if a court encourages the patient to enter into a behavioral contract and to make a public commitment to comply, the chances of compliance are likely to be enhanced. . . . [A] court composed of a single judge is arguably better able to apply these psychological health care compliance principles than is an administrative Psychiatric Security

Review Board, such as the type that exists in the state of Oregon. How, one might ask, might a British Mental Health Review Tribunal fare in using the health care compliance principles? DAVID B. WEXLER & BRUCE J. WINICK, ESSAYS IN THERAPEUTIC JURISPRUDENCE 318 (1991) (footnote omitted).

10 383 U.S. 375, 378 (1966) ('the conviction of an accused person while he is legally incompetent violates due process').

11 *But see* Dan M. Kahan, *What Do Alternative Sanctions Mean?*, 63 U. CHI. L. REV. (1996). Relatedly, homogeneity/heterogeneity may also make a difference in the operation of the psychological principles of health care compliance. *See supra* note 24. For example, 'if a court encourages the patient to enter into a behavioral contract and to make a public commitment to comply, the chances of compliance are likely to be enhanced. But, in a comparative exercise, we should ask whether a public commitment is more likely to yield compliance in rural or homogeneous societies than in urban or heterogeneous ones. DAVID B. WEXLER & BRUCE J. WINICK, ESSAYS IN THERAPEUTIC JURISPRUDENCE 318 (1991). The stigma of seeking mental health treatment (and perhaps the corresponding need for a psychotherapist/patient privilege) may also vary according to the size and homogeneity of the community. At the 1996 annual convention of the American Academy of Psychiatry and Law, held in San Juan, Puerto Rico, I met the sole psychiatrist of a tiny Caribbean nation. To avoid stigmatizing his patients, he characterizes his practice (on his business cards and otherwise) as one involving 'general and psychological medicine'.

12 Other cautionary examples might involve the duty to warn and the civil commitment system. With respect to the former, Wexler has argued that a rule requiring psychotherapists to warn a particular victim of a patient's potential dangerousness may be therapeutically sound: if patients overwhelmingly threaten intimates and family members, which they do in the United States, a warning rule may operate to bring the potential victim into family therapy. In a comparative context, we should of course be interested in learning whether the pattern of threatening intimates holds in other jurisdictions. If it does not, 'transplantation' of the rule might work more therapeutic harm than good. DAVID B. WEXLER & BRUCE J. WINICK, ESSAYS IN THERAPEUTIC JURISPRUDENCE at 317–18. With regard to civil commitment, I have been given anecdotal evidence by psychologist colleagues in Puerto Rico that an American-style civil commitment code does not function well on the island. This is apparently so because in Hispanic culture, a mother, instead of invoking the commitment law, will care for a mentally ill adult child at home, regardless of the emotional toll to her and to other family members. Only when the mother dies, it is said, will the mentally ill person be committed-or consigned to the streets. Perhaps a creative respite care law should be designed to fit this situation.

13 GLENDON ET AL., *supra* note 13, at 12. Yet, the comparatists may benefit from the behavioral science perspective of therapeutic jurisprudence scholars, for, as a leading comparatist has noted, 'we [comparatists] talk about legal systems but not about the people living and breathing under those systems.' Inga Markovits, *Hedgehogs or Foxes: A Review of Westen's and Schleider's Zivilrecht im Systemvergleich*, 34 AM. J. COMP. L. 113, 134 (1986).

14 On the judicial absorption of social facts, see Peggy Davis, *There is a Book Out. An Analysis of Judicial Absorption of Legislative Facts*, 100 HARV. L. REV. 1539 (1987). *See also* REFORMING THE LAW: IMPACT OF CHILD DEVELOPMENT RESEARCH (Gary B. Melton, ed. 1987). On the diffusion of 'innovation' generally, see EVERETT M. ROGERS, DIFFUSION OF INNOVATIONS (3d ed. 1983).

15 GLENDON, ET AL., *supra* note 13, at 1 (quoting EMILE DURKHEIM, THE RULES OF SOCIOLOGICAL METHOD 139 (8th ed. 1964)). Therapeutic jurisprudence, with an interest in empirical and comparative law issues, parallels developments in the 'new evidence law' scholarship. *See generally* Richard Lempert, *The New Evidence Scholarship: Analyzing the Access of Proof*, 66 B.U. L. REV. 439, 477 (1986), and J. F. Nijboer, *Common Law Tradition in Evidence Scholarship Observed from a Continental Perspective*, 41 AM. J. COMP. L. 299, 338 (1993). Perhaps law itself will someday have a comparative dimension, so that there will no longer be comparative law, only law.

REFERENCES

Ashworth, A. (1993). Victim Impact Statements and Sentencing. *Crim. L. Rev.*, 498.

Carson, D. (1995). Therapeutic Jurisprudence for the united Kindom?. *J. Forensic Psychiatry, 6*, 43.

Carson, D. (1996). Therapeutic Jurisprudence: An Alternative Approach to Issues Affecting the Criminal Justice System. In: J. McGuire (Ed.), *Does Punishment Work?* (p. 72).

Carson, D., & Wexler, D.B. (1996). New Approaches to Mental Health Law: Will the UK Follow the US Lead, Again? In: D.B. Wexler & B.J. Winick (Eds.), *Law in a Therapeutic Key* (chapter 31).

Davis, P. (1987). There is a Book Out. An Analysis of Judicial Absorption of Legislative Facts. *Harv. L. Rev., 100*, 1539.

Durkheim, E. (1964). *The Rules of Sociological Method* (p. 139).

Gendreau, P. (1996). Offender Rehabilitation: What We Know and What Needs to be Done. *Crim. Just. & Behav., 23*, 144.

Glendon, M.A., et al. (1994). *Comparative Legal Traditions: Text, Materials and Cases 1.*

Goleman, D. (1995). *Emotional Intelligence.*

Greer, A., O'Regan, M., & Traverso, A. (1996). Therapeutic Jurisprudence and Patients' Perception of Procedural Due Process of Civil Commitment Hearings. In: D.B. Wexler & B.J. Winick (Eds.), *Law in a Therapeutic Key,* (chapter 47).

Herbst, M.D. (1996). Treatment Outcomes for Methadone Clients Receiving Lump-Sum Payments at Initiation of Disability Benefits. *Psychiatric Services, 47*, 119.

Jacob, H. et al. (1996). *Courts, Law and Politics in Comparative Perspective.* (342–47).

Kahan, D.M. (1996). What Do Alternative Sanctions Mean? *U. Chi. L. Rev., 63.*

Kahn-Freund (1974). On Uses and Misuses of Comparative Law. *Mod. L. Rev., 37*, 1.

Kavanagh, K. (1996). Don't Ask, Don't Tell: Deception Required, Disclosure Denied. In: D.B. Wexler & B.J. Winick (Eds.), *Law in a Therapeutic Key,* (chapter 17).

Lehman, J.J. (1995). The Movement Toward Therapeutic Jurisprudence: An Inside Look at the Origin and Operation of America's First Drug Courts. *NJC Alumni, 10*, 13.

Lempert, R. (1986). The New Evidence Scholarship: Analyzing the Access of Proof. *B. U. L. Rev., 66*, 439–477.

Markovits, I. (1986). Hedgehogs or Foxes: A Review of Westen's and Schleider's Zivilrecht im Systemvergleich. *A. J. Comp. L., 34*, 113–134.

Markovits, I. (1989). Playing the Opposites Game: On Mirjam Damaska's The Faces of Justice and State Authority. *Stan. L. Rev., 91*, 1313.

Massaro, T.M. (1991). Shame, Culture, and American Criminal Law. *Mich. L. Rev., 89*, 1880–1882.

Melton, G.B. (1987). *Reforming the Law: Impact of Child Development Research.*

Moskovitz, M. (1995). The O.J. Inquisition: A United States Encounter with Continental Criminal Justice. *Vand. J. Transnat'l L., 28*, 1121.

Nijboer, J. F. (1993). Common Law Tradition in Evidence Scholarship Observed from a Continental Perspective. *Am. J. Comp., 41*, 299, 338.

Petrila, J. (1996). Paternalism and the Unrealized Promise of essays in Therapeutic Jurisprudence. In: D.B. Wexler & B. J. Winick (Eds.), *Law in a Therapeutic Key* (chapter 34).

Rogers, E.M. (1983). *Diffusion of Innovations.*

Rubin, G.R. (1996). Section 146 of the Criminal Justice and Public Order Act of 1994 and the 'Decriminalization' of Homosexual Acts in the Armed Forces. *Crim. L. Rev.* (p. 393).

Schopp, R.F. (1996). Therapeutic Jurisprudence and Conflicts Among Values in Mental Health Law. In: D.B. Wexler & B.J. Winick (Eds.), *Law in a Therapeutic Key* (chapter 37).

Shiff, A.R., & Wexler D.B. (1996). Teen Court: A Therapeutic Jurisprudence Perspective. In: D.B. Wexler & B. J. Winick (Eds.), *Law in a Therapeutic Key* (chapter 14).

Tomlinson, E.A. (1983). Nonadversarial Justice: The French Experience. *MD. L. Rev., 42*, 131.

Watson, A. (1993). *Legal Transplants: an Approach to Comparative Law*

Wexler, D.B. (1996). Therapeutic Jurisprudence and the Criminal Courts. In: D.B. Wexler & B.J. Winick (Eds.), *Law in a Therapeutic Key: Developments in Therapeutic Jurisprudence* (chapter 9).

Wexler, D.B. (1996). Reflections on the Scope of Therapeutic Jurisprudence. In: D.B. Wexler & B.J. Winick (Eds.), *Law in a Therapeutic Key* (chapter 41, p. 822).

Wexler, D.B. (1996). Justice, Mental Health, and Therapeutic Jurisprudence. In: D. B. Wexler & B. J. Winick (Eds.), *Law in a Therapeutic Key* (chapter 36, p. 728).

Wexler, D.B. (1996). Some Thoughts and Observations on the Theaching of Therapeutic Jurisprudence. *Revista de Derecho Puertorriqeno, 35,* 273:285–86.

Wexler, D.B., & Winick, B.J. (1991). *Essays in Therapeutic Jurisprudence* (pp. 317–320).

Wexler, D.B., & Winick, B.J. (1996). Patients, Professionals, and the Path of Therapeutic Jurisprudence: A response to Petrila. In: D.B. Wexler & B.J. Winick (Eds.), *Law in a Therapeutic Key* (chapter 35).

Wiebe, R.P. (1996). The Mental Health Implications of Victims' Rights. In: D.B. Wexler & B.J. Winick (Eds.), *Law in a Therapeutic Key* (chapter 12).

Winick, B.J. (1996). The Jurisprudence of Therapeutic Jurisprudence. In: D.B. Wexler & B.J. Winick (Eds.), *Law in a Therapeutic Key* (chapter 32).

Chapter 16

RESTITUTION AND MEDIATION AS FORMS OF RESTORATIVE JUSTICE: A VIABLE ALTERNATIVE TO REVENGEFUL JUSTICE

Elmar G.M. Weitekamp

INTRODUCTION

Historically, restorative justice approaches have been widely used as alternatives to punishment. Today, supporters of restorative justice approaches, particularly restitution and mediation programs, have claimed that these are valuable alternatives to incarceration and the more revengeful approaches of current criminal justice systems. However, evaluations of such programs show that this is not the case. Quite the contrary to the goals and aims of restitution and mediation, existing programs lead to higher rates of incarceration, use too rigid selection criteria, and only serve first-time offenders, property offenders, and offenders who come from a middle class background. This paper will show the results of a study in Philadelphia, in which restitution orders were given to hard core criminals, and were considered to be more effective than incarceration. We will further use the results of the National Crime Severity Study to show that the American public evaluates and classifies damages caused by violent offenders in terms of money, sometimes very little. Thus, the American public supports our argument that restorative justice approaches such as restitution and mediation programs can be very well used in cases of serious violent crimes.

RESTORATIVE JUSTICE: RECENT RATIONALE, PURPOSE AND ISSUES

In the early 1970s, the approach of restorative justice in the forms of restitution and victim-offender mediation were rediscovered. We can identify five reasons for which such methods became popular. The first was that the victims of crimes were completely left out and felt isolated by existing criminal justice programs and procedures. They were actually the losers in the justice process. The second was that restitution and victim offender mediation led to less severe and more humane sanctions for the offender. These approaches were in this context considered to be a viable alternative to incarceration. Not only did the offender in particular, and probably his family benefit from this approach, but the society also benefited in general. Third, restitution and victim offender mediation enhanced the reintegration of the offender into the community. This was considered more rehabilitative than other correctional measures because it was related rationally to the amount of damages done, with the victim as the central key player in the restorative process. It also forced the offenders to take the responsibility for their actions, and provided them with a fair way to repair the damage done. Fourth, restitution and mediation seemed to provide a fairly easy-to-administer tool for the criminal justice system. These programs, it was argued, could be used at the pre-trial stage in the prosecutor's office, or at community correctional facilities, as part of probation or parole sentences, and as part of diversion programs. Finally, it was argued that society at large would benefit from a more humane approach in that it would lead to a reduced need for vengeance and retribution. If society saw that the offender took an active step to undo the harm he had done, and that the victim was actively involved in the criminal justice process, people might develop different attitudes towards offenders. These five reasons are not mutually exclusive and may not be complete. They are, in practice, defined more concretely by specific restitution and victim offender mediation programs. Nevertheless, these ideas led to a booming business in the creation and operation of restitution and mediation programs in the 1970s.

So far, these programs under the umbrella term 'restorative justice' sound great in theory. Nevertheless, many of the subsequently implemented programs during the 1970s and 1980s were plagued by shortcomings in practice that almost caused again the disappearance of restorative justice approaches.

First, despite prolific legislation with regard to the implementation of restitution schemes and victim offender reconciliation programs, they were applied in a very unsystematic manner, at the discretion and initiative of criminal justice administrators who supported such programs on very different levels. Second, almost all restorative justice programs used restitution or mediation only for property offenses and/or first-time offenders. There was no reason why these programs were restricted to these offenders. One looks in vain to the literature to find a theoretical explanation. Encountering such limitations, we are not surprised that restitution and mediation programs as alternatives to incarceration for serious violent offenders, although heavily advocated by proponents of restorative justice, were nearly non-existent.

Further, research showed that restitution and mediation programs were very selective and admitted only a disproportionately small number of minorities. The majority of restitution and mediation programs were applied to juvenile offenders, and to offenders coming from a white, middle-class background. The question still remains as to whether or not restitution and mediation programs in their various forms have reduced the recidivism rate. Finally, the major problem with the policy perspective seems to lie in the planning, implementation and evaluation of such programs.

In this paper, we will examine the results of a study of court cases in Philadelphia in which restitution was used on a large scale, as well as the results of the National Crime Severity Study. This will allow us to examine whether restorative justice measures such as restitution and mediation can be used as reasonable alternatives to incarceration.

RESTITUTION FOR A NORMAL POPULATION OF CRIMINALS: THE PHILADELPHIA STUDY

The purpose of this study was to examine the criminal cases of the Honorable Lois Forer of the Philadelphia Court of Common Pleas from 1974 to 1984. The data from this study are unique and valuable because other studies on restitution have usually only examined special programs in which eligible offenders were seriously screened before they were able to participate. Such screening processes led usually to the inclusion of only first time offenders, property offenders, and predominantly white, middle class offenders. This study, on the other hand, has used data from a large metropolitan court of Common Pleas where the cases were assigned randomly to the judge. She imposed restitution sentences when she felt it was appropriate, and long before it had become fashionable. In order to enforce such sentences, she had to rely on existing criminal justice agencies. Thus, this study has examined a different type of offender: coming from a large metropolitan area most of the offenders belonged to a minority group, and over 50% of their crimes were violent.

Of the 605 offenders in our study 198 were incarcerated, 173 received restitution sentences, 196 received probation, 26 were found not guilty, and 10 were found not guilty by reason of insanity. In two cases we were unable to determine the outcome. 57.7% of the persons studied had prior arrest records, and 28.6% had been incarcerated before. The offender in this group were charged with homicide (5.1%), rape (4%), robbery (23.1%), aggravated assault (20.2%), burglary (15%), larceny (9.4%), auto theft (3.3%), arson (2.5%), kidnapping (0.8%), fraud (3.3%), and other offenses (13.3%). A weapon was used in 45.6% of the cases, and the victim was injured in 46.6%. Females constituted only 9.8% of the group, and the mean age was 27.6. With regard to race, 74.2% of the offenders were black, 20.3% were white, 4.5% were Hispanic, 0.7% were

Asian, and 0.2% were American Indian. Race was unknown for 0.2% of the cases. The majority of the offenders were single (55%), and were high-school dropouts, while 23.6% were illiterate or semiliterate and 39% were unemployed.

To determine which offender received a particular sentence, we constructed three different sub-samples: an incarceration group, a probation/restitution group and a probation group that constituted our dependent variable. We created a model containing variables that described the criminal histories of the offenders, including prior offense(s), juvenile record(s), adult record(s), the number of prior arrests, the number of prior convictions, and previous incarceration(s). A second independent set of variables was created to describe the type of offense committed and the resulting damage. Homicide, rape, robbery, aggravated assault, burglary, larceny, auto theft, arson, kidnapping, fraud, and other offenses constituted the offense variables. Pleas, pretrial detentions, gang memberships, weapon use, the existence of a co-defendant, victims' injuries, and victims' property loss comprised the independent variables for determining which offender received a particular sentence. In addition, we created a third set of variables describing the offenders' demographic backgrounds. It included age, gender, marital status, education, occupation, number of children, literacy, whether the offenders lived with parents or relatives, and whether or not their earnings were sufficient.

We employed various forms of statistical measures to analyze the data. Besides univariate descriptive measures, we used discriminant and logistic regression analysis to predict group membership and to determine the best predictors.

The logistic regression analysis for the criminal history model showed that only the existence of a prior arrest had a significant effect on receiving an incarceration sentence rather than a restitution one. The odds of being incarcerated were three times higher for the offenders who had prior arrest(s). By comparing incarceration with probation, we found again that if an offender had a prior arrest, he was 2.5 times more likely to receive an incarceration sentence. No other variables were significant. We also found no significant effects when we compared the criminal history variables with whether an offender received restitution or probation.

For the offense-related model, we found that pretrial detention, the involvement of property valued from $101 to $500, and that valued at over $1,000 had a significant effect on whether an offender received an incarceration sentence or a restitution sentence. An offender who was detained before trial was more than two times as likely to be imprisoned. An offender who committed a property offense valued from $101 to $500 was twice as likely to receive a restitution sentence. An offender who committed a property offense valued at over $1,000, on the other hand, was three times as likely to be incarcerated. By comparing the effects of these variables on incarceration and probation, we found that in the cases of rape, robbery, and aggravated assault, the offenders were more than twice as likely to receive incarceration sentences. This was also true in the cases involving pretrial detention and gang-membership. An offender who committed a property crime valued from $501 to $1,000 was twice as likely to receive a probation sentence. By comparing the effects of these variables on restitution and probation, we found that an offender who committed a property crime valued from $1 to $100 was 2.3 times as likely to receive a restitution sentence, while a property crime valued from $501 to $1,000 doubled an offender's chance of receiving a probation sentence.

A comparison of the effects of the demographic background variables on incarceration, restitution and probation showed that the only significant effect was being illiterate or semiliterate.

Looking at the results of the two-year follow-up period of the offenders who were placed on probation or parole, we found that the restitution group had the highest percentage of probation revocation (51%), followed by the probation (30.8%) and incarceration (27.8%) groups.

However, we must be cautious about the results for the two latter groups because a great deal of information was missing. Reasons for probation revocation for the restitution group included commission of a new crime (35.4%), and technical violations (45.6%). However, in 32.7% of these cases a new probation term was imposed, and 61.7% of the offenders served their new term successfully.

To summarize our results, the implications of this study are that restitution can and should be used in large metropolitan courts for more serious and violent offenses. Although the data comprising this study comes from the files of a single judge in a Philadelphia court, which might limit generalization, we believe the results are encouraging. They should lead to a wider use of restitution as an alternative to incarceration for serious violent offenders.

In order to determine whether the public could or would go along with such an alternative to incarceration, and how they perceive and evaluate damages caused by serious violent crimes, we examined the results of the

National Crime Severity Study of the USA. This seems to be crucial since opponents of restorative justice approaches doubt that one can find an objective method to determine the damage caused by serious violent crimes. They therefore reject restitution and mediation, as well as other forms of restorative justice for such crimes altogether.

THE DEVELOPMENT OF THE NATIONAL SURVEY OF CRIME SEVERITY

Criminologists and criminal justice researchers have been interested in methods of determining the seriousness of criminal events for many years. Postulated differential seriousness for infractions against the law have remained assumed rather than systematically demonstrated until recently. Until 1964, the year in which Sellin and Wolfgang published their pioneering study 'The Measurement of Delinquency,' in which they introduced the Sellin-Wolfgang Index, the measurement of the severity of crimes and penalties remained intuitive and primitive. Through the application of a psychophysical scaling technique, Sellin and Wolfgang obtained a scale of the severity of offenses. (For a detailed description of the Sellin-Wolfgang Index see: Sellin, T. and Wolfgang M.E. 'The Measurement of Delinquency' 1964/1978; Wolfgang, M.E., Figlio, R.M., Tracy, P.E. and Singer, S. 'The National Survey of Crime Severity' 1985; and also for an excellent critique Alemika, E.O. 'Continuities in the Research on the Measurement and Scaling of the Perceived Severity of Crime and Delinquency' 1983.)

Sellin and Wolfgang viewed delinquent events and non-delinquent juveniles as their major focal points for establishing an index of delinquency. They constructed a sample of descriptions of offenses which represented the stimuli which were presented to the surveyed population for rating. In all, they constructed 141 offense descriptions which were given to an unrepresentative sample group of police officers, college students, and juvenile court judges. Sequence or order effects were controlled through the randomization of the order in which the stimuli were presented. Although the developing, conducting and compiling of the results of the severity study was a complex process using highly sophisticated mathematical techniques, the process of rating for the respondents was relatively simple. They were given a description of a crime; 'a person steals a bicycle parked on the street,' and told that the seriousness of this crime was 10. They were then given a list of other crimes and told to compare them in seriousness to the bicycle theft. For example, if a crime seemed to be three times as serious as the bicycle theft, the participants were to rate it at 30, if it seemed to be half as serious, they were to rate it at 5, and so on.

Sellin and Wolfgang used magnitude and category scales in their study and constructed the final Sellin-Wolfgang Index on the scores of the magnitude scales. (For a discussion of the advantages and disadvantages of magnitude scales see: Sellin and Wolfgang 1978, Figlio 1979, Bridges and Lisagor 1975, Shelly and Sparks 1980 and Alemika 1983). These magnitude scores were then transformed into ratio scales.

In 1977, Wolfgang and colleagues had the chance to replicate the crime severity study on a grand scale. Their survey of the seriousness of crime was conducted as a supplement to the National Crime Survey. The survey, which included 60,000 persons 18 years of age or older, was the largest ever made of how the general public ranks the seriousness of a wide range of crimes. The National Crime Survey, a stratified random sample representative of the entire USA, was conducted over a six month period beginning in July 1977. The 60,000 participants in the survey each rated 25 specific criminal events. Twelve different forms were used, each with a different set of items, adding up to 204 different crime descriptions. Some descriptions appeared on more than one form and five appeared on all forms. Each of the descriptions in the survey was quite specific as to the details of the crime and its consequences. These consequences strongly affected the ratings, meaning that the ratings differed tremendously if one asked about the facts of a crime but changed the consequences of the facts. For example, crime descriptions scoring 72.1, 43.9, 33.0 and 24.5 were all for the same crime; planting a bomb that goes off in a public building. The consequences of the crime descriptions, though, ranged from 20 people being killed, one person being killed, one person being injured but with no medical treatment required, and no one being injured.

RESULTS OF THE NATIONAL SURVEY OF CRIME SEVERITY

In order to pursue our question on how revengeful the public is, and if there exists a cry for severe punishment, one can look at the ratings of the crime descriptions and how and in which context the public ranked them. One has to keep in mind that the descriptions did not entail any information about the relationship of the victim to the participants or 'raters.' The victim was never an acquaintance, family member, or friend; they were always 'neutral' fellow citizens. Also, one cannnot distinguish between raters who were never victimized themselves, or raters who had been victims of one or more of the crimes they were rating. In addition, we have no information as to whether family members of the participants had ever been victimized.

Assuming that a substantial number of participants (or close family members thereof) had been victimized themselves, as the results of the National Victim Survey indicate, one could expect that these participants assigned higher scores to the items they were asked about in general; particularly those of which they were victims. On the other hand, one can assume that the participants who were never victimized themselves, and who did not have family members who were victimized, assigned lower scores to the crime descriptions they had to rate. Therefore, one can safely assume that all things even out quite nicely. In other words, the ratings of the 60,000 participants in the survey accurately represent the general public with regard to its perception of how serious a crime is, and how that seriousness compares to the bicycle theft. This ranking procedure implies also how punitive the public is, how revengeful and how severe the punishment should be. An examination of the results of the National Survey of Crime Severity therefore allows us to answer the crucial question of how punitive the public is, and if restitution or reparative justice programs have to be restricted to first-time, juvenile, and/or property offenders, or if they can be applied to serious, even violent criminals.

In order to achieve this, we assigned each of the 204 offense descriptions a number. #1 represents the offense that was considered the least serious, i.e., a person under 16 years old plays hooky from school with a ratio score of 0.25. Instead, #204 represents the crime that was considered the most serious: a person plants a bomb in a public building, the bomb explodes and 20 people are killed with a ratio score of 72.10. Since the offense descriptions on the National Survey of Crime Severity always entailed information about the damage or injury caused by the crime, one can compare offenses which indicate loss or damage in terms of dollar amounts with crimes that led to injuries of differing severity, or even death.

One crucial aspect of the offense description is whether the assessment of the circumstances of the crime and the intent of the offender had an influence on the participant's perception of the seriousness of the offense, or if external aspects (amount of injury, theft, or damage) were more influential. Riedel (1975) analyzed this problem in a replication study of the Sellin-Wolfgang Index and came to the conclusion that offense severity will continue to be looked upon as a measure of the costs to the victim, be that victim an individual, a group or society in general.

In an examination of the results obtained in the National Survey of Crime Severity, one finds in general a rather interesting trend: crimes of violence, even those leading to severe injuries or death, correspond to property crimes of relatively low values.

The offense description: 'A person robs a victim. The victim is injured but not hospitalized' ranked #54 on the severity scale, and corresponds to: 'A person picks a victim's pocket of $100,' ranked # 55 on the scale. This means that the damage done by a robbery with an injury is equal to theft of $100, according to the Crime Severity Scale. In terms of restitution and mediation, this would mean that a robbery with an injury could be compensated through a restitution payment of $100, since the public ranks and perceives the severity of these crimes equally.

At first glance this may sound strange, but when we examine the arguments of the restitution and mediation debate, and the definition of restitution, this makes a lot of sense. Once more, according to its definition, restitution is an act of restoring; restoration of anything to its rightful owner; the act of making good on or giving the equivalent to any loss, damage or injury; and indemnification. While it is easy to assess the amount of damage in cases of property damage or loss, and to agree upon making good by repaying that sum, it is quite difficult to assess in terms of dollar values the damage or injury caused by a violent crime. This might be precisely the reason why criminal law professionals always argue that restitution and mediation programs are not feasible for such offenses. They assert that finding an equivalent dollar amount which might be suitable to restore the damage or injury caused by a violent crime is close to impossible. The above mentioned example from the National Survey of Crime Severity enables us to do just that: to give an estimate of how the public perceives the severity of a violent crime in relation to a property crime. This therefore gives us an idea as to how to determine the damage of an injury in terms of a dollar value, which then could be used as an estimate to determine the amount of restitution the offender has to repay.

Based upon the crime severity scale, one can construct a great number of comparisons between offense descriptions that include dollar values, and others in which the damage is physical. This gives us a better understanding about the severity of these crimes, and also helps us to estimate the value that needs to be restored. The offense description: 'A person, armed with a gun, robs a bank of $100,000 during business hours. No one is physically hurt' ranked #164 on the severity scale. We can compare it to: 'Knowing that a shipment of cooking oil is bad, a store owner decides to sell it anyway. Only one bottle is sold and the purchaser dies,' which ranked #166 on the severity scale. Taking the above established logic, this would mean that in order to restore the death of a person, we lie in the vicinity of a dollar amount of $100,000, which seems to be reasonably cheap. Another comparison reveals that 'A person (who) intentionally shoots a victim with a gun. The victim requires hospitalization,' ranked #185 on the severity scale, is almost equal to 'A person intentionally sets fire to a building causing $100,000 worth of damage,' ranked #186. The latter offense description corresponds also to 'A woman stabs her husband. As a result, he dies' which ranked #191 on the severity scale. Once again, we find that the public ranks a murder or death in the vicinity of a crime in which the dollar amount of the damage lies around $100,000.

To give some additional examples, we found other similarly ranked offenses: 'A teenage boy beats his mother with his fists. The mother requires hospitalization,' ranked #154 on the severity scale, 'A person robs a victim of $ 1,000 at gun point. The victim is wounded and requires treatment by a doctor but not hospitalization,' ranked #156, and 'A person, using force, robs a victim of $ 1,000. The victim is hurt and requires hospitalization,' ranked #158. These offenses were rated even a bit lower than an offense like 'A legislator takes a bribe of $ 10,000 from a company to vote for a law favoring the company,' which ranked #160. The point in these examples is to show that the public perceives crimes which involve serious injuries, often in combination with a monetary loss of $ 1,000, in the vicinity of a crime in which no injury occurs, and the monetary damage involved does not exceed $ 10,000.

POLICY IMPLICATIONS AND CONCLUSIONS FROM THE PHILADELPHIA STUDY AND THE NATIONAL CRIME SEVERITY STUDY

As we pointed out earlier, one of the main obstacles for extending restitution and mediation programs is the argument that they are not suitable for serious, violent offenses. Even though the historical application of restorative justice does not know such a limitation, current opponents and even proponents argue this idea.

The Philadelphia study clearly indicates that without outside interference, a judge can impose restitution sentences (and as we argue this can be extended to mediation orders as well) in combination with probation on a large scale. Further, that the official establishment of restitution programs might have had negative effects on their implementation because of too rigid screening. We found in this study that restitution, contrary to its current use, can be applied successfully in a large metropolitan court in which the majority of the offenders belong to a minority group, have previous criminal records, and commit mostly violent offenses.

An evaluation of the results indicates that in terms of the criminal background of the offenders, only prior arrests made a difference in whether an offender was imprisoned or given a restitution sentence. If we look at the offense-related model, we find that only pretrial detention made a difference between incarceration and restitution. Weapon use, whether in violent offenses, in those involving property damage or loss, in crimes related to gang membership, or in which the victim was injured, made no difference. Because these variables are usually used to determine the seriousness of a crime and the penal sanction, it was surprising that they made no difference in this study. These results indicate that today we can return to the ancient concept of restorative justice such as restitution for very serious crimes. That prior arrest and pretrial detention made a difference in determining who was incarcerated and who received a restitution sentence was expected. However, the number of prior arrests, the fact of being previously convicted, the number of prior convictions, the fact of being previously incarcerated, and the number and length of previous incarcerations had no effect on the imposition of an incarceration sentence. We can therefore argue that we should overlook the obstacle of a prior offense and pretrial detention, since the latter variables indicate a much less serious behavior.

The analysis further revealed that the amount of money involved in property offenses affected imprisonment and restitution. While a value from $101 to 500 led to a restitution sentence, a value of over $1,000 led to imprisonment. These results are astonishing if we compare them to the victim's injuries. The extent of the injuries had no effect on the imposition of the sentence. It is no surprise that a more costly property offense is punished more severely, but if bodily injuries and even death make no difference, why should property values make such a difference?

To no one's surprise, the only demographic variables that had an effect on incarceration were being male and being illiterate or semiliterate. It is well known that males commit more crimes of a more serious nature, and are more likely to have fewer marketable skills. Before the illiterate or semiliterate offenders could make restitution, they would have to learn how to read and receive job training.

The results of this study clearly favor a wider use of restitution for more serious offenders than is now the case. Although the restitution group in the present study had the highest percentage of probation revocations (51%), 61.2% served their probation terms successfully. The high number of revocations can be explained through the net-widening effect of restitution. Because restitution is an added, although just, burden to the offender, it is controlled by representatives of the criminal justice system. Failure to make restitution payments can lead to the revocation of probation. However, the net-widening effect, viewed negatively in the past because it led to more social control, can now be viewed positively in the context of restitution. In the context of this study, the offender also profited from the imposition of an restitution sentence and the extended social control, since he was not incarcerated. Despite their high number, most of the probation revocations led to the imposition of new probation terms, emphasizing to the offenders the need to make restitution payments.

An additional reason for applying restitution, mediation and other forms of restorative justice measures is the fact that one can easily estimate the amount of damage caused by property offenders, as well as by violent offenders. Thus, the amount to be restored is easily calculable. Up to now, people, mainly criminal law officials, have been fishing in the darkness to evaluate damage done, especially in violent crimes and more importantly, appropriate punishments for such offenses. Is an armed robbery of a pedestrian who gets wounded in the incident worth 2 or 15 years in prison? We seem to sentence such an offender in a rather arbitrary manner, and dismiss the idea of a restorative sentence in which we would have to attach a monetary value to the damage done. A prison sentence seems more appropriate in this case, according to the criminal law officials, without a reasonable explanation as to why a restorative justice sentence has to be dismissed.

An examination of the results of the National Survey of Crime Severity revealed surprising results. 60,000 respondents in the USA ranked a robbery in which the victim was injured as severe as a pick-pocketing of $100. Serious robberies with injuries and aggravated assaults which led to hospitalization of the victims were considered as severe as taking a bribe worth $10,000, and intentionally causing the death of a person. Killing a person was considered as severe as burning down a house worth $100,000.

In transferring these results to the application of restitution or restorative justice sentences, one can establish quite easily some monetary values for serious and/or violent offenses. These values were obtained by the ranking of criminal acts through the public, who seems neither revengeful nor interested in severe punishment as is claimed by criminal law officials. A sentencing practice based upon the National Crime Severity Scale seems to have a solid basis. At least this sentencing practice is based upon the opinion and perceived seriousness of the public, rather than that of criminal law officials, as is the current standard. Finally, the current sentencing practice sends criminals of serious offenses behind bars. After serving the prison sentence, they come out usually worse than they were before, and their victims receive nothing. If one on the other hand based the sentencing practice on the Crime Severity Study, and implemented the sentences within a restorative justice model, the offenders would be forced to make good on the damage or injury they had caused, and the victims would not lose in the process. They would receive some payment for the losses suffered, even though some of the amounts determined seem to be quite low. We could consider doubling the amount of money, in order to adjust the inflation rate for the past twenty years, but the amounts would still be reasonably low. However, the sentencing practice would become a system that the public could and would support, since they ranked the offenses themselves according to their perceived severity. We have shown that the argument 'one cannot apply restorative justice in cases of serious, violent crimes' is false and misleading. One should look ahead and try to figure out how a restorative justice model could be shaped for the future. There are several authors who favor large scale restorative justice models, and want to replace existing criminal justice systems by a full-fledged restorative justice model. However, they are often considered to be 'too idealistic.' On the other hand, did realism ever change the world? The gruesome picture of the criminal justice system in the United States of America should remind us that the retributive approach only leads to disaster, and causes us to wonder when they will stop these insane developments. As the results of the Philadelphia study and the analysis of the National Crime Severity Study revealed, restorative justice models seem by far the better answer to the crime problem, and have a solid basis for application.

REFERENCES

Alemika, E.O. (1983). *Continuities in the Research on the Measurement and Scaling of the Perceived Severity of Crime and Delinquency.* University of Pennsylvania, Philadelphia, PA, unpublished paper

Austin, J., & Krisberg, B. (1982). The Unmet Promise of Alternatives to Incarceration. *Crime and Delinquency, 28,* 374–409.

Barnett, R. (1980). The Justice of Restitution. *American Journal of Jurisprudence, 25,* 117–132.

Berrini, B. (1921). La giustizia. *Problemi giudiziari italiani.* Not published.

Black, H.C. (1968). *Black's Law Dictionary.* St. Paul: West Publishing.

Braithwaite, J. (1989). *Crime, Shame, and Reintegration.* Cambridge: University of Cambridge Press.

Braithwaite, J. (1991). Diversion, Reintegrative Shaming and Republican Criminology. Paper presented at the International Symposium on Diversion and Social Control: Impacts on Justice, Delinquents, Victims and the Public. Bielefeld, Germany.

Christie, N. (1978). Conflicts as Property. *British Journal of Criminology, 17,* 1–15.

Coates, R.B. (1990). Victim Offender Reconciliation Programs in North America. In: B. Galaway & J. Hudson (Eds.), *Criminal Justice, Restitution, and Reconciliation* (pp. 245–265). Mounsey: Criminal Justice Press.

Coates, R.B., & Gehm, J. (1988). An empirical Assessment. In: M. Wright & B. Galaway (Eds.), *Mediation and Criminal Justice: Victims, Offenders, and Communities* (pp. 253–265). London: Sage.

Coates, R.B., & Gehm, J. (1985). *Victim meets Offender: An Evaluation of Victim Offender Reconciliation Programs.* Valparaiso: PACT Institute of Justice.

Cohen, I.E. (1942). The Integration of Restitution in the Probation Service. *Journal of Criminal Law, Criminology, and Police Science, 33,* 315–321.

Daniels, R.A. (1988). Making Things Right: An Evaluation of a Victim Restitution Program. Paper presented at the ASC Meeting. Chicago, IL.

Del Vecchio, G. (1975). The Problem of Penal Justice. In: J. Hudson & B. Galaway (Eds.), *Considering the Victim* (pp. 85–101). Springfield: Charles C Thomas.

Edelhertz, H. (1977). Legal and Operational Issues in the Implementation of Restitution within the Criminal Justice System. In: J. Hudson & B. Galaway (Eds.), *Restitution in Criminal Justice* (pp. 63–76). Lexington: DC Heath Company.

Eglash, A. (1958a). Creative Restitution: A Broader Meaning for an Old Term. *Journal of Criminal Law, Criminology, and Police Science, 48,* 619–622.

Eglash, A. (1958b). Creative Restitution: Some Suggestions for Prison Rehabilitation Programs. *American Journal of Corrections,* 226–232.

Eglash, A. (1959). Creative Restitution: Its Roots in Psychology, Religion, and Law. *British Journal of Delinquency, 10,* 114–119.

Eglash, A. (1977). Beyond Restitution: Creative Restitution. In. J. Hudson & B. Galaway (Eds.), *Restitution in Criminal Justice* (pp. 91–100). Lexington: DC Heath and Company.

Figlio, R.M. (1975): The Seriousness of Offenses: An Evaluation by Offenders and Non-offenders. *Journal of Criminal Law, Criminology, and Police Science, 66,* 189–200.

Galaway, B. (1977a). Is Restitution Practical? *Federal Probation, 41,* 3–8.

Galaway, B. (1977b). Restitution as an Integrative Punishment. In: R. Barnett & J. Hagel (Eds.), *Assessing the Criminal* (pp. 331–348). Cambridge: Ballinger.

Galaway, B. (1977c). Toward the Rational Development of Restitution Programming. In: J. Hudson & B. Galaway (Eds.), *Restitution in Criminal Justice* (pp. 77–90). Lexington: DC Heath and Company.

Galaway, B. (1985). Victim-Participation in the Penal Corrective Process. *Victimology, 10,* 617–630.

Galaway, B., & Hudson, J. (1974). Using Restitution in the Rehabilitation of Offenders. *International Social Work, 16,* 44–50.

Galaway, B., & Hudson, J. (1975a). Issues in the Correctional Implementation of Restitution to Victims of Crime. In: J. Hudson & B. Galaway (Eds.), *Considering the Victim* (pp. 351–360). Springfield: Charles C Thomas.

Galaway, B., & Hudson, J. (1975b). Restitution and Rehabilitation: Some Central Issues. In: J. Hudson & B. Galaway (Eds.), *Considering the Victim* (pp. 255–264). Springfield: Charles C Thomas.

Garofalo, R. (1914). *Criminology,* Boston: Little Brown.

Gehm, J. (1990). Mediated Victim Offender Restitution Agreements: An Exploratory Analysis of Factors Related to Victim Participation. In: B. Galaway & J. Hudson (Eds.), *Criminal Justice, Restitution, and Reconciliation* (pp. 348–360). Mounsey: Criminal Justice Press.

Gehm, J., & Coates, R.B. (1986). *The Indiana Community Corrections Act: Process, Practice, and Implications.* Valparaiso: PACT Institute of Justice.

Geis, G. (1977). Restitution by Criminal Offenders: A Summary and Overview. In: J. Hudson & B. Galaway (Eds.), *Restitution in Criminal Justice* (pp. 147–164). Lexington: DC Heath Company.

Harland, A.T. (1981a). Court-Ordered Community Service in Criminal Law: The Continuing Tyranny of Benevolence. *Buffalo Law Review, 29,* 425–486.

Harland, A.T. (1981b). *Restitution to Victims of Personal and Household Crimes.* US Department of Justice. Washington, DC: Government Printing Office.

Hudson, J., & Galaway, B. (1974). Undoing the Wrong. *Social Work*, *19*, 313–318.

Hudson, J., & Galaway, J. (1980). A Review of the Restitution and Community-Service Sanctioning Research. In: J. Hudson & B. Galaway (Eds.), *Victims, Offenders, and Alternative Sanctions* (pp. 173–194). Lexington: DC Heath Company.

Hudson, J., & Galaway, B. (1989). Financial Restitution: Toward an Evaluable Program Model. Canadian *Journal of Criminology*, 31, 1–18.

Hudson, J., Chesney, S. (1978). Restitution Program Model. In: B. Galaway & J. Hudson (Eds.), *Offender Restitution in Theory and Action* (pp. 131–148). Lexington: DC Heath Company.

Hudson, J., Galaway, B., & Novack, S. (1980). *National Assessment of Adult Restitution Programs: Final Report*. Duluth: University of Minnesota, School of Social Development.

Marshall, T. (1989). The Power of Mediation. *Mediation Quarterly*, *vol. 8*, 115–124.

Marshall, T. (1991). Criminal Justice in the New Community: Bending to the Trends in Politics, Society, Economics and Ecology. Paper presented at the British Criminology Conference, York. Great Britain.

Marshall, T. (1992). Grassroots Initiatives Towards Restorative Justice: The New Paradigm? Paper presented at the Fulbright Colloquium at the University of Sterling, Great Britain.

Michalowski, R.J. (1985). *Order, Law, and Crime*. New York: Random House.

Mowrer, O.H. (1978). Applications and Limitations of Restitution. In: B. Galaway & J. Hudson (Eds.), *Offender Restitution in Theory and Action* (pp. 67–72). Lexington: DC Heath Company.

Pepinsky, H., Quinney, R. (1991). *Criminology as Peacemaking*. Bloomington: Indiana University Press.

Schafer, S. (1968). *The Victim and His Criminal*. New York: Random House.

Schafer, S. (1970a). *Compensation and Restitution to Victims of Crime*. Montclair: Patterson Smith.

Schafer, S. (1970b). Victim Compensation and Responsibility. *Southern California Law Review, 43*, 55–67.

Schafer, S. (1974). Compensation of Victims of Criminal Offenses. Criminal *Law Bulletin*, 605–636.

Schafer, S. (1975a). The Proper Role of a Victim Compensation System. *Crime and Delinquency, 21*, 45–49.

Schafer, S. (1975b). The Restitutive Concept of Punishment. In: J. Hudson & B. Galaway (Eds.), *Considering the Victim* (pp. 102–115). Springfield: Charles C Thomas.

Sellin, T., Wolfgang, M.E. (1964/1978). *The Measurement of Delinquency*. Montclair, Patterson Smith.

Sessar, K. (1992). *Wiedergutmachen oder Strafen*. Pfaffenweiler, Centaurus Verlag.

Shapiro, A. (1990). Is Restitution Legislation the Chameleon of the Victims' Movement? In: B. Galaway 6 J. Hudson (Eds.), *Criminal Justice, Restitution, and Reconciliation*. Mounsey: Criminal Justice Press.

Shelly, P.L., Sparks, M.F. (1980). Crime and Punishment. Paper presented at the Annual Meeting of the American Society of Criminology in San Francisco, CA.

Spencer, H. (1975). Prison Ethics. In: J. Hudson & B. Galaway (Eds.), *Considering the Victim* (pp. 71–84). Springfield: Charles C Thomas.

Sutherland, E.H., & Cressey, D.R. (1960). *Principles of Criminology*, 6th edition. Chicago: Lippincott.

Tallack, W. (1900). *Reparation to the Injured and the Rights of Victims of Crime Compensation*. London: Wertheimer, Lea and Co.

Turner, S. (1978). Introduction. In: T. Sellin. & M.E. Wolfgang (Eds.), *The Measurement of Delinquency*. Montclair: Patterson Smith.

Umbreit, M.S. (1985). *Crime and Reconciliation: Creative Options for Victims and Offenders*. Nashville: Abingdon.

Umbreit, M.S. (1986). Victim Offender Mediation: A National Survey. *Federal Probation, 50*, 53–56.

Umbreit. M.S. (1988). *The Meaning of Fairness to Victims in Victim Offender Mediation*. Minneapolis: University of Minnesota. Unpublished manuscript.

Viano, E.C. (1978). Victims, Offenders, and the Criminal Justice System. In: B. Galaway & J. Hudson (Eds.), *Offender Restitution in Theory and Action* (pp. 91–100). Lexington: DC Heath Company.

Waller, I. (1990). Implementing the Victims Declaration of the United Nations. Paper presented at the VIIth International Course on Victims and the Criminal Justice System. Dubrovnik, Croatia

Weitekamp, E.G. M. (1989). *Restitution: A New Paradigm of Criminal Justice or a New Way to Widen the Net of Social Control?* Ann Arbor: University Microfilms.

Wolfgang, M.E., Figlio, R.M., Tracy, P. E., Singer, S.I. (1985). *The National Survey of Crime Severity*. US Department of Justice, Bureau of Justice Statistics, Washington, DC.

Wright, M. (1991). *Justice for Victims and Offenders*. Milton Keynes: Open University Press.

Zehr, H., & Umbreit, M.S. (1982). Victim Offender Reconciliation: An Incarceration Substitute? *Federal Probation, 46,* 63–68.

Chapter 17

FROM JUROR TO JURY MEMORY OF THE EVIDENCE

Ramòn Arce, Francisca Fariña, Carlos Vila and Santiago Real

INTRODUCTION

Several studies have considered the unreliability of a single juror's memory in contrast to the reliability of a jury's group memory. The collective jury memory is said to counteract deficiencies in an individual memory (Hartwick, Sheppard & Davis, 1982; Hastie et al., 1983; Vila, 1996). Group memory is defined as the group's positive recall of the evidence, even if only one of the jurors has correctly done so. Hastie et al. (1983) have reported that a single juror's recall of evidence is not optimum. It is estimated to be approximately 30% for the judge's instructions and 60% for the factual evidence. Corresponding percentages for group memory were 80% and 90% respectively. Consequently, it has been argued that as a group, the jury is capable of fulfilling its duties by correcting individual errors in the recall of evidence. It is frequently assumed that this will automatically occur during the deliberation process. Kaplan and Miller (1978) considered the effects of favorable and unfavorable emotional states on single jurors, as well as on the jury as a group. They found that while changing emotional states did have an effect on decisions made individually, the group as a whole compensated for any deficiency in single juror efficiency.

Research concerning the comprehension of the instructions given by a judge has shown that certain instructions do not influence the juror's decision. These include instructions concerning the evidence, attitudinal characteristics, and the elimination of inadmissible evidence. However, instructions concerning the verdict, the background of the defendant, and the trial publicity do have a bearing on the juror's decisions (Gerbasi, Zuckerman & Reis, 1977). Two hypotheses have been advanced to explain this discrepancy:

a) the jury does not understand the formal legal language of the judge (Charrow & Charrow, 1979; Elwork, Alfini & Sales, 1982; Severance, Greene & Loftus, 1984),

b) instruction given at the end of a trial may undermine efficiency, since jurors may have already come to a decision (Kassin & Wrightsman, 1979).

Previous studies have substantiated both hypotheses and have underlined their compatibility (Arce, Fariña & Vila, 1994). Considering the first hypothesis, it appears jurors may not understand the judge's instructions. A possible solution to this problem that has been put forth is the elimination of jurors who are unable to process such information correctly (Graciano, Panter & Tanaka, 1990). Graciano et al. propose that by eliminating such jurors the jury would be free of bias and free from error.

Nevertheless, many questions remain unanswered. For example, how can errors be corrected if the decision rule, as is the case of a simple majority, does not require discussion? Further, if only one or a minority of jurors recalls an event correctly, what likelihood is there that their interpretation will prevail to correct any possible errors? Moreover, the deliberation process may in itself also give rise to new errors.

Another problem to be considered is the poor recollection of individual jurors. Pennington (1981) and Diamond (1993) have indicated that the errors may arise in the confirmation of the verdict. If this is the case, bearing in mind that in nine out of ten cases, juries arrive at a verdict based on the initial majority, (Kalven & Zeisel, 1966), it would appear that many decisions are erroneous. This study aims to clarify the above mentioned issues.

METHOD

Subjects
A total of 680 fully competent subjects were selected from the electoral register. These subjects were randomly divided into a total of 80 juries under eight conditions:

- Six subjects that had to reach a unanimous decision.
- Six subjects that had to reach a 2/3 majority decision.
- Nine subjects that had to reach a unanimous decision.
- Nine subjects that had to reach a 2/3 majority decision.
- Twelve subjects that had to reach a unanimous decision.
- Twelve subjects that had to reach a 2/3 majority decision.
- Seven subjects that had to reach a qualified majority decision;
(4–7 for a not-guilty decision, 6–7 for a guilty decision).
- Seven subjects that had to reach a combined decision; (a unanimous decision, and a 5–7 majority decision after 30 minutes of deliberation).

Materials
The juries were shown one of two videotapes of a re-enactment of a real life trial. One case involved a rape and subsequent murder, while the other

was a trial of grievous bodily harm (GBH). Both cases included pleas made by the prosecution and the defense, testimony given by witnesses and legal experts, closing arguments of both the defense and prosecution, and the judge's summation.

In the rape and murder case, the defendant was a young man and the victim a young girl. There were no direct eyewitnesses, though there were witnesses who testified that the defendant had been the last person to be seen accompanying the young girl. The defendant tried to coax one witness into supporting his alibi, but the witness refused. A forensic expert reported the existence of hematomas around the genital organs of the defendant, though he also stressed that the lesions could not be directly attributed to rape. The defense council pleaded not guilty and argued that the prosecution's case rested entirely on conjecture. The prosecution accused the defendant of both crimes, and asked that he be sentenced accordingly.

The second case (GBH) involved two people engaged in a fight in a public bar. The issue was to determine whether the aggression was in self-defense or not.

After the closing arguments, the judge instructed the jury on the legal definition of self-defense.

Procedure

Subjects participated voluntarily in the experiment and were instructed as to their duties before being randomly assigned to a particular jury. This was done in order to ensure an equal distribution of socio-demographic factors such as gender, age, profession and economic status. Thereafter, the subjects were shown one of the two re-enactment videotapes. After viewing the video, subjects were asked to complete a pre-deliberation questionnaire.

For the purpose of this study, the questionnaire was designed to evaluate the juror's decision regarding the verdict, the sentence, and to measure their recall of the trial evidence and judge's instructions. The recall measurement questionnaire consisted of four options for each question: a correct answer; an incorrect answer in favor of the accused; an incorrect answer against the accused; and an incorrect neutral answer.

Possible alternatives were suggested by the research team in a brainstorming session in order to ensure that these were plausible responses. In fact, all of the possible alternatives were at some time chosen by the jurors. Thereafter, the juries deliberated according to the previously mentioned decision rules. The deliberation was recorded on video in order to obtain information regarding the correction of errors during the deliberation.

Analysis of the deliberation

Three encoders evaluated the deliberation in search of errors as well as corrections. For this purpose codifiers were familiarized with the trials and supplied with a list, for each deliberation, of the most frequent errors made in the pre-deliberation questionnaire. Moreover, the three encoders were allowed to consult the trial evidence whenever necessary.

This procedure allowed the gathering of two types of information. First, the real scope of group memory as opposed to deliberation memory. In other words, we considered subjects who knew the correct answer to an item on the questionnaire who then influenced a group decision, as opposed to the arrival at a correct answer by the group as a whole. Second, we examined new errors that were committed during the deliberation and registered any possible correction.

Reliability

In order to ensure consistency, a cross-validation was carried out between and within the three encoders through a re-codification process one month later. The statistical treatment applied was the agreement index (see Table 1).

The results show inter- and intra- consistency. The encoders have been shown to be consistent in other contexts (Arce, Fariña & Novo, 1995; Arce, Fariña, Vila & Real, 1995; Arce, Fariña & Novo, 1996); thus, our results are reliable (Wicker, 1975).

Table 1: Average consistency of codes. errors

Inter	1
Intra	1

AI = Agreement/ (Agreements + Disagreements)

RESULTS

Recall

Bearing in mind that the juror's pre-deliberation memory recall was evaluated using a questionnaire with four options, our aim was to determine the following: a) if jurors favoring a guilty verdict process the evidence more rigorously than jurors favoring a verdict of innocence; b) if the verdict biased the juror's recall of the evidence. In other words, if jurors favoring guilt commit more errors in favor of guilt, and those favoring innocence commit errors in favor of innocence (Pennington, 1981; Diamond, 1993); as suggested by the story model described by Hastie et al. (1983).

The results reveal that jurors in favor of a guilty verdict correctly recalled more evidence [$X^2(1) = 100,63$; p <,01] than jurors in favor of a not-guilty verdict. Furthermore, our findings indicate that the verdict does not lead to biased errors [$X^2(1) = 0,52$; NS]. Thus, the results indicate that arriving at a guilty verdict involves profound cognitive activity, and that the juror's final decision is not based on a cognitive deformation of the information. A possible explanation is that jurors process the trial information automatically. Therefore, they consciously check key issues in order to avoid errors which would have undesirable consequences on the defendant (Reason, 1979).

We should point out, however, that we do not assert that jurors in favor of innocence do not consciously verify the evidence. They may, however, verify the evidence according to the importance they ascribe to it. It is possible that there is a greater tendency to consciously verify evidence indicating guilt than that indicating innocence, due to the material and emotional implications involved.

The average recall demonstrated by jurors was quite poor. The average recall of evidence was 59% and 66% for the GBH case and the rape and murder case respectively. As for the judge's instructions, the recall was even poorer—42% and 53% for the rape and murder case and the GBH case respectively.

Group recall of factual evidence and judge's instructions

To determine if the size of the jury influences the group memory, an analysis of variance, with the Bonferroni protection level was undertaken. Here, group memory is intended as the sum of the individual recollections before deliberation.

The results show that jury size did not influence the group memory of factual evidence in either the rape and murder case [1] [$F(3,36) = ,97$ MS = 160; NS], or the GBH case [$F(3,36) = 1,07$; MS = ,15; NS]. Furthermore, the recall of the judge's instructions was not influenced by jury size. For the rape and murder case, the results are [$F(3,36) = ,0$; MS = ,0; NS]. For the GBH case, a slight difference was observed; the results are [$F(3,36) = 2,45$; MS = ,9; p<,07]. The collective group memory and the individual juror memory were compared to determine if the former improved the latter.

Individual jurors recalled on average 59% and 66% of the factual evidence, and 52% and 42% of the judge's instructions in the GBH and rape and murder cases, respectively.

The recall of factual evidence for the group improved to between 90% and 100% for factual evidence and, on average, 80% to 100% for the judge's instructions in the GBH and rape and murder cases respectively.

Errors during the deliberation

Examinations were carried out on the eight experimental conditions and the re-codified phenomenological variables (i.e., jury size and decision rule) in unanimous versus non-unanimous juries. The unanimous juries also included the combined rulings since they also involved unanimity. Significant differences were observed among the eight conditions and between the unanimous and non unanimous decision rulings. More errors were corrected in the unanimous conditions (see Tables 2 and 3).

Table 2: Error frequency in each condition

	6U	9U	12U	6M	9M	12M	7QD	7CD
Corrected Errors	22	26	38	6	12	12	7	23
Non Corrected Errors	20	18	8	40	33	30	39	15

7CD = Combined decision rule; 7QD = Qualified decision rule. $X^2 (7) = 88,13; p <, 001$.

Table 3: Error frequency in unanimous and non-unanimous decision rulings

	Unanimous	Non-Unanimous
Corrected Errors	109	37
Non-Corrected Errors	61	142

$X^2 (1) = 67, 84; p <, 001$.

Significant differences were found between our category of reference (the condition of 12 jurors with a unanimous decision ruling) and the other conditions. More errors were corrected in the 12 unanimous decision ruling condition (see Table 4).

Table 4: Error comparison with 12U condition

Condition	X^2	P
6 jurors and unanimous rule	9.25	.01
9 jurors and unanimous rule	6.05	.05
6 jurors and majority rule	44.61	.001
9 jurors and majority rule	28.76	.001
12 jurors and majority rule	26.13	.001
7 jurors and combined rule	5.10	.05
7 jurors and qualified majority rule	41.80	.001

12U = the condition of 12 jurors and unanimous decision rule.

The main decision errors, that is, those on which the construction of the events hinge, only appear in non-unanimous juries (see Table 5).

Table 5: Main decision errors

Condition		
6	Majority	5(4)
9	Majority	6(4)
12	Majority	8(5)
7	Combined	3(2)
7	Qualified	6(5)

Defense of a verdict based on errors (number of juries). (*) Only when a unanimous verdict was not reached.

A detailed analysis of the results illustrated in Table 5 highlights that main decision errors only appear when there are two readings of the evidence without the need for a conversion.

For this reason, the probabilities sometimes appear doubled since an erroneous reconstruction of guilt can lead to an erroneous interpretation of innocence. The impression of the three encoders indicates that this is mainly due to attempts to 'assimilate' the other faction. This interpretation seems to be valid since it is always the majority who introduces the source of errors that are sometimes challenged with other errors by the minority. Thus, the introduction of an error can lead to a 'counter-error' by the other faction.

DISCUSSION

Individual recall was not very high and one may infer that the individual decision was of low quality. The group decision does not always exceed individual limitations. Two phenomenological factors (jury size and decision rule) could influence the quality of jury recall, though in our study the group size did not provoke differences in the group memory. This is not to say that with other evidence this is not possible. It is worth highlighting that the aim of the deliberation is to improve the group memory; in this sense, unanimity favors the correction of errors during the deliberation. A closer examination of the reliability of the evidence favors a unanimous jury composed of 12 members.

Conversely, in non-unanimous juries in which there are two final readings of the evidence, jurors not only correct fewer errors, but also introduce new ones. We believe that this is done to assimilate the other faction. On the other hand, we have observed that individual juror's recollection is not determined by errors 'aimed at' confirming the verdict.

NOTES

1   As the dependent variable was the percentage of collective memory in order to carry out a variance analysis, this variable was transformed into proportions and converted into a continuum
using the arcosine method.

REFERENCES

Arce, R., Fariña, F., & Novo, M. (1995). *The mixed or escabinato jury vs. the lay jury: A critical analysis.* 5th International Conference on Social Justice Research, Reno.

Arce, R., Fariña, F., Vila, C., & Real, S. (1995). Empirical assessment of the escabinato jury system. *Psychology, Crime, and Law, 2,* 131–141.

Arce, R., Fariña, F., & Novo, M. (1996). *Cognition and judicial decision making.* XXVI International Congress of Psychology, Montreal.

Arce, R., Fariña, F., & Vila, C. (1994). Sobre la calidad y ubicación de las instrucciones judiciales al jurado. *Revista de Psicología Social Aplicada, 4*(3), 105–119.

Charrow, R., & Charrow, V. (1979). Making legal language understandable: A psycholinguistic study of jury instructions. *Columbia Law Review, 79,* 1306–1374.

Diamond, S.S. (1993). Instructing on death: Psychologists, juries, and judges. *American Psychologist, 48,* 423–434.

Elwork, A., Alfani, J. J., & Sales, B. D. (1982). Toward understandable jury instructions. *Judicature, 65,* 432–433.

Gerbasi, K.C., Zuckerman, H., & Reis, H.T. (1977). Justice needs a new blindfold: A review of mock jury research. *Psychological Bulletin, 84,* 323–345.

Graciano, S.J., Panter, A.T., & Tanaka, J.S. (1990). Individual differences in information processing strategies and their role in juror decision making and selection. *Forensic Reports, 3*(3) 279–301.

Hans, V.P., & Vidmar, N. (1986). *Judging the jury.* New York: Plenum Press.

Hartwick, J., Sheppard, B.H., & Davis, J.H. (1982). Group remembering: Research and implications. In: R. Guzzo (ed.), *Improving group decision making in organizations: Working from theory.* New York: Academic Press.

Hastie, R., Penrod, S., & Pennington (1983). *Inside the Jury.* Cambridge, Mass.: Harvard University Press.

Kalven, H., & Zeisel, H. (1966). *The American jury.* Boston, Mass.: Little Brown.

Kaplan, M.F., & Miller, J.H. (1978). Reducing the effects of juror bias. *Journal of Personality and Social Psychology, 36,* 1443–1455.

Kassin, S.M., & Wrightsman, L.S. (1979). On the requirements of proof: The timing of judicial instructions on mock jury verdicts. *Journal of Personality and Social Psychology, 37,* 1877–1887.

Pennington, N. (1981). *Causal reasoning and decision making: The case of juror decisions.* Unpublished Doctoral Dissertation, Harvard University.

Reason, J. (1979). Actions not as planned: The price of automatization. In: G. Underwood, & R. Stevens (Eds.), *Aspects as consciousness, Vol 1: Psychological issues.* London: Academic Press.

Severance, L.J., Greene, E., & Loftus, E.F. (1984). Toward criminal jury instructions that jurors can understand. *The Journal of Criminal Law and Criminology, 1.*

Vila, C. (1996). *Formación de juicios en jurados Legos e incidencia de variables fenomenológicas en la deliberación de jurados legos* Unpublished Doctoral Thesis, Universidad de Santiago de Compostela.

Wicker, A.W. (1975). An application of a multiple-trait/multi-method logic to the reliability of observational records. *Personality and Social Psychology Bulletin, 4,* 575–579.

Chapter 18

POLYGRAPHY IN POLAND

Józef Wójcikiewicz

THE PAST

American spies arrested in the early 1950s by Polish intelligence confessed during interrogations that before their training they had been examined with a type of 'clearance' device. When it was determined that it had been a polygraph, that machine was bought without delay by the intelligence (Krzyoscin, 1996a). At about the same time, the then director of the Institute of Forensic Research, Dr. Jan Sehn, in his paper read in 1950 at a conference at the Ministry of Justice, compared 'pneumo, sfigmo and pletysmographic lie detectors' to 'magic wands' and 'fortune teller's predictions' (Sehn, 1951, p. 14).

The intelligence monopoly lasted until the early 1960s when Professor Horoszowski, a forensic scientist from Warsaw University, during his scholarship in the United States, bought a polygraph on sale. Despite his limited knowledge and meager experience, he started to provide opinions for public prosecutors and the courts.

The first evidential use of a polygraph in a Polish criminal case took place in 1963 in Olsztyn. Professor Horoszowski used the polygraph to examine two men who were suspected of stabbing a relative during a quarrel (Horoszowski, 1965). Needless to say, the results were far from perfect. However, the district court approved of the examinations as admissible evidence, and sentenced the accused to fifteen years in prison. Only later did it turn out to have been a miscarriage of justice. In another case, the same expert performed the test in the courtroom, against the objections of the defense counsel who had requested him to provide a psychological opinion and not one derived from polygraph results (Krzyoscin, 1996a).

The Olsztyn case (III K 177/64) opened up an opportunity for the Supreme Court to express its attitude concerning the admissibility of polygraph examinations in criminal trials. Unfortunately, the Court did not take a stand (Daszkiewicz, 1965). This case, however, evoked a prolonged and heated legal dispute over the admissibility of polygraph examinations in Polish criminal justice. The first phase of it, from 1964 to 1967, was mainly characterized by the debaters' ignorance. The second stage, in the 1970s, was completely different.

In 1969 a psycho-physiological laboratory was established at the Military Police Headquarters. From 1969 to 1989, military experts examined 4,226 persons in 943 cases (Bieñkuñski, 1997). A real breakthrough in the status of the polygraph occurred in the seventies when it entered university forensic science departments in Kraków, Toruñ, Wroclaw and Katowice. Many research projects were carried out in the field, and even a habilitation thesis on the diagnostic value of polygraph examination was written by Widacki (1977). It was Professor Widacki (later the Deputy Minister of the Interior and the ambassador to Lithuania), together with Professor Konieczny (later the Minister of the Interior), who created a leading polygraph center at the Department of Criminalistics at the Silesian University in Katowice in 1977. 407 persons in 44 criminal cases were examined there in the three year period from 1977 to 1980 (Widacki 1982). In the decade 1969 to 1979, over 2,000 persons were subjected to polygraph examinations in Poland (Krzyoscin, 1982).

It was symptomatic that police administrators expressed a rather unfavorable attitude toward the polygraph, while the police almost never engaged in organizing a polygraph laboratory (Krzyoscin, 1996a, 1996).

A growing number of cases in which a polygrapher had been called upon as an expert witness compelled the Supreme Court to take a position on this question. In 1976, the Court passed a judgment (II KR 171/76) in which it ruled, erroneously, that the polygraph examination must be treated only as 'accessorial' and not 'independent' evidence. Since Polish law does not recognize such a classification of evidence, the judges' term 'accessioral' was interpreted as circumstantial evidence. Nevertheless, it was the first approval by the Supreme Court of the evidential use of polygraph examination results (Daszkiewicz, Jez-Ludwichowska, 1979). In subsequent judgments (I KR 136/77, III KR 211/80, II KR 6/82) the Court, accordingly, erroneously emphasized the necessity of the participation by physicians in polygraph examinations (Waltos, Widacki 1979), and rightly pointed out that the expert's opinion was the only legal form of this type of evidence (Gurgul, 1981). It further stated that the polygraph examination was admissible, albeit unnecessary and only recommended with great caution (Waltose, Widacki, 1984; Daszkiewicz, 1984).

The present author (Wójcikiewicz, 1978) took a survey on the polygraph involving 195 representatives of different legal professions. It was revealed that the subjects had a very limited knowledge of the issue. Only 8 (4%) knew some basic facts about the polygraph examination. Nevertheless, they were able to formulate definite answers as to the question of whether this apparatus should be applied in criminal cases. It turned out that there were as many adherents as opponents—43%. Whereas the judges and public prosecutors surveyed were almost equally divided, the policemen were generally in favor of the use of the polygraph, and defense counsels generally against it.

The scientific community had likewise remained heterogeneous. The main argument of the opponents was that the polygraph excludes freedom of statements and, according to Art. 157 par. 2 of the previous Code of Criminal Procedure, 'the testimony or statements given in such conditions could not be regarded as evidence' (Gaberle & Doda, 1995). In spite of that, numerous public prosecutors have called upon polygraphers as expert witnesses. Only in the period 1994–1995 did military experts examine 197 persons in 97 cases. In 1994, 33 persons were examined in 23 non-military cases. In 1995, 101 people were subjected to the test in 52 such cases. The majority of the cases (50) were homicides. All examinations were carried out using the Control Questions Technique (Bieńkuński, 1997). One of the most famous cases in which polygraph evidence was accepted was the recent (1997) trial for the alleged murderers of the former Polish Prime Minister Piotr Jaroszewicz and his wife.

The discrepancy between theory and practice, however would be in the long run harmful for the criminal justice system.

It seemed that all was clarified, and that the opponents had scored a victory over the advocates when the draft Code of Criminal Procedure was elaborated (Wójcikiewicz, 1996). Its Art. 168 par. 4 sec. 2 banned the application of any chemical or technical means which influence the psychological processes of an interrogated person. Further, any aim at monitoring the unconscious reactions of such a person in connection with the interrogation was also prohibited. Statements or testimony given in the above conditions would have to be excluded as inadmissible evidence. These methods were even forbidden during an examination carried out by an expert! Fortunately, the latter ban was later withdrawn from the Bill. Otherwise, some far less controversial psychological tests like projective techniques would also have to be ruled out, and medical treatment of the accused during his or her psychiatric observation would also be forbidden!

Nevertheless, the reasons for Bill and the subsequent Act have remained unchanged, as well as the arguments against the polygraph. They indicate a mixture of ignorance and prejudice. Clearly, they involve the humanistic resistance to an intrusion into the subconsciousness, the fear that the influence of an expert witness on the court might be excessive, and the unreliability of an examination on a nervous, innocent suspect. One must also consider that Polish society is one that holds on firmly to the past. In doing so, according to the reasons, it maintains a negative attitude toward procedures even indirectly connected with the police.

Paradoxically, although the Act was not yet in force, its grounds were. First of all it concerned the argument of violation of the court's prerogatives of free appraisal of evidence by a polygrapher. On that ground, the courts and public prosecutors often rejected defendants' motions for polygraph examinations. As an example, we can consider a robbery case (II Akr 268/93) tried by the Poznañ Court of Appeal (Wójcikiewicz, 1995.) The Court ruled that the polygraph examination of the accused, requested by the defense counsel 'for the evaluation of the reliability of his statements,' was inadmissible because it limited the principle of free appraisal of evidence. This was an overt misinterpretation of the polygraph examination, which obviously and absolutely does not limit a judge's prerogative by being itself the subject of evidence evaluation. The polygraph examination should not be treated as 'lie detection' or 'truthfulness verification.' Rather, it should simply be considered a detection of emotional memory traces (Widacki, 1982; Krzyoscin, 1982), even if the final aim is the verification of a defendant's statements and other pieces of evidence.

THE PRESENT

On 6 June, 1997 the Polish Parliament passed a new Code of Criminal Procedure which has been in force since 1 September, 1998. Its Art. 171 par. 4 sec. 2 duplicates art. 168 par. 4 sec. 2 of the draft. It states the inadmissibility of the use of technical means which influence psychological processes of an interrogated person, or that would aim at monitoring the unconscious reactions of such a person in connection with the interview. The sanction is expressed in par. 6:

> Testimony or statements given in conditions excluding the ability of free statements, or obtained in contradiction to the ban from par. 4 may not be given into evidence.

Some authors maintain that these bans do not concern the polygraph examination, since the polygraph neither registers unconscious reactions (Bieñkuñski, 1997; Krzyoscin, 1997), nor excludes the ability of free statements by the person examined (Kmiecik, Skretowicz, 1996). In addition, Art. 171 obviously concerns only the formal interrogation, and not the expert witness opinion.

Despite the categorical, and very emotional, arguments formulated on the grounds of the Act, the polygraph examination has not been eliminated from the Polish criminal procedure. It is still allowed (or more precisely, not forbidden) as an expert witness' tool. Such its use was approved by the Supreme Court in a decision from 21 December 1998, (IVKO 101/98; Widacki, 1999) and the Kraków Court of Appeal in a judgement form 19 August, 1999 (II Aka 147/99; Widacki, 2000). Both techniques, the CQT and the GKT, are used. The former is used more frequently, although the advantages of the latter are evident (Ben-Shakhar & Furedy, 1990; Kulicki, 1994). It cannot be overlooked that the polygraph can also act in favor of an innocent suspect (Jaworski, 1996). The following case may serve as an example:

> A vagrant was apprehended as a suspect in a series of rapes. Two victims recognized him during the identification process, but he passed a polygraph test and was released. Later, the police arrested the actual offender (Krzyoscin, 1996b).

On the other hand, the polygraph examination, especially a failed one, can induce a suspect to confess. Such a confession should however, be carefully evaluated (Gudjonsson, 1992). A witness may also be subjected to polygraph examination, but like a suspect, only with his or her consent.

Polygraph tests are carried out both for investigative purposes, and in expert work done by university scientists. It is used by the Military Police, State Protection Office officials, and even by a private company which offers employee testing. However, extra-forensic use of the polygraph, without any legal basis, has been the subject of much controversy (Sajnug & Szubiela, 1995).

In 1994 the Polish Polygraphers' Association was established. It maintains contact with the American Polygraph Association (Krzyoscin, 1996b; Bieńkuñski, 1997).

THE FUTURE

Polygraphy is certainly not 'junk science' (Gianelli, 1993). Although it has not yet gained general acceptance within the scientific community, it has reached the scientific level, which justifies its investigative and even evidential use (Vrij, 2000). Therefore, withdrawal of the ban on calling upon a polygrapher as an expert witness from the Code of Criminal Procedure deserves approval. Undoubtedly, a clarification of the legal status of the polygraph examination would contribute significantly to the development of polygraphy in Poland.

Besides the legal and ethical problems, a social context of polygraphy also deserves exploration. Saks (1992, p. 186) wondered why the polygraph 'receives the brunt of judicial resistance, while so many other kinds of psychological expertise, based on lesser knowledge, are routinely admitted.' It seems that this resistance results from ignorance. The fear that an expert could usurp the role of a lawyer is mostly caused by the perception of the polygraph as a 'lie detector,' or as 'La Bocca della Verità.' As a matter of fact, it is an *a priori* piece of evidence just as valid as any other. Moreover, the danger of its overestimation, resulting in a miscarriage of justice, is relatively low. This is especially true in cases in which 'hard' scientific evidence does not exist. The courts in these cases are usually much more suspicious of such 'fishy' evidence. It occurs more frequently that a specialized forensic expert influences a verdict, rather than a polygrapher. Often, the courts become overwhelmed by such new and highly sophisticated scientific evidence presented by experts (Moenssens, 1993). The Birmingham Six case, or the recent Polish case of a police expert who faked 64 physicochemical opinions are significant examples. The only solution is to increase criminal justice practitioners' knowledge of forensic science and psychology. The scientists and experts from the Institute of Forensic Research in Kracków have been working toward that goal by organizing many courses and seminars for public prosecutors and judges.

REFERENCES

Ben-Shakhar, G., & Furedy, J.J. (1990). *Theories and Applications in the Detection of Deception. A Psychophysiological and International Perspective*. New York: Springer Verlag.

Bieńkuński, J. (1997). Rola badań poligraficznych w dzialaniach wykrywczych organów œcigania i wymiaru sprawiedliwoœci. *Problemy Kryminalistyki 216*, 41–49.

Daszkiewicz, W. (1965). Glosa do wyroku Sadu Najwyzszego z 11 XI 1964, III K 177/64, *OSPiKA 10*, 456–462.

Daszkiewicz, W. (1984). Glosa do wyroku z 11 II 1982, II KR 6/82. *Państwo i Prawo 1*, 140–147.

Daszkiewicz, W., & Jez-Ludwichowska, M. (1979). Glosa do wyroku z 25 IX 1976, II KR 171/76. *Państwo i Prawo 5*, 173–179.

Doda, Z., & Gaberle, A. (1995). *Dowody w procesie karnym*. Warszawa: ABC.

Gianelli, P.C. (1993). „Junk Science': The Criminal Cases. *The Journal of Criminal Law and Criminology, 84*, 1, 105–127.

Gudjonsson, G.H. (1992). *The Psychology of Interrogations, Confessions and Testimony*. Chichester: John Wiley and Sons.

Gurgul, J. (1981). Glosa do wyroku Sadu Najwyzszego z 8 lipca 1980 r., III KR 211/80 (dot. problematyki badań poligraficznych w procesie karnym). *Problemy Praworzadnosci, 3*, 81–85.

Horoszowski, P. (1965). Eksperymentalno-testowa metoda wariograficzna w seledczej i sadowej ekspertyzie psychologicznej, *Przeglad Psychologiczny, 9*, 55–75.

Jaworski, R. (1996). Wyniki badań poligraficznych jako dowód odciazajacy. *Prokuratura i Prawo, 6*, 50–58.

Kmiecik, R., & Skretowicz, E. (1996). *Proces karny. Czeosac ogólna*. Kraków-Lublin: Kantor Wydawniczy Zakamycze.

Krzyoscin, A. (1982). Istota kryminalistyczna badania poligraficznego. *Nowe Prawo, 3–4*, 145–150.

Krzyoscin, A. (1996a). Letter to the author of 6th February.

Krzyoscin, A. (1996b). Wykorzystanie poligrafu w procesie karnym, *Przeglad Sadowy, 3*, 86–98.

Krzyoscin, A. (1997). Poligraf prawde powie?. *Gazeta Sadowa, 18*, 14, 19.

Kulicki, M. (1994). *Kryminalistyka. Wybrane zagadnienia teorii i praktyki seledczo-sadowej.* Toruń: Uniwersytet Mikolaja Kopernika.

Moenssens, A.A. (1993). Novel Scientific Evidence in Criminal Cases: Some Words of Caution. *The Journal of Criminal Law and Criminology 84*, 1, 1–21.

Sajnug, D., & Szubiela J. (1995). Prawdomównoseac w luce prawnej. *Gazeta Wyborcza -Magazyn, 21*, 16–17.

Saks, M. J. (1992). Normative and Empirical Issues About the Role of Expert Witnesses. In: D.K. Kagehiro & W.S. Laufer (Eds.), *Handbook of Psychology and Law* (pp. 185–203). New York: Springer Verlag.

Sehn, J. (1951). *Obecny stan kryminalistyki w Polsce. In: Stan kryminalistyki i medycyny sadowej* (pp. 5–26). Warszawa: Ministerstwo Sprawiedliwoœci.

Vrij, A. (2000) *Detecting dies and Deceit. The Psychology of Lying and the Implications for Professional Practice.* Chichester: John Wiley & Sons.

Waltose, S., & Widacki, J. (1979). Glosa do wyroku z dnia 14 grudnia 1977 r. (I KR 136/77). *Nowe Prawo, 7–8*, 227–233.

Waltose, S., & Widacki, J. (1979). Glosa do wyroku z 11 II 1982, II KR 6/82. *Państwo i Prawo, 1*, 136–140.

Widacki, J. (1977). *Wartosac diagnostyczna badania poligraficznego i jej znaczenie kryminalistyczne.* Kraków: Uniwersytet Jagiellońsji.

Widacki, J. (1982). *Analiza przeslanek diagnozowania w badaniach poligraficznych.* Katowice: Uniwersytet Slaski.

Widacki, J. (1999). Glosa do postanowienia Sadu Najwyzszego z 21 grudnia 1998r., *Palestra 3–4*, 237–239.

Widacki, J. (2000). Glosa do wyroku Sadu Apelacyjnego w Krakowie z 19 sierpnia 1999r., *Palestra 2–3*, 251–253.

Wójcikiewicz, J. (1978). Poligraf w sewietle wypowiedzi przedstawicieli niektórych zawodów prawniczych, *Studia Kryminologiczne Kryminalistyczne i Penitencjarne 8*, 241–254.

Wójcikiewicz, J. (1995). Glosa do wyroku Sadu Apelacyjnego w Poznaniu z dnia 2 grudnia 1993 r., II Akr 268/93. *Palestra 1-2*, 239-242.

Wójcikiewicz, J. (1996). Psychological Issues in the Draft Polish Code of Criminal Procedure. In: G. Davies, S. Lloyd-Bostock, M. McMurran & C. Wilson (Eds.), *Psychology, Law and Criminal Justice. International Developments in Research and Practice* (pp. 585–590). New York: Walter de Gruyter.

Chapter 19

THE ASSESSMENT OF FITNESS TO STAND TRIAL IN AUSTRALIA: A PROPOSED ASSESSMENT TOOL

Astrid Birgden and Donald M. Thomson

In the criminal justice process, a defendant must be fit to stand trial so that the criminal procedure is dignified, the results are reliable and the punishment is morally justified, i.e., a fair trial (Grisso, 1988; Melton, Petrila, Poythress & Slobogin, 1987).

In Australia there are special rules and procedures, as in other parts of the world, to determine whether a defendant is not fit to be tried due to mental impairment. If the defendant is found unfit by a jury empanelled for the purpose, the trial is prevented from continuing. Within Australian Criminal codes and state and federal legislation, an unfit defendant must be kept in strict custody until the Governor's pleasure is known. The problem with this is that the courts have no power to recall the defendant for trial resulting in the possibility of an indefinite sentence. Defendants with intellectual disability, head injury or dementia who are unlikely to recover mental capacity are particularly likely to be detained indefinitely.

Although it is unjust to try individuals who are so mentally impaired that they cannot understand the proceedings or instruct their lawyers about their defence, the converse is that since the issue of fitness is not raised for fear of indefinite sentence, the presence of mental impairment amongst defendants is understated.

In Australia, fitness to stand trial is rarely raised because of the possibility of lengthy incarceration. It is unknown what percentage of defendants in Australia have the issue of fitness to stand trial raised but it is considered extremely small. Some data has been collated in three states in Australia

Data regarding fitness to stand trial in Australia.

NEW SOUTH WALES

Office of the Director of Public Prosecutions
Nov 1990- March 1992: 29 fitness to stand trial matters out of 3552 trials = 0.8%.

April 1992 and March 1994 = 68 fitness to stand trial matters.
Ref: New South Wales Law Reform Commission (1994).

Mental Health Review Tribunal
October 1991: of 86 forensic patients reviewed,
10% unfit to stand trial.
Ref: Hayes, Sterry, Ovadia, Boerma, & Greer (1991).

May 1993: of 101 forensic patients,
26% found unfit.
Ref: Hayes, Langley, & Greer (1993).

WESTERN AUSTRALIA
Survey of trials in the Supreme Court over 1970–1985:
six cases where fitness was raised.
Ref: Law Reform Commission of WA (1991).

VICTORIA
Review of DPP files 1936–1988:
24 received Governor's pleasure (including Not Guilty on the Grounds of
Insanity).
Of 78 defendants, two (3%) had been found unfit to plead.
Ref: Van Groningen (1989).

The rarity of the issue being raised has implications for any research into
its definition and assessment.

The issue of fitness to stand trial has been considered by several law
reform commissions in Australia but they have focussed upon procedural
issues rather than questioning the current definition and assessment
methods used by mental health professionals; there are no detailed statu-
tory guidelines for the assessment of fitness to stand trial.

DEFINITION OF FITNESS TO STAND TRIAL

In Australia, the most influential case has been that of *R. vs. Presser 1958*
where the Presser criteria were outlined by Justice Smith. These criteria
are similar to those outlined by *R. vs. Pritchard 1836* in the UK and *R. vs.
Dusky 1960* in the USA. The criteria are based on a common notion of
the ability to understand, comprehend and assist in order to ensure meaningful participation in the criminal trial process.

A Model Bill (Unfitness to Stand Trial, Mental Impairment and Disposition) was developed in 1994 by the Attorney Generals of all the Australian states based upon the Presser criteria:

Model Bill- Unfitness to stand trial, mental impairment and disposition
1. Not able to understand the nature of the charge; or
2. Unable to plead to the charge or to exercise the right of challenge; or
3. Unable to understand the nature of the proceedings; or
4. Unable to follow the course of the proceedings; or
5. Unable to understand the substantial effect of any evidence that may be given in support of the prosecution; or
6. Unable to make a defense or answer the charges.

Mental impairment = senility, intellectual disability, mental illness, brain damage and severe personality disorder.

The criteria are extremely general and what they actually mean and to what extent each criterion has to be met (and whether indeed they all need to be met) has not been specified. Only one criterion mentions the word 'substantial' and the remainder do not indicate the level of adequacy or sufficiency required (Freckelton, 1995). The criteria only state what characteristics a defendant requires in order to be considered fit to stand trial once the trial is underway, but do not indicate what mental health professionals should consider when assessing defendants prior to entry into the courtroom.

What is evident from case law however, is that the threshold for fitness is a minimum standard with a reasonable and common-sense application; defendants need to understand the evidence against them but do not need to understand the technicalities of the court or the law (e.g., *Keseverajah vs. R. 1994; Ngatayi vs. R. 1976*). Thus the law provides little guidance about the level of understanding required, although it need not be sophisticated or technical, and there are no empirical norms, the layperson's understanding of trials, with which to make comparisons.

THE ROLE OF MENTAL HEALTH PROFESSIONALS

Fitness to stand trial is a legal, not a clinical decision; the mental health professional offers an opinion and the court decides. Determining fitness is considered a moral, social and legal matter to be determined by legislation and the courts using the common-sense viewpoint of laypersons (Morse, 1978). The courts should not shift responsibility to mental health professionals to define what fitness is when they do not have the specific ability to decide the legal issue (Bonnie, 1993). Grisso (1988) warns against mental health professionals seeking to reformulate legal policy in the image of psychological theory. This aspect needs to be noted when developing an assessment tool.

ASSESSMENT OF FITNESS TO STAND TRIAL

The following paper attempts to outline some of the difficulties faced by mental health professionals in the assessment of fitness to stand trial and the methodology that is proposed as part of PhD research in an attempt to overcome some of these problems.

No standardized assessment tool exists in Australia. Several assessment tools for both the intellectually disabled and mentally ill defendants have been developed by researchers in the USA. Some difficulties with these tools concern inadequate validity and reliability data, little systematic research, high false positives, value laden questions that may idealize the criminal justice system and poor guidelines for scoring responses. Some tools have used small standardization samples of defendants. Not all test items are applicable to an Australian context.

Another major problem is that research and descriptive literature indicate that mental health professionals tend to assess mental status or intellectual capacity alone. However, there is no empirical evidence of a relationship between these assessments and fitness to stand trial (Grisso, 1988). The assessment of fitness should be conducted to determine the functional ability of defendants to be involved in their defence related to the particular circumstances of their case (Roesch & Golding, 1980). Bonnie (1992, 1993) feels that counsel are in the best position to determine whether the defendant is fit to stand trial and may need assistance by mental health professionals on determining how to respond to the impairment. What is required is an assessment tool that directly assesses the defendants knowledge of the upcoming trial, together with counsel who have an understanding of the elements of law, rather than a measure of mental status or intellectual capacity alone.

In addition, fitness is described as an open-textured construct, i.e., a poorly defined concept made up of unrelated criteria varying across cases. Fitness depends upon the seriousness and complexity of the charges, the challenges facing the defendant in a particular case, the defendant-lawyer relationship, the ability of the defendant to adequately instruct counsel, the ability of counsel to successfully communicate and so on (Bukatman, Foy & Degrazia, 1971; Freckelton, 1995; Melton et al, 1987). The defendant may be fit for some aspects of the trial and not others (Bennett & Sullwold, 1984; Grisso, 1986, 1988). Fitness is context-dependent and therefore needs to be decided upon a case-by-case basis. This makes the development of a standardised assessment tool extremely difficult, if not impossible.

The aim of the PhD research is to develop psychological measures of the legal criteria to assist in the assessment process. Ideally the assessment of fitness needs to be functional in that it is related to legal rather than clinical criteria, it is as context-dependent as possible in that it is applicable to the individual situation of the defendant, and pragmatic in that it has practical application (Grisso, 1988). In addition, it must focus upon the defendant's ability to communicate with counsel; the defendant needs to be able to make informed decisions depending upon the situation and weigh up the risks and benefits of each decision (Bonnie, 1992, 1993; Grisso, 1988).

Ancillary research

Firstly, a retrospective study to determine what psychological methods mental health professionals have been using when assessing fitness and whether they relate them to the legal criteria is currently being conducted.

Because the number of defendants who have been found unfit in Victoria and the number of mental health professionals who assess them are so low, the following information is presented as broadly as possible to avoid identification.

In relation to the 11 males who have been found unfit to stand trial in Victoria, offenses include murder and physical assault, injury and sexual offenses including rape and indecent assault against adults and children. One half of the defendants had committed a violent offense and one defendant was found guilty of damaging property. Almost one half had an intellectual disability and one fifth both an intellectual disability and a mental illness; none had a head injury. Fitness is most often raised by the defense despite the negative consequences. In terms of age, half of the defendants were in their 30's when fitness was raised and two were in their 70–80's. Sixty three percent of defendants remained as security residents while the prosecution charges for two were dismissed. Two intellectually disabled defendants were retried and found fit to stand trial.

Data gathered from 51 sources of information including court reports, court transcripts and yearly reviews through the Public Prosecution's Office, the Adult Parole Board and the Intellectual Disability Review Panel indicated that the majority of assessments are conducted by psychiatrists (92%). Almost 60% of the assessments are conducted by mental health professionals within public agencies, the majority of these through Forensic Psychiatry Services, Department of Human Services. Half of the assessments were conducted using clinical interviews regarding mental status and/or intellectual level together with the legal (Presser) criteria. Nevertheless, 20% of interviews were conducted on a clinical basis alone and only 6% used standardised tests of intelligence or comprehension. Only one assessment was conducted together with a solicitor. Seventy eight percent of the assessments concluded that the defendant was unfit to stand trial and 20% concluded that the defendant was fit to stand trial with disagreement on occasion, while 18% of this last group went on to predict the unlikelihood of improvement in the future.

Overall, when legal criteria were addressed by mental health professionals, very little evidence was required for the court that the defendant did or did not understand the criteria. For example, court transcripts indicated that the clinician would state 'yes,' the defendant was unable to plead to the charge without any more substantial evidence given. The court appeared to be satisfied with this. The assessments were context-dependent in that they related to the defendants' individual circumstances, but they were not standardized and responses are assumed to have been compared to some subjective norm. It is unknown whether the responses were any less informed than that of the general population.

As in New South Wales, the Director of Public Prosecutions in Victoria does not identify the fitness issue as a distinct category on its database. Currently, attempts are being made to locate the files of defendants where fitness was raised but who were subsequently found fit to stand trial.

Future research
Please note that the methodology outlined below has been altered substantially in the past year in order to attempt to address the contextualized nature of assessment to stand trial.

Phase 1
Initially, the legal criteria were to be operationalized into psychological measures and an initial assessment battery made up of currently available

tools. A diverse range of assessments other than those available for fitness assessments were reviewed taking into consideration individual and group administration, evidence of reliability and validity, Australian norms, the level of literacy required, appropriateness for adults with mental impairment, and the time taken to administer. Assessment tools reviewed included measures of problem solving, verbal competence and oral comprehension, critical thinking and so on. No applicable tools could be found as they tended to be measures of cognitive ability like any other standardized test of intellectual capacity.

As a result, the development of an assessment tool specifically to assess fitness is now being considered.

Phase 2

A draft vignette outlining a criminal offense with a number of open-ended questions based upon the legal criteria was administered to 114 Legal Studies university students at LaTrobe University in May 1996. The aim was to place the respondents within a legal context. It appears from the initial administration of the assessment tool that the minimum standards regarding the legal criteria may be met except for knowledge about 'challenging the jury.' The respondents still had some difficulty despite being Legal Studies students and so it is expected that general population respondents will perform more poorly.

The results from the questionnaire have been grouped around the Model Bill criteria but in the future two assessment procedures will occur one assessing the understanding of the legal criteria and the second being as contextual as possible. The intention is to develop a three-tiered system of assessment, followed by a fourth lawyer-defendant colloquy when appropriate:

1. An initial brief screening tool assessing general population respondents' basic knowledge necessary to participate in the criminal trial process will be administered allowing for the development of standardized norms. These norms will involve knowledge about the legal criteria outlined in the Model Bill (1994). The tool will be used to screen for those defendants who are clearly unfit to stand trial and will be simple to administer.

The initial screening tool and the assessment tool will be administered first to general population respondents in order to develop a baseline of abilities before assessing those with mental impairment. It is unknown in Australia whether even the general community would be able to satisfactorily meet the legal criteria. The initial screening tool is yet to be developed.

2. For those more borderline cases regarding fitness such as an individual with a dual diagnosis (both intellectual disability and mental illness), an additional assessment tool addressing the ability to understand the evidence, make decisions and communicate to counsel will be developed. The tool will be based upon the elements required for defendants to understand the evidence against them and the implications of the evidence without necessarily having to understand the rules of law. Vignettes outlining legal situations such as theft or murder, as previously administered, will be developed in an attempt to contextualize the situation as much as possible. In a real-life situation, the involvement of counsel would be required at this point.

Because the assessment tool is designed to be eventually used for adults with mental impairment, it is intended that the vignettes be developed into a storybook that would outline the scenario and then use pictures to assist the respondent to indicate his or her ability to comprehend the legal process and assist a lawyer. An additional problem solving framework that has been developed for adults with an intellectual disability may assist in the decision-making aspects outlined by Bonnie (1992; 1993). It is hoped that this method will overcome poor literacy, concentration and memory. The intention is to assess comprehension of the legal process rather than intellectual capacity, i.e., not a test of verbal comprehension or memory.

3. The screening tool will be administered to respondents with mental impairment (intellectual disability, mental illness, dementia or head injury) to compare them to the results of general population respondents. For those respondents who demonstrate a basic understanding, i.e., who score within two standard deviations of the general population, the second assessment tool using vignettes in the form of storybooks will be administered in order to determine whether the defendant has the capacity to relate the evidence to the elements required in court.

Because the issue of fitness to stand trial is so rarely raised in Australia, the requirements for methodology differ greatly from that of test construction in, for example, the USA. Because of the small number of unfit defendants, this phase will need to involve mentally impaired respondents who have not necessarily had contact with the criminal justice system. Brief assessments of intellectual capacity and mental status will also be conducted in order to determine correlations.

4. A fourth level involves the lawyer communicating with defendants about their individual circumstances where the responses cannot be standardized. However, if defendants perform successfully on the first and second level but cannot perform at the third level in applying the information to their own situation, then it is doubtful that they are fit to stand trial.

CONCLUSION

In conclusion, a finding of unfitness to stand trial entails unnecessary indeterminate sentencing resulting in costs to the individual in particular and society in general. This may be avoided by identifying strategies that may assist the defendant in the criminal justice process.

The assessment of fitness to stand trial in Australia requires the development of a tool that is reliable and valid in order to assist the courts. What is required is an assessment tool that directly assesses the defendants knowledge of the upcoming trial, together with counsel who have an understanding of the elements of law, rather than a measure of mental status or intellectual capacity alone.

Difficulties in relation to this include developing a tool that is related to legal rather than clinical criteria, is pragmatic in its application, and is as contextualized as possible. Where possible, the asssessment process will be placed within the individualized legal context of mentally impaired defendants with possible administration of it by both lawyers and mental health professionals. In addition, it will assist the defendant's ability to communicate with counsel. However, it is acknowledged that no standardized assessment will ever be able to match the actual offense of the defendant or the sequence of events that are likely to occur in court.

Future development will require standardized administration, Australian norms, assessment of reliability and validity.

REFERENCES

Ausness, C.W. (1978). The identification of incompetent defendants: Separating those unfit for adversary combat for those that are fit. *Kentucky Law Journal*, 66, 666–706.

Bennett, G.T., & Sullwold, A. F. (1984). Competence to proceed: A functional and context-determinative decision. *Journal of Forensic Science*, 29, 1119–1126.

Bonnie, R.J. (1992). The competence of criminal defendants: A theoretical reformulation. *Behavioural Sciences and the Law*, 10, 291–316.

Bonnie, R.J. (1992). The competence of criminal defendants: Beyond Dusky and Drope. *University of Miami Law Review*, 47(3), 539.

Bukatman, B.A., Foy, J.L., & Degrazia, E. (1971). What is competency to stand trial? *American Journal of Psychiatry*, 127, 1225–1229.

Campbell, I. (1988). *Mental disorder and the criminal law in Australian and New Zealand*. Butterworths: Sydney, Wellington.

Freckelton, I. (1995). *Assessment of fitness to stand trial*. (Unpublished).

Grisso, T. (1986). *Evaluating competencies: Forensic assessments and instruments*. New York: Plenum.

Grisso, T. (1988). *Competency to stand trial evaluations: A manual for practice*. Professional Resource Exchange Inc.

Melton, G.B., Petrila, J., Poythress, N.G., & Slobogin, C. (1987). *Psychological evaluations for the courts: A handbook for mental health professionals and lawyers*. The Guilford Press: NY and London.

Morse, S. (1978). Crazy behaviour, morals and science: An analysis of mental health law. Southern *California Law Review*, 51, 527–654.

New South Wales Law Reform Commission. (1994). *People with an intellectual disability and the criminal justice system*. DP 35, NSWLR: Sydney.

Roesch, R., & Golding, S.L. (1980). *Competency to stand trial*. Urbana: Univ. of Illinois Press.

Ward, W.C., Frederiksen, N., & Carlson, S. B. (1980). Construct validity of free-response and machine-scorable forms of a test. *Journal of Educational Measurement*, 17(1), 11–29.

Index